D0606748

KITCHENS

Santa Fe
KITCHENS

Santa Fe KITCHENS

THE MUSEUM OF
NEW MEXICO FOUNDATION
MEMBERS AND FRIENDS

Ancient City Press
Santa Fe

First Edition
09 08 07 06 05   5 4 3 2 1

Text © 2005 Museum of New Mexico Foundation
Photographs as noted throughout

All rights reserved. No part of this book may be reproduced by any means
whatsoever without written permission from the publisher, except brief
portions quoted for purpose of review.

Published by
Ancient City Press
An imprint of Gibbs Smith, Publisher
P.O. Box 667
Layton, Utah 84041

Orders: 1.800.748.5439
www.gibbs-smith.com

Designed by TTA Design
Printed and bound in Hong Kong

Library of Congress Cataloging-in-Publication Data
Santa Fe kitchens / Museum of New Mexico Foundation members and
friends.—
1st ed.
     p. cm.
  ISBN 1-4236-0018-5
  1. Cookery, American—Southwestern style. I. Museum of New Mexico
Foundation.

TX715.2.S69S28 2006
641.5979—dc22

2005021724

Contents

Introduction

For centuries, Santa Fe has charmed visitors and captured the imagination and spirit of its residents. A central ingredient in the making of Santa Fe's charm has been the kitchens of the city and the surrounding area. Whether in the home or in restaurants, Santa Fe kitchens reflect the diversity of its residents and visitors. Blending the diverse cultures of New Mexico, Native American, Hispanic, Anglo and others, Santa Fe kitchens daily create a unique and compelling cuisine that is both local and worldly in its tastes and appeal.

The Museum of New Mexico Foundation sought recipes from its membership, local chefs, artists and dignitaries to help create this cookbook, *Santa Fe Kitchens,* which you now hold. Out of over 700 recipes submitted for consideration, the experts on the Museum of New Mexico Foundation's Cookbook Committee selected more than 350 for this book. The recipes in the cookbook reflect the balance of Santa Fe's cultures and lifestyle; the simple and the complex, artistic and basic, fun yet challenging, and of course spicy yet with some unbelievable sweets. Where else could you enjoy both Stuffed Tuna Jalapenos and Red Chile Chocolate Chip Cookies but from a unique cookbook that reflects the Santa Fe kitchen?

No book produced by the Museum of New Mexico Foundation on Santa Fe kitchens would be complete without a discussion of the wonderful cultural institutions that the Foundation supports. Throughout the book specific artwork from the Museums of New Mexico are shown and display the depth and quality that can be seen at these museums. Below is a brief description of the Museums and Foundation. We urge you to support the Museums not only by purchasing this cookbook, but also by visiting them often when in Santa Fe.

THE MUSEUM OF NEW MEXICO FOUNDATION

The Foundation is a private, nonprofit organization dedicated to the four museums and six historical state monuments that comprise the Museum of New Mexico.

We envision a Museum of New Mexico that will have ever-increasing financial resources and support, stronger private-public partnerships, and broader community participation. Our philanthropy, stewardship and leadership will help strengthen the Museum of New Mexico's ability to create engaging cultural experiences for all New Mexico residents and visitors.

We promote excellence at the Museum of New Mexico through effective fund-raising, innovative entrepreneurial ventures, community collaboration and essential support services.

THE PALACE OF THE GOVERNORS

The Palace of the Governors, of the Museum of New Mexico, built in 1609 and 1610, is the state history museum for New Mexico and is housed in the oldest continuously occupied public building in the United States. Exhibits, collections and archives at the Palace of the Governors reflect the Spanish colonial (1540–1821), Mexican (1821–1846), U.S. Territorial (1846–1912) and statehood (1912–present) periods of New Mexico history. The collection consists of more than 15,000 catalogued objects, many of which were donated to the Museum of New Mexico in the 1970s by the Historical Society of New Mexico. For more information about the Palace of the Governors, visit www.palaceofthe-governors.org.

THE MUSEUM OF FINE ARTS, SANTA FE

The Museum of Fine Arts was founded in 1917 as the Art Gallery of the Museum of New Mexico. Housed in a spectacular Pueblo Revival building designed by I. H. and William M. Rapp, it was based on their New Mexico building at the Panama-California Exposition (1915). The museum's architecture inaugurated what has come to be known as "Santa Fe Style."

The building combines aspects of several Southwestern regional styles including elements of the facades of the Spanish mission churches of Acoma, Laguna and San Felipe Pueblos. For more than eighty-five years the Museum has collected and exhibited work by artists from New Mexico.

When the Museum of Fine Arts opened its doors in 1917, it was also a collecting institution. The earliest donations of works to the Museum of New Mexico include paintings by artists who were active in the early days of the Taos and Santa Fe art communities.

Today, the Museum of Fine Arts' holdings number more than 23,000 objects, focusing on the areas of photography and works on paper; paintings, sculpture and furniture from the twentieth century; and contemporary art. There is particular emphasis on work produced in or related to New Mexico. For more information about the Museum of Fine Art visit their Web site at www.mfasantafe.org .

THE MUSEUM OF INTERNATIONAL FOLK ART

The Museum of International Folk Art opened to the public in 1953 and has gained national and international recognition as the home of the world's largest collection of folk art. The collection of more than 130,000 artifacts forms the basis for exhibitions in four distinct wings: Bartlett, Girard, Hispanic Heritage and Neutrogena.

The Girard Wing's popular permanent exhibition, Multiple Visions: A Common Bond, showcases folk art, popular art, toys and textiles from more than 100 nations. The late Alexander Girard, who contributed his immense collection to the museum, designed this unorthodox and delightful exhibition, which opened in 1982.

The Hispanic Heritage Wing introduces the culture of northern New Mexico, and its permanent exhibition, Familia y Fe/Family and Faith, focuses on two of the strongest currents that continue to shape regional life today. Spanning four centuries from the Spanish colonial period to the twentieth century, the exhibition presents hide paintings, tinwork, furniture, jewelry, straw appliqué, horse gear, weavings, santos, three-dimensional bultos and painted retablos. A changing gallery features artists representing living artistic traditions from vibrant and varied Hispano/Latino cultures.

The Bartlett Wing, named in honor of museum founder Florence Dibell Bartlett, has two galleries that offer rotating exhibitions based on the museum collections and on field studies of specific cultures or art forms. Exhibitions in this wing have ranged from Turkish, Tibetan and Swedish traditions to New Deal era art in New Mexico, recycled objects and mayólica. Recent exhibitions include 100 Aspects of the Moon: Japanese Woodblock prints by Yoshitoshi; Dressing Up: Children's Clothes from Around the World; and Vernacular Visionaries: International Outsider Art in Context.

The Neutrogena Wing encompasses the Cotsen Gallery and Lloyd's Treasure Chest. The gallery provides an ideal setting for exhibitions featuring textiles from the museum's renowned collection which now includes the Neutrogena Collection, a gift to the museum from Lloyd Cotsen and the Neutrogena Corporation in 1995. This international collection contains exquisite textiles and garments as well as objects. The Treasure Chest invites visitors to explore what goes on behind-the-scenes in a museum and attracts all ages. The Neutrogena

Wing opened in 1998, expanding upon an ongoing public-private partnership that has characterized the museum's profile since its inception. For more information on the Museum of International Folk Art, visit www.moifa.org.

THE MUSEUM OF INDIAN ARTS AND CULTURE

At The Museum of Indian Arts and Culture, one can encounter Native cultures of the Southwest from ancestral to contemporary times. You can see art, material culture and archaeology from a collection of over 100,000 pieces, which includes some of the area's most treasured jewelry, baskets, pottery and weaving. More than 65,000 visitors come to the Museum of Indian Arts and Culture each year, of which 30 percent hail from New Mexico, 50 percent from other states, and 20 percent from foreign countries. It is the Museum of Indian Arts and Culture's mission to provide cross-cultural education to the many visitors to Santa Fe who take part in our programs and to New Mexican residents throughout the state. It is especially important that MIAC serves the Indian communities in our state and throughout the Southwest whose contemporary and ancestral cultures are represented in the museum's collections. For more information on the Museum of Indian Arts and Culture, visit www.miaclab.org.

Appetizers

Picture of Calla Lily, 1932, by Marsden Hartley, oil on canvas, 27 x 32 inches, Museum of Fine Arts.

Spicy New Mexico Roasted Nuts

Makes 4 cups

SPICE MIX:

2 tablespoons white sugar

1 tablespoon hot taco mix
   (in packets)

2 tablespoons red pepper flakes

1 teaspoon salt

2 cups raw almonds

1 cup pecan halves

1 cup raw peanuts, no shells

4 tablespoons olive oil

2/3 cup white sugar

Put spice mix in a large mixing bowl and set aside. In a large frying pan, sauté nuts in olive oil until roasted. Add sugar to nuts and stir until sugar liquefies and turns amber. Avoid overcooking after sugar liquefies or the nuts will taste burned. Add nuts to spice mix and toss well. Spread nuts out on large baking sheet and separate nuts, if needed. Let nuts dry and cool for a few hours. Then pack in an airtight container. This recipe makes a nice hostess gift and keeps for months in a tight container.

Do not double this recipe.

The Absolutely Best Cocktail Mix

Makes 16 cups

8 ounces pecan halves

1 (6-ounce) package small
   cheese crackers

2 (6-ounce) packages corn chips

2 (4-ounce) cans toasted coconut
   chips, essential

1 (8-ounce) can walnuts

1 (8-ounce) can almonds

1 (3 1/2 -ounce) package popcorn,
   popped

1 tablespoon New Mexico red
   chile powder

1/2 pound melted butter

1 teaspoon garlic salt

1 clove garlic, crushed

1/2 teaspoon salt

1 teaspoon curry powder

1 tablespoon Worcestershire sauce

1 tablespoon olive oil

1/2 teaspoon cinnamon

1 teaspoon sugar

Preheat oven to 250 degrees. In a large bowl, mix together first seven ingredients and set aside. Mix remaining ingredients in a saucepan. Pour over dry mixture and mix well. Bake on a large baking sheet for 1 hour. Stir every 15 minutes. Keep in an airtight container.

Divine Chicken Liver

Makes 3 cups

8 slices bacon, diced

1 pound chicken livers

1/2 cup brandy

3/4 cup heavy cream or whipping cream

1 medium yellow onion, chopped

1/4 cup mayonnaise

1 teaspoon dried thyme

Large pinch ground nutmeg

Salt and freshly ground black pepper, to taste

1/2 cup walnuts, coarsely chopped

3 tablespoons fresh Italian parsley, chopped

One day before serving, fry bacon in a medium skillet until crisp. Remove from pan and drain. Sauté livers in bacon fat over medium-high heat until brown. Remove from pan and reserve. Pour the brandy into the skillet over medium heat, stir and scrape bottom of pan, add the cream and heat to boiling. Reduce heat and simmer until reduced to about 1 cup. In food processor, chop the livers, onion and reduced cream until smooth. Add mayonnaise, thyme, nutmeg, salt and pepper. Process mixture in a food processor until smooth. Add diced bacon, walnuts and parsley, and process until blended. Do not over process, as you want texture. Place liver mixture in a crock or service dish. Cover and refrigerate overnight to allow the flavors to blend. Garnish paté with crumbled bacon and parsley or walnuts and parsley. Serve with crusty bread or assorted crackers.

Gorgonzola Wafers

Makes 36

1/4 pound unsalted butter, room temperature

1/2 pound Gorgonzola or other blue cheese

1 cup unbleached all-purpose flour

3/4 cup pine nuts, lightly toasted

Dash salt

Preheat oven to 350 degrees. Combine butter and cheese in a food processor. Add flour, nuts, and salt and blend briefly. Do not puree nuts. Form into two 1 1/2-inch cylinders. Wrap in foil or waxed paper and chill overnight. Slice dough 1/8 inch thick and place on lightly greased baking sheets. Bake until golden brown, about 12 minutes. Cool on wire racks.

Sherried Cheese Crock

Makes 4 cups

2 (8-ounce) packages cream cheese
1 pound sharp cheddar cheese
   (Kaukauna Klub)
1/4 pound soft butter
1/4 cup dry sherry
2 tablespoons dry vermouth

1/2 teaspoon dry mustard
1/2 teaspoon Worcestershire sauce
2 to 3 drops Tabasco sauce
1/2 teaspoon seasoned salt
1/2 teaspoon celery salt
1/4 teaspoon oregano

Mix cheese with butter until thoroughly blended. Add remaining ingredients and stir until well mixed. Pack in crocks, cover and refrigerate. Bring to room temperature to serve with crackers. This recipe makes a great hostess or Christmas gift. It is also good as a stuffing for celery.

Green Chile Guacamole

Makes 3 cups

6 large ripe avocados
2 large ripe tomatoes, unpeeled and
   diced into small squares
1 teaspoon table salt, divided
1 large fresh lemon

2 dozen large New Mexico green
   chiles (hot), finely chopped
2 large cloves garlic, pureed
Salted blue corn, white corn and
   yellow corn tortilla chips

Follow each preparation step carefully so that ingredient flavors meld additively. Slice avocados in half, remove pit, scoop avocado from skin into bowl, mash avocados with fork. Blend 1/3 teaspoon salt into avocados. Blend 1/3 teaspoon salt into tomatoes. Blend tomatoes into avocados. Slice lemon in half and squeeze juice (2 teaspoons) onto avocado mixture. Blend green chile, pureed garlic, and 1/3 teaspoon salt and stir into avocado mixture.

Earth and Water, 1950, by Rebecca Salisbury James, oil on glass, 19 x 16 inches.
Museum of Fine Arts, bequest of Helen Miller Jones.

Chile Cheese Cookies

Makes 60 cookies

2 cups all-purpose flour

1 teaspoon (or less) cayenne pepper

Pinch salt

1 cup butter

2 cups sharp cheddar cheese, shredded

1/3 cup green chiles, chopped

Preheat oven to 350 degrees. Combine dry ingredients. Cream butter and cheese thoroughly. Stir in dry ingredients and chiles. Roll teaspoonful of dough in small balls (1 inch or less) and place on ungreased baking sheet. Then flatten slightly with heel of hand. Bake 15 to 18 minutes and cool on racks. Cookies are a snap to make, freeze well and are delicious with drinks. Cookies are particularly good if warmed slightly before serving.

Chipotle Hummus

Makes 3 cups

3 cups garbanzo beans (canned okay)

1/2 cup tahini

Juice of 1 lemon

2 cloves garlic

2 tablespoons tamari or other soy sauce

2 to 3 canned chipotle peppers (or to taste)

2 tablespoons adobo sauce (or to taste)

Toasted pita triangles or crackers

Drain garbanzo beans, reserving 1/4 cup liquid. Add drained beans and remaining ingredients to bowl of food processor. Using metal blade, process until smooth. If hummus is too thick, add some reserved garbanzo bean liquid to thin.

Garnish with a drizzle of good olive oil. Serve with toasted pita triangles or crackers. Also makes a good sandwich with tomato, red pepper, sprouts, etc. Hummus will keep in refrigerator for a week.

Roasted Red Pepper and Artichoke Tapenade

Makes about 1 1/2 cups

1 (7-ounce) jar roasted red bell peppers, drained, coarsely chopped

1 (6-ounce) jar marinated artichoke hearts, chopped and drained

1/2 cup minced fresh parsley

1/2 cup freshly grated Parmesan cheese

1/3 cup olive oil

1/4 cup drained capers

4 cloves garlic

1 tablespoon fresh lemon juice

Combine all ingredients in a food processor. Process using on/off turns until mixture is well blended and finely chopped. Transfer mixture to a medium bowl. Season to taste with salt and pepper. Serve with slices of baguette or focaccia bread. This is better made 1 day in advance. Cover and refrigerate.

Kathryn Huelster, professional cooking instructor

Home in Las Campanas. Photography: Daniel Nadelbach, photographic styling: Gilda Meyer-Niehof.

White/Green Chile Con Queso

Makes 3 cups

1 tablespoon oil

1 yellow onion, minced

1 tomato, minced

1 (16-ounce) carton frozen medium or
  hot green chile, thawed, drained
  and minced

3 cloves garlic, crushed

2 (8-ounce) packages
  cream cheese

Tostada chips

Heat oil, add onion, tomato, green chile, and garlic and cook until soft. Drain in colander. Place items back in pan. Melt cream cheese in mixture and serve in fondue pot to keep warm. Serve with chips.

Optional: 1 pound sausage, cooked, crumbled and drained, may be added.

Santa Fe Caviar

Makes 4 to 8 servings

1 avocado, chopped

3 tomatoes, chopped

1 purple onion, minced

2 cups chopped peppers
  (red, orange, yellow, green)

1/4 cup cilantro, chopped

1 to 4 jalapeno peppers, chopped
  (to taste)

1 (14-ounce) can chick peas

2 (14-ounce) cans black beans, rinsed

1 can black olives

1 (14-ounce) can red kidney beans

1 can kernel corn, rinsed and drained

1 cup green olives

1/2 cup lime juice (fresh or bottled)

Splash balsamic vinegar

1 teaspoon salt

1 teaspoon cumin, crushed

Splash olive oil, just before serving
  (optional)

Chop all fresh vegetables; you may remove seeds from peppers and tomatoes. Add all canned ingredients, green olives, lime juice, vinegar and spices. Toss until all ingredients are mixed. Serve with chips or crackers.

Marigold Arts—Barbara Marigold, proprietor

Cowboys Going to Dinner, *Mora County, New Mexico, ca. 1897.*
Courtesy of the Palace of the Governors Photo Archives. Negative 5324.

Chef's Choice Vegetable Dip

Makes about 2 cups

1 cup mayonnaise

1/2 cup sour cream

1/2 teaspoon crushed oregano

1/2 teaspoon crushed dried basil

1/4 teaspoon crushed dried thyme

1/4 teaspoon salt

1/8 teaspoon curry powder

2 teaspoons chopped and drained
   capers

1 1/2 teaspoons fresh lemon juice

1 1/2 teaspoons Worcestershire sauce

1 tablespoon grated onion

1 tablespoon fresh parsley, chopped

Blend all ingredients in a small bowl. Cover and refrigerate until serving time. Serve with fresh celery, grape tomatoes, red peppers, green onions, cucumbers, zucchini, blanched cauliflower, broccoli and carrots.

To blanch vegetables: Bring water to boil in saucepan. Have a deep bowl of ice cubes and ice water ready. Drop prepared vegetable into boiling water for only 2 to 3 minutes. Time carefully. Remove vegetables with slotted spoon and plunge them into iced water. Remove vegetables and drain on paper towels. Repeat with remaining vegetables. They will be easier to eat and retain their bright colors.

Kathryn Huelster, professional cooking instructor

Stuffed Tuna Jalapenos

Makes 6 to 12 servings

1 (12-ounce) can tuna

1/4 cup mayonnaise

1/8 teaspoon prepared mustard

1/4 teaspoon garlic powder

1 tablespoon dried parsley

2 green onions, finely chopped

1/8 cup fresh celery leaves or a pinch
   of celery seed

1 medium can whole jalapenos

Prepare tuna with all ingredients except jalapenos. Mash finely with a fork. Cut whole jalapenos in half and seed. Fill with tuna mixture. Arrange in starburst pattern on plate.

Prosciutto-Topped Brie

Makes 4 to 6 servings

1 whole 8-ounce Brie (firm), chilled

3 tablespoons finely chopped oil-packed tomatoes, sun-dried, drained (reserve oil)

1 ounce thinly sliced prosciutto

2/3 cup pine nuts, lightly toasted

Preheat oven to 350 degrees. Cut Brie in half horizontally. Place one half of Brie, cut side up, in a greased, shallow baking dish, about 6 inches in diameter, just slightly larger than the cheese. Spread with tomatoes. Cover with the other half of the cheese, cut side down. Mix prosciutto with 1 tablespoon of the reserved oil and distribute over top of cheese. Bake uncovered until cheese melts at edges and center is warm, about 12 minutes. Sprinkle pine nuts on top and serve with garlic bagel chips or crackers.

Hot Shrimp Cheese Dip

Makes 5 cups

4 tablespoons butter

2 tablespoons chopped onion

4 tablespoons chopped green pepper (or chile)

4 tablespoons flour

2 cups stewed tomatoes, undrained

1 teaspoon dry mustard

1/2 cup milk

2 eggs, beaten

4 cups (1 pound) Old English cheese, cubed or grated

2 cups (1 pound) chopped shrimp, cooked

Salt and pepper, to taste

Melt butter in saucepan and add onion and green pepper (can substitute green chile, if desired). Sauté until semi-soft. Stir in flour, mix well. Add stewed tomatoes. Mix dry mustard with milk and add to saucepan. Stir in beaten eggs. Stir in cheese until melted and mixture begins to thicken. Stir in shrimp and add salt and pepper, to taste. Serve warm in chafing dish accompanied by toast rounds, tortilla chips, corn chips or pita chips.

Smoked Trout Spread

Makes 2 cups

1 pound smoked trout, skinned and boned

1/2 cup green onion, sliced

1/4 cup fresh dill

3 tablespoons fresh lemon juice

1/4 teaspoon pepper

1 cup heavy cream

Salt and pepper, to taste

Combine trout, onion, dill, lemon juice and pepper in food processor. With processor running slowly, pour cream through the feed tube and blend well. Taste and adjust seasonings with salt and pepper. Chill several hours or overnight. Serve with melba toast, crackers or Belgium endive spears.

Seviche

Makes 12 servings

4 pounds very fresh fish fillets, cut into bite-size pieces (flounder, halibut or red snapper)

2 cups lemon or lime juice

1 bay leaf

2 medium onions, finely chopped

4 medium tomatoes, chopped

1/4 cup olive oil

1/2 cup chopped cilantro

3 tablespoons chopped parsley

20 stuffed olives, sliced

2 serrano chiles or to taste, chopped and seeded

1 teaspoon dried oregano

1/2 teaspoon dried thyme

Salt and pepper, to taste

1/2 cup ketchup

Hot sauce, to taste

Arrange fish in one layer in a large, shallow glass or stainless-steel container. Pour in enough lemon juice to cover fish completely. Add bay leaf, cover tightly, and refrigerate for 4 to 5 hours, or until the fish is opaque rather than transparent. Drain and discard bay leaf. Combine onions, tomatoes, olive oil, cilantro, parsley, olives, chiles, seasonings, ketchup and hot sauce. Mix well and toss with fish. Transfer to a serving bowl, cover and chill for several hours. Serve with tortilla chips or crackers.

Untitled, 1938?, by Gerald Nailor (Toh Yah), Navajo, tempera on board 12 3/4 x 14 inches. The Dorothy Dunn Collection in the Museum of Indian Arts and Culture.

Jalapeno Pie

Makes 8 to 12 servings

1 (12-ounce) jar jalapenos, drained
    and seeded, split and flattened
1 (10 to 12-ounce) package sharp
    cheddar cheese, grated

4 eggs, beaten
Dash garlic powder

Preheat oven to 275 degrees. This recipe is flexible. Don't be afraid of a little less or more jalapenos or cheese. Drain jalapenos and arrange in bottom of buttered glass or 9-inch square pan. Sprinkle cheese evenly over peppers. Beat eggs slightly and pour slowly and evenly over cheese and jalapenos. Allow to settle 1 to 2 minutes. Bake for 45 minutes, or until eggs set. Serve hot or at room temperature. This dish also freezes well.

Chile Con Queso

Makes 7 cups

2 tablespoons margarine
2 medium white onions, chopped
2 small cans chopped green chile;
    or 5 to 6 pods of New Mexico-
    grown roasted green chile,
    chopped; or 8 ounces frozen
    green chile, drained

1 (10-ounce) can original Rotel
    tomatoes, drained
2 pounds Monterey Jack or
    Muenster cheese, shredded
1 pound Velveeta cheese, with or
    without jalapenos, cubed
1 teaspoon garlic salt

Melt margarine in a large nonstick skillet. Wilt chopped onions in melted margarine. Add chopped chile and tomatoes. Cover and simmer for 10 minutes. Gradually fold in grated Jack cheese. When fully melted, stir in small cubes of Velveeta cheese, a few pieces at a time. Stir to desired consistency. If too thick, add a little milk.

Chile Cheese Squares

Makes 30 to 40 servings

10 large eggs
1 teaspoon salt
1 teaspoon baking powder
1/3 cup flour
2 dashes Tabasco sauce

2 cups cottage cheese
1 pound Monterey Jack cheese, grated
1/2 cup butter, melted
16 green chiles, diced and well drained, mild or hot

Preheat oven to 400 degrees. Beat eggs lightly with a whisk in a large bowl. Blend in salt, baking powder, flour and Tabasco. Add cottage cheese, Jack cheese and melted butter to mixture. Mix until blended. Stir in chiles by hand. Pour mixture into 9 1/2 x 13-inch baking pan. Bake for 15 minutes. Reduce temperature to 350 degrees and continue to bake for 35 to 40 minutes. The top should be golden brown and a toothpick inserted should come out clean. Cheese squares may need more baking time at higher altitudes. Cut into bite-size squares. Serve hot or at room temperature. This recipe freezes well.

Caprese Bruschetta

Makes 12 servings

1 baguette
6 medium Roma tomatoes
2 cloves garlic
Handful fresh basil
3 to 4 tablespoons olive oil

Salt and pepper, to taste
12 ounces fresh mozzarella, Buffalo is best
Whole, fresh basil leaves for garnish

Slice baguette into 24 slices, approximately 1/2 inch thick. Toast until golden and cool on rack. Halve the Roma tomatoes and remove seeds, chop finely. Peel and chop garlic and add to tomatoes. Chop basil, and add it along with olive oil to tomatoes. Sprinkle with salt and pepper, to taste. Slice the mozzarella thinly. Sprinkle a small amount of olive oil on each slice of toasted bread. Arrange mozzarella on bread and cover the surface with tomato mixture. Garnish with small whole basil leaf.

Hot Southwest Dip

Makes 4 cups

1 (10 1/2-ounce) can refried beans
1 cup sour cream
1/2 cup jalapeno peppers, chopped
1/2 cup black olives, sliced
1 cup tomatoes, peeled and chopped
1 cup Monterey Jack cheese, grated

TOPPING:
1/2 cup salsa
1/2 cup green onions, chopped

Preheat oven to 375 degrees. In an ovenproof dish, layer ingredients, beginning with beans and ending with cheese. Bake until heated through and cheese is melted. Top with salsa and green onions. Serve with tortilla chips.

Bruschetta with Smoked Salmon, Avocado and Tomato Salsa

Makes 12 servings

3 large plum tomatoes, seeded and chopped

1/2 yellow bell pepper, seeded and chopped

3 tablespoons chopped onion

1 jalapeno chile, seeded and chopped

1 tablespoon fresh lime juice

1 teaspoon olive oil

1/2 avocado, peeled and cubed

3 tablespoons fresh basil

Salt and pepper, to taste

Baguette, sliced 1/2 inch thick

Olive oil

1/2 pound smoked salmon, thinly sliced

Combine first 9 ingredients for salsa. Preheat broiler, brush 1 side of bread slices with oil, and sprinkle with black pepper. Toast/broil both sides until golden brown, about 2 minutes per side. Arrange bread oil side up on work surface. Top with salmon, then top with salsa mixture.

Chile Relleno Green Hots

Makes 6 1/2 dozen

1 pound lean ground beef

1/2 small onion, finely diced

1/2 teaspoon salt

1 cup sugar

1 pint fresh green chile or frozen, thawed and well drained, diced

1/2 cup currants

1/2 cup pine nuts

1/2 teaspoon nutmeg

1/2 teaspoon cinnamon

1/3 cup white wine

2 cups flour

4 eggs, separated

2 cups shortening or oil

Pinch salt

Sauté ground beef only until no longer pink. Drain. Add finely diced onion and cook until meat is fully cooked. Add salt, sugar, diced green chile, currants, nuts, nutmeg and cinnamon. Cook for 30 minutes, stirring frequently. Drain any excess moisture. Add wine, cool and set aside. Coat hands generously with flour. Place heaping teaspoons of cooled meat mixture into floured hand. Mold into walnut-size balls, being careful not to incorporate too much flour into the mixture. Set balls on a baking sheet. Beat egg whites with pinch of salt until stiff and dry. Fold in yolks. Dip each floured ball into egg batter. Fry in 2 inches of hot oil, 420 degrees, until golden brown. Drain on paper towels. Serve Hot. Can be frozen and reheated.

Seed Jar, Nampeyo, from the collection of the Museum of Indian Arts and
Culture/Laboratory of Anthropology.

Chile Cheesecake

Makes 20 servings

2 (8-ounce) packages cream cheese, softened to room temperature

2 cups sharp cheddar cheese, shredded

1 (1 1/2-ounce) package taco mix

3 large or jumbo eggs

1 (16-ounce) package sour cream, divided

1/2 cup roasted green chiles, chopped, or 14-ounce can of chopped green chiles, drained

1/2 cup red bell pepper, diced

1/2 cup salsa, hot or mild; homemade or commercial

AVOCADO SAUCE:

1 teaspoon lemon juice

1 large avocado, pitted, peeled and mashed

1/2 cup sour cream

Combine lemon juice with avocado and sour cream and blend until smooth.

Preheat oven to 350 degrees. Combine cream cheese, cheddar cheese and taco mix. Beat well on high with electric mixer. Add eggs, one at a time. Beat 2 minutes after each of the first 2 eggs and 5 minutes after the last one. Stir or fold in 8 ounces of sour cream. Fold in chiles and red pepper. Lightly grease and flour a 10-inch spring-form pan. Pour cheesecake mixture into pan and bake for 35 minutes. Remove from oven. Combine 8 ounces of sour cream with salsa. Spread over cheesecake; return to oven and bake for 5 minutes. Remove from oven and cool on a wire rack, then carefully remove from pan.

Cover and chill for at least 8 hours. Spread with Avocado Sauce; garnish and serve with chips, chopped fresh tomato, sliced ripe olives or shredded cheddar cheese.

Thai Chicken Wings

Makes 12 servings

2 dozen chicken wings or drumettes

1/2 cup tamari or other soy sauce

1/2 cup honey

1 tablespoon minced garlic

1 tablespoon fresh ginger, grated

1 tablespoon chile flakes

Toasted sesame seeds

1 (12-ounce) can rice noodles

Cilantro leaves, chopped

Mix soy sauce and honey in skillet. Add wings or drumettes and garlic. Cook slowly, turning as necessary. Add water if sauce reduces to nothing before chicken is cooked. Add grated ginger and chile flakes and cook until chicken is well glazed. Sauce will become very thick and sticky. Toss with sesame seeds. Serve on a bed of noodles with cilantro as garnish.

New Mexico Wontons

Makes 24

2 pounds lean ground beef
2 medium onions, chopped
1 clove garlic, minced
1 1/2 teaspoons salt
1/2 teaspoon oregano

1 teaspoon ground cumin
4 cups cheddar cheese, shredded
24 fresh green chiles, roasted and
   peeled
24 egg roll wrappers

Brown beef slowly. Drain off fat. Add onion, garlic and seasonings. Cook and stir until onions are golden. Remove from heat. Cool slightly and add cheese. Blend well. Spread open chiles and remove seeds. Fill each chile with 2 tablespoons of meat mixture. Roll up chiles like a jelly roll. Place filled chile diagonally on individual egg roll wrapper. Lift lower triangle flap over chile and tuck the point under it. Bring left and right corners toward the center and roll, sealing edges with a few drops of water. Deep fry at 325 degrees until golden brown. Drain on paper towels and serve immediately with guacamole to dip.

Spanish Chorizos and Olives

Makes 6 to 8 servings

12 Spanish chorizos
1/4 to 1/2 cup olive oil
2 large onions, thinly sliced

2 large (12-ounce) jars
   stuffed Spanish olives

Cut the Spanish chorizos into 4 pieces each. In a large skillet, heat oil over medium heat until fragrant. Brown chorizos with the sliced onions until almost tender, then add the two drained jars of stuffed olives until the olives are hot. Serve hot with toothpicks.

Tempura-Style Herb-Stuffed Squash Blossoms

Makes 12

12 squash blossoms (zucchini flowers)
9 ounces goat cheese
2 tablespoons fresh basil, chopped
1/2 tablespoon thyme, chopped
1/2 tablespoon rosemary, chopped
1 teaspoon garlic, chopped
Pinch salt and pepper

TEMPURA:

1/4 cup cornstarch
1/2 cup flour
1/2 tablespoon kosher salt
2 cups soda water
4 cups vegetable oil

Mix together goat cheese, basil, thyme, rosemary, garlic, salt and pepper. Place mixture in a pastry bag. Gently open blossom and squeeze 2 ounces of mixture into each squash blossom petal. Allow to chill for 2 hours.
Tempura: mix cornstarch, flour, salt and soda water until all is combined. Heat vegetable oil in a sauté pan until hot. Coat (dip) squash blossom in tempura batter and place in hot oil to fry. Turn squash blossom in pan until all sides seem crispy. Once cooked, allow squash blossom to cool for 2 minutes before serving.

Las Campanas Country Club—Brad Gallegos, chef

Banks, San Pedro Tlaquepaque,
Jalisco, Mexico.
Painted earthenware, watermelon 10 3/4
inches long, ca. 1960. Girard Collection.
Museum of International Folk Art.
Photo by: Michel Monteau.

Empanadas

Makes 3 dozen

DOUGH:

2 cups sifted flour

2 teaspoons baking powder

1/2 teaspoon salt

2/3 cup shortening

1/4 cup sugar dissolved in 1/2 cup milk

1/2 teaspoon anise oil, optional

SWEET FILLING:

1 1/2 cups pumpkin or mashed sweet potatoes

1/2 cup sugar

1/2 cup pine nuts or almonds

1/2 cup raisins

1/2 teaspoon allspice

1/2 teaspoon cloves

1/2 teaspoon anise oil, optional

MEAT FILLING:

1/2 cup boiled pork

1/2 cup dried, diced apricots

1/4 teaspoon cloves

1/4 teaspoon allspice

1/2 cup sugar

1/2 teaspoon cinnamon

1/2 cup raisins and currants

1/2 cup almonds, chopped

1/2 cup meat stock

Preheat oven to 375 degrees. Dough: sift dry ingredients and cut in shortening. Add sweetened milk and anise. Stir until dough follows fork around bowl. Knead 2 or 3 times on floured board and roll out about 1/4 inch thick. Cut into 4-inch circles. Now make either sweet or meat filling: put all ingredients in a bowl and mix well. Place 1 tablespoon of filling on half of the circle of dough. Fold over and crimp edges with fork. Brush pies with canned milk or egg white. Bake on greased baking sheet for 15 minutes, or until golden brown. Sprinkle with sugar and cinnamon, or powdered sugar.

Crab Toasties

Makes 32

3 strips bacon, cooked and crumbled

1 pound crabmeat, cleaned of all shell and cartilage

3 green onions, chopped

1 can water chestnuts, drained

1 teaspoon lemon juice

3/4 cup mayonnaise

1/2 cup shredded cheddar cheese

1/4 green or red pepper, chopped

Tabasco sauce, to taste

4 English muffins, split

Mix ingredients together. Lightly toast English muffins, spread with crab mixture. Broil for 5 to 10 minutes. Cut into quarters. May also use toasted rye or pumpernickel.

Caramelized Onion Quesadillas

Makes 9 servings

2 large white onions, thinly sliced

3 tablespoons oil

5 teaspoons dried basil

4 tablespoons honey

1 cup chicken stock

Salt, to taste

3 large flour tortillas

2 cups Monterey Jack cheese

Preheat oven to 350 degrees. Sauté onions in oil until softened, but not brown. Sprinkle in basil and continue stirring over medium heat for 15 minutes. Stir in honey and cook 5 minutes. Add stock and heat on medium so stock barely simmers until evaporated. Salt to taste. Remove from heat. Sprinkle cheese onto tortillas and spoon on onion mixture. Fold each tortilla in half, creating half-moon shape. Bake 8 minutes. Remove from oven and slice in thirds. Serve immediately with salsa.

Stuffed Jalapeno Poppers

Makes 6 to 8 servings

12 to 16 jalapenos

1 (8-ounce) package cream cheese, softened

1 pound cooked, crumbled bacon

2 teaspoons bacon grease

2 cups shredded Mexican cheese

1 teaspoon chile powder

1 teaspoon garlic powder

1 teaspoon cumin

Salt and pepper, to taste

1/2 cup dried bread crumbs

Preheat oven to 350 degrees. Slice jalapenos in half lengthwise and remove seeds and membrane. Mix remaining ingredients, except bread crumbs. Spoon mixture into halved jalapenos until full. Sprinkle jalapenos with bread crumbs on top of cheese mixture. Bake on a baking sheet for 20 to 40 minutes. The longer the baking time, the milder the pepper.

Beverages

Trees at Canoncito, *1937, by Will Schuster, oil on canvas, Museum of Fine Arts.*

Almond Tea

3 tea bags

1 cup sugar

1 teaspoon vanilla extract

1 1/2 teaspoons almond extract

Juice of 3 lemons, or 6 tablespoons concentrated lemon juice

6 cups water

In a saucepan, bring 2 cups of water to a boil. Reduce the heat to a simmer. Add tea bags and steep for 5 minutes. Remove tea bags. Add sugar, extracts and lemon juice. Simmer and stir until sugar is dissolved. Remove from heat. Add 6 cups cold water and chill. Serve over ice.

Territorial Frozen Tea

Makes 2 gallons

3 lemons

2 oranges

9 family-size tea bags

1 cup fresh mint leaves, chopped

3 cups sugar

1/2 cup maraschino cherry juice

Fresh mint, for garnish

Maraschino cherries

Squeeze lemons and oranges. Chill juices and reserve lemon hulls. Boil 2 quarts water, remove from heat and add tea bags, mint leaves and reserved lemon hulls. Steep for 30 minutes. Strain, add sugar and stir until dissolved. Refrigerate up to 24 hours. When mixture is thoroughly cooled, add lemon, orange and cherry juices, plus 1 1/2 quarts more cold water. Stir well, and freeze to slushy consistency. You may add less sugar, but tea will freeze more solid. When serving, garnish with fresh mint and maraschino cherry.

Chimayo Cocktail

Makes 6 servings

1 (12-ounce) can frozen apple juice concentrate

3/4 cup light or dark rum

1 small apple, cored but not peeled

1 tablespoon lemon juice

Place all ingredients in a blender. Add enough ice to fill container. Blend until slushy.

Mint Tea

Makes 1 quart

3 teaspoons tea
6 sprigs mint

1/2 cup lemon juice
1 cup sugar

Pour 2 cups boiling water over tea and mint sprigs, let stand 15 minutes. Pour 2 cups boiling water over lemon juice and sugar, let stand 15 minutes. Mix together when cool. Chill and serve over ice in tall glasses.

Desert Breeze Punch

Makes 12 servings

2 cups cranberry juice, chilled
1 cup grapefruit juice, chilled
1 cup vodka, chilled
Juice of 1 lime

1 tablespoon superfine sugar
1 liter bottle sparkling wine, chilled
Lime slices
Grapefruit slices

In a 2-quart pitcher or punch bowl, combine cranberry juice, grapefruit juice, vodka, lime juice and sugar. Stir until sugar is dissolved. Add sparkling wine. Pour over crushed ice and garnish with lime and grapefruit slices.

Sparkling Peach-Lime Nectar

Makes 4 drinks

Fresh lime
Sugar in a shallow bowl
Peach or apricot nectar
Strawberry puree frozen into ice cubes (made at least a day in advance.)

Sparkling water
Rum, optional

With a wedge of lime, moisten the rims of fancy cocktail or wine glasses. Turn the glasses over and coat rims with sugar. Fill the glasses half full with fruit nectar. Squeeze in a generous amount of lime juice. Add one strawberry puree ice cube to each glass. Fill glass with sparkling water. Add rum, if you want alcohol. Decorate rim of glass with a circular, thin slice of lime. Chill all liquid ingredients first.

Barela's Bloody Marys

Makes 8 to 10 drinks

1/8 teaspoon garlic powder

1 teaspoon onion powder

1 1/4 teaspoons celery salt

1 (46-ounce) can Clamato juice

3 tablespoons lime juice

2 ounces taco sauce

1 teaspoon Tabasco sauce

2 tablespoons Worcestershire sauce

2 cups lemon vodka

Celery stalks

In a large pitcher, combine all ingredients, except celery. Stir until well blended. Chill overnight in refrigerator. When ready to serve, pour into tall glasses, over ice, and garnish with celery stalk.

Home of Allison Tinsley in Galisteo, New Mexico. Interior design by Sher Colquitt Designs. Photography: Daniel Nadelbach, photographic styling: Gilda Meyer-Niehof.

Santa Fe Sunrise

Makes 1 serving

3 to 4 tablespoons gold tequila

1/2 cup orange juice

1 teaspoon grenadine syrup

Slice of fresh lime

Club soda, optional

Fill a tall glass with ice. Stir tequila into orange juice and pour into glass. Pour grenadine into the glass, letting it settle. Squeeze lime into the drink and serve. You may add a splash of club soda, if desired.

Mansion Drive Punch

Makes 3 quarts

1 1/2 cups confectioners' sugar

1/2 cup triple sec or other orange-flavored liqueur

1/2 cup cognac

1/2 cup maraschino cherry juice

Maraschino cherries, optional

2 bottles chilled champagne

1 orange, sliced

1 lemon, sliced

1 quart pineapple sorbet

Combine sugar, liqueur, cognac, cherry juice, and cherries, if desired. Pour into a punch bowl. Just before serving, add chilled champagne, orange and lemon slices, and sorbet. Stir to mix.

Frozen Daiquiri Punch

Makes 12 servings

1 fifth (25 ounces) rum

2 (6-ounce) cans frozen pink or regular lemonade

1 (6-ounce) can frozen limeade concentrate

4 cups water

1/2 cup grenadine syrup, optional

Mix all ingredients, cover and freeze overnight. When ready to serve, spoon out into a punch bowl. This is a great party punch.

Mexican Mocha

Makes 4 servings

1 cup coffee

6 ounces semisweet chocolate

1 cup water

2 cups scalded milk

1/2 cup heavy cream

1/4 cup brandy or Kahlua

1 cup cream, whipped with

   2 teaspoons sugar

1 teaspoon orange extract

Cinnamon sticks

Combine coffee, chocolate and water in pan. Heat just to boiling. Remove and pour into blender. Add hot scalded milk and heavy cream. Beat until frothy. Add brandy. Whip cream, adding sugar and orange extract. Pour chocolate mixture into cups and top with whipped cream. Put a cinnamon stick in each cup. Serve warm.

Sangria Blanca

Makes 6 servings

4 cups chilled white wine
1/2 cup orange-flavored liqueur
1/4 cup brandy
1/4 cup sugar
1 (10-ounce) bottle club soda, chilled

1 lemon, sliced
2 limes, sliced
1 green apple, unpeeled, cut into
    wedges

In a glass pitcher, combine the wine, liqueur, brandy and sugar. Blend. Stir in club soda and garnish with fruit.

Lamy Lemonade

Makes 1 quart

1 (12-ounce) can
frozen pink lemonade concentrate

Tequila, to fill the lemonade can
Mint sprig, lemon slices or cherries

Put lemonade concentrate and tequila in a blender filled with crushed ice. Blend at high speed until frothy. Pour into pitcher and serve. Garnish with mint sprig, lemon slices or cherries.

Santa Fe Plaza in the 1880s, *ca. 1880, by Francis Grosshenney, oil on canvas, 36 1/4 x 60 1/2 inches, Museum of Fine Arts.*

Speedy Sangria

Makes 6 servings

1 (.750 liter) bottle red wine
1 (8-ounce) can frozen lemonade, thawed

Orange and lemon slices
8 ounces club soda

Mix wine and lemonade in pitcher. Add a couple of orange and lemon slices. Add club soda to pitcher just before serving. Serve in tall glasses over ice.

Margaritas Olé

Makes 1 quart

3 cups margarita mix
1 cup tequila, gold or silver

1/2 cup orange liqueur
3 fresh limes, cut in wedges

Pour all ingredients into a blender filled with crushed ice. Blend at high speed. Pour into glasses and garnish with lime wedge. If you like salt on rim of glasses, dip glasses upside down in bowl of lime juice, and then dip into bowl of salt.

Peach Daiquiri

Makes 4 servings

4 ounces rum
2 ounces Rose's Lime Juice
1/3 to 1/2 cup sugar

4 ripe peaches, peeled
2 cups frozen peach slices

Mix ingredients together in a blender. Add ice cubes and blend until slushy. One tablespoon of amaretto can be added.

Cafe Mexicano

Makes 1 serving

1 ounce tequila
1/4 ounce Kahlua
6 ounces hot, fresh coffee

Whipped cream
Lemon zest

Pour tequila and Kahlua into an 8-ounce mug and fill with coffee. Top with whipped cream and lemon zest. Serve immediately.

My Gate on the Camino, *1928, by Andrew Dasburg, oil on*
canvas, Museum of Fine Arts.

Sangria

Makes 6 servings

1 cup orange juice
1/2 cup lemon or lime juice
1/2 cup sugar

1 quart red wine
1/2 cup brandy or amaretto
1 can 7-Up
Orange or lime slices

In a large pitcher, pour orange and lemon juices with sugar. Stir until sugar is dissolved. Add wine and brandy. When ready to serve, add 7-Up. Garnish each glass with an orange or lime slice. Chill all liquid ingredients before mixing and serve over ice cubes.

Zozobra Slush

Makes 6 to 8 servings

1 1/2 to 3 1/2 cups bourbon whiskey, as desired
1 (12-ounce) can frozen lemonade concentrate

2 tablespoons frozen orange juice concentrate
Mint sprigs or maraschino cherries

In an electric blender, combine bourbon, lemonade and orange juice concentrates, and 4 1/2 cups water. Place in freezer for 1 to 3 hours, until mixture freezes. Just before serving, mix in the blender. Pour into cocktail glasses. Add a sprig of mint or cherry, to garnish.

Hammer Borracho

Makes 6 to 8 servings

1 (2-ounce) jigger banana liqueur
3/4 jigger Kahlua
1/2 jigger brandy

3/4 jigger triple sec
1 quart french vanilla ice cream
Straws, to serve

Mix all liqueurs and blend with ice cream in blender. Freeze. Serve in any attractive bar glass.

Brunch

Cui Bono, ca. 1911, by Gerald Cassidy, oil on canvas, 93 1/2 x 48 inches, Museum of Fine Arts.

Gift of the artist.

Ojai Manor Granola

Makes 4 1/2 quarts

6 cups regular rolled oats
1 cup soy flour
1 cup nonfat powdered milk
1 cup wheat germ
1 cup pumpkin seeds
1 cup almonds, chopped
1 cup sunflower seeds

1 cup hazelnuts, chopped
1 cup Canola oil
1/4 cup maple syrup
1/2 cup honey
2 cups raisins
1/2 teaspoon cinnamon
1/2 teaspoon nutmeg

Preheat oven to 250 degrees. Mix the first 8 ingredients together in a large bowl. Place oil, syrup and honey together in a small bowl, and whisk. Add wet mixture to dry ingredients in 1/3 amounts, mix well, break up lumps and incorporate until well mixed. Divide into 2 roasting pans or similar containers and bake for 2 hours. Stir mixture every 20 minutes and change oven location, upper/lower rack position to cook evenly. Granola will be lightly golden brown. Remove from oven and add 1 cup raisins to each pan, mix in. Sprinkle cinnamon and nutmeg on granola, mix thoroughly. Cool. Store in glass jars.

Muesli for Breakfast

Makes 3 cups

1/2 cup raisins
1/2 cup old-fashioned oats
1 1/2 cups quick oats
1/3 cup brown sugar
1/4 to 1/2 teaspoon cinnamon
2 cups milk

FRESH FRUIT
AND NUTS:
Use 1/4 cup of each or all:
Walnuts
Apples
Bananas
Fresh berries
Coconut

Mix all ingredients except fruit and let sit in refrigerator overnight. Add fresh fruit when you are ready to serve. Keeps in refrigerator for 4 to 5 days.

Tomato, Bacon and Basil Salad

Makes 8 servings

5 cups halved cherry or
    grape tomatoes
8 slices lean bacon, cooked
    crisp and crumbled
1/3 cup fresh basil
2 tablespoons red wine vinegar

2 teaspoons sugar
1/2 teaspoon dry mustard
1 small clove garlic, crushed
Salt and pepper, to taste
4 tablespoons extra-virgin olive oil

Toss together tomatoes, bacon and basil. In a separate bowl, mix rest of ingredients thoroughly until blended. Pour over tomato mixture and toss lightly.

Granola Bars

Makes 16 bars

1/2 cup butter or margarine
1 cup brown sugar
1/4 cup white sugar
2 tablespoons honey
1/2 teaspoon vanilla
1 egg or 1/4 cup egg whites

1 cup flour
1/2 teaspoon baking powder
1/4 teaspoon salt
1 1/2 cups regular rolled oats
1 heaping cup shredded coconut
1 cup butterscotch chips
1 cup pecans or almonds, chopped

Preheat oven to 375 degrees. Mix together the first 9 ingredients. Stir in the last 4, but *do not* beat heavily. Grease a 9 x 13-inch pan with a little oil (such as Canola or Wesson). Press mixture firmly into pan; bars will be about 1/4 inch thick. Bake for 25 to 28 minutes. *Do not overbake.* Remove from oven and let cool to room temperature. Cut into bars. Store in airtight container after cooling thoroughly.

VARIATIONS:
Chocolate chips can be substituted for the butterscotch chips and 1 1/4 cups Rice Krispies can be added, if desired.

Blue Corn Porridge

Makes 2 to 4 servings

1/2 cup toasted blue cornmeal
1/2 teaspoon natural sea salt
2 cups cold water

Real butter
Brown sugar
1/2 teaspoon cinnamon
1/2 teaspoon powdered clove

In a saucepan, stir cornmeal and salt into cold water. Place on stove and slowly bring to a boil while stirring to avoid clumping. Remove from heat when mixture begins bubbling. Stir into a smooth porridge. When serving, top with a tab of butter and brown sugar. Sprinkle with cinnamon and powdered clove.

Douglas Johnson, artist
Represented by Nedra Matteucci Galleries

Baked Chile Bacon

Makes 8 servings

1 cup brown sugar
1/4 cup red chile powder

2 teaspoons cinnamon
1 pound lean bacon

Preheat oven to 350 degrees. Mix together sugar, chile powder and cinnamon. Place on a flat plate. Dip each slice of bacon into mixture, pressing down on both sides. Place on rack and bake for 30 minutes, watching carefully. More or less time may be required. Remove from oven and cool slightly.

Zuni Polychrome Stew Bowl, from the Collection of the Museum of Indian Arts and Culture/Laboratory of Anthropology.

Lime Honey Dressing for Fruit

Makes 1 2/3 cups

1/3 cup lime juice
1/3 cup honey
1 cup vegetable oil
1/2 teaspoon paprika
1/2 teaspoon prepared mustard
1/2 teaspoon salt
Grated peel of 1 lime

FRUIT CHOICES:
Bananas
Blueberries
Raspberries
Peaches
Oranges
Pears
Watermelon
Cantaloupe

Blend all ingredients thoroughly. Serve with tray of fresh fruit.

Marzipan Apricots

Makes 14 to 16 servings

1 pound or 14-ounce can
    whole apricots
8 ounces almond paste
16 whole almonds
1 tablespoon cornstarch
1 cup orange sections,
    coarsely chopped

1/4 cup toasted sliced almonds
1 teaspoon grated orange rind
2 teaspoons Cointreau or
    Gran Marnier

Preheat oven to 325 degrees. Drain apricots, reserving liquid. Slit each apricot on one side only, to remove pit, if necessary. Divide almond paste into 14 to 16 pieces. Insert one whole almond into each piece of almond paste. Roll into ball and insert into each apricot. Arrange in a 6 x 12-inch baking dish. Bake for 25 minutes. Measure apricot liquid and add water to make 2 cups. Combine with cornstarch and heat to boiling over medium heat, stirring constantly. Add oranges, reduce heat and simmer for 2 minutes, stirring constantly. Stir in toasted almonds, orange rind and liqueur. Pour over apricots and serve warm.

Naranja Crème Fruit Dip

Makes 2 cups

2 tablespoons fresh orange juice
7 ounces marshmallow crème
8 ounces cream cheese, softened
1/2 teaspoon pure orange extract

1/2 teaspoon freshly
    grated orange rind
Fruit pieces, such as strawberries,
    grapes, pineapple and bananas

In a food processor or blender, mix all ingredients except fruit pieces. Chill until ready to use. Serve with the fruit pieces.

Corrales Ginger Fruit Cup

Makes 8 servings

1 cup sour cream
1/2 cup fresh strawberries
1 medium banana
2 tablespoons crystallized ginger, chopped
1 tablespoon light brown sugar, packed

1 tablespoon rum
3 cups bananas, sliced
2 cups strawberries, halved
2 cups seedless green grapes
Fresh mint

Combine first 6 ingredients in a blender or food processor. Blend until smooth. Refrigerate overnight. In a large bowl, combine bananas, strawberries and grapes. Toss fruit with dressing and garnish with mint.

Gnocchi a la Romaine

Makes 12 to 15 servings

1 quart milk
1/2 cup butter
1 cup hominy grits, not the quick-cooking kind
1 teaspoon salt

1/4 teaspoon pepper
1/2 cup melted butter
1 cup grated Gruyère
1/3 cup grated Parmesan

Preheat oven to 375 degrees. Bring milk to a boil with 1/2 cup butter. Stir in grits. Bring to a boil and then simmer over lowest heat, stirring often for 15 to 20 minutes. Remove from heat; add salt and pepper and cool for 5 to 10 minutes. Then beat with electric mixer for 5 minutes. Pour into greased loaf pan, cover and chill overnight. Turn out on bread board and slice 1/2 inch thick. Place, like fallen dominoes, in buttered shallow 8 1/2 x 11-inch casserole dish. Pour melted butter over and sprinkle with grated cheeses. Bake for 30 to 35 minutes.

Fruit Clafouti

Makes 4 to 6 servings

1 1/2 cups fresh fruit: blueberries, raspberries, peaches, apricots
1/2 cup white flour, Wondra works without sifting
1/3 cup sugar

1/4 teaspoon salt
4 eggs, beaten lightly
1 cup milk or soy milk
Powdered sugar

Preheat oven to 350 degrees. Butter a 9-inch round, shallow pie pan. Lay fruit on bottom of pan. Sift flour into a bowl, add sugar and salt, and stir. Make a well; add the combined eggs and milk by whisking until smooth. Pour batter over fruit. Bake for 40 minutes. Remove from oven, cool slightly. Invert on plate and dust with powdered sugar. Serve immediately.

Piñon Orange Glazed Bananas

Makes 6 servings

6 firm bananas, peeled
  and halved lengthwise
3/4 cup fresh orange juice
1/4 cup Gran Marnier

3 tablespoons unsalted butter
1/3 cup pine nuts
1/3 cup packed brown sugar
Sour cream

Preheat oven to 400 degrees. Arrange bananas in shallow baking dish. Combine orange juice and Gran Marnier and pour over bananas. Dot with butter and bake 5 minutes, basting occasionally. Remove from oven and preheat broiler. Sprinkle bananas with pine nuts and brown sugar, and broil until sugar is melted and nuts are toasted, about 5 minutes. Serve warm with sour cream.

Skeleton Orchestra, *crafted for annual Day of the Dead celebrations. Painted plaster and wire. State of Mexico, ca. 1956. Museum of International Folk Art, Girard Foundation Collection. Photo: Michel Monteaux.*

Big Dutch Baby

Makes 1 to 2 servings

1/4 cup butter
3 eggs

3/4 cup milk
3/4 cup all-purpose flour
Honey, syrup or jam

Preheat oven to 425 degrees. Take a 2 to 3-quart pan with straight sides (a fry pan with iron handle will do). Put butter in pan and place in oven. While butter melts, (don't let it burn) whip three eggs, high speed, for 1 minute in a blender, then slowly add milk, then flour. When butter is melted, add mixture and put back in oven for about 25 minutes, or until brown and puffy on top. Serve with honey, syrup or jam.

Gary Niblett, artist
Represented by Nedra Matteucci Galleries

French Breakfast Puffs

Makes 12 puffs

1/3 cup butter
1/2 cup sugar
1 egg
1 1/2 cups flour
1 1/2 teaspoons baking powder
1/2 teaspoon salt
1/2 teaspoon nutmeg
1/2 cup milk

TOPPING:
1/2 cup sugar
1 teaspoon cinnamon
6 tablespoons melted butter

Preheat oven to 350 degrees. Beat butter and sugar until well mixed. Beat in egg until light and fluffy. Sift dry ingredients: flour, baking powder, salt and nutmeg. To butter mixture, add dry ingredients alternately with milk. Begin and end with dry ingredients. Don't overmix. Fill well-greased muffin tins 2/3 full. Bake for 20 to 25 minutes. Combine sugar and cinnamon for topping. Roll warm muffins in melted butter and then in cinnamon-sugar mixture.

Mushroom Strudel

Makes 24 servings

1 1/4 pounds finely minced
   mushrooms
2 tablespoons shallots, finely
   chopped
1 teaspoon salt
1/4 teaspoon ground pepper
1 tablespoon sherry

4 tablespoons butter or margarine
1 cup sour cream
2 tablespoons bread crumbs
1 pound package phyllo or strudel
   dough
1/2 cup melted butter
3/4 cup bread crumbs

Preheat oven to 375 degrees. Sauté mushrooms, shallots, salt, pepper and sherry in butter until liquid evaporates; about 15 minutes. Set aside until cool. Then add sour cream and 2 tablespoons bread crumbs. Spread out cool damp cloth to work on. Unwrap dough but keep covered. Lay out 1 layer of dough on towel, brush with melted butter and sprinkle with bread crumbs. Repeat 3 times. Spoon 1/4 mushroom mixture about 2 to 3 inches wide at short end. Turn long sides in 1 inch. Roll like jelly roll, starting at short side. Repeat with other 3 sheets. Place on greased baking sheets. Bake for 25 to 30 minutes. Let sit about 5 minutes and slice into 1-inch roundels.

Baked French Toast

Makes 6 servings

1 loaf french bread
6 eggs
1 1/2 cups milk
1/2 cup half-and-half
1 teaspoon vanilla
1/2 teaspoon cinnamon

1/4 teaspoon nutmeg
1/4 cup butter, softened
1/2 cup brown sugar
1/2 cup chopped pecans
1 tablespoon light corn syrup

Preheat oven to 350 degrees. Butter 9 x 13-inch baking dish. Slice bread 1 inch thick. Place in pan, overlapping layers. Combine eggs, milk, half-and-half, vanilla, cinnamon and nutmeg. Pour evenly over bread in pan. Cover and refrigerate several hours or overnight. Liquid should be fully absorbed in bread. Mix softened butter, brown sugar, pecans and corn syrup. Dot butter mixture on top of bread mixture. Bake for 35 to 40 minutes.

Cheese Grits with Green Chiles

Makes 8 to 10 servings

6 cups water

1 1/2 cups quick-cooking grits, uncooked

2 teaspoons salt

1 teaspoon paprika

1 teaspoon ground red pepper

3 large eggs

4 cups (1 pound) shredded sharp cheddar cheese

1 (4 1/2-ounce) can green chiles, chopped and undrained

Red bell pepper curls

Preheat oven to 300 degrees. Bring water to a boil in saucepan: stir in grits and salt. Return mixture to a boil; cover, reduce heat, and simmer, stirring frequently, 10 minutes or until thickened. Stir in paprika and ground red pepper. Beat eggs in a large bowl. Gradually stir about 1/4 of hot grits mixture into eggs; add to remaining hot grits, stirring constantly. Stir in cheese and chiles; pour into a lightly greased 11 x 7 x 1 1/2-inch baking dish. Bake for 45 minutes or until set. Serve immediately, or spoon grits into 10 lightly greased 6-ounce custard cups, and cool. Invert cooled grits onto a greased baking sheet; remove custard cups. Bake for 5 minutes or until thoroughly heated.

Zucchini Blinis

Makes 8 servings

1 1/4 cups grated zucchini

1 small grated onion

2 eggs

1/4 cup flour

1/2 teaspoon salt

Pepper, to taste

Herbs of choice may be added

Mix and fry all ingredients in hot skillet with butter or oil. A quarter cup batter is an ideal size for each blini. Topping suggestions: sour cream, sour cream with caviar, chopped chiles and salsa.

The Puertas at Los Santeros. Photography: Daniel Nadelbach, photographic styling: Gilda Meyer-Niehof.

Breakfast Bread Pudding

Makes 6 servings

6 croissants
6 ounces cream cheese
1/2 cup orange marmalade
5 large eggs
1 cup milk
1/2 cup heavy cream
1 teaspoon vanilla
1/2 teaspoon ground cinnamon
1/2 teaspoon ground nutmeg

ORANGE SYRUP:
1 stick (1/2 cup) butter
1/2 cup orange marmalade
3/4 cup fresh orange juice
1/2 cup light brown sugar

Preheat oven to 350 degrees. Slice croissants in half lengthwise. Butter a 13 x 9 x 2-inch baking dish. Mix cream cheese and marmalade in a small bowl. Spoon a generous tablespoon of mixture in bottom half of croissant, and arrange top piece over filling. Place in prepared pan, overlapping slightly. Whisk together eggs, milk, cream, vanilla and spices until combined well. Pour evenly over bread. Cover bread mixture and chill overnight. Bring bread mixture to room temperature. Bake bread mixture uncovered until puffed and golden, about 45 minutes. Serve hot, sprinkled with powdered sugar and Orange Syrup.

To make Orange Syrup: Melt butter and stir in remaining ingredients.

Tortilla Espanola

Makes 4 servings

3 large boiling potatoes

1 Spanish onion

2 to 3 cloves garlic

2 whole cloves

2 bay leaves

4 tablespoons olive oil, divided

4 to 5 eggs

1 teaspoon salt

2 teaspoons green chile powder, optional

2 teaspoons red chile powder

1 teaspoon pimenton (Spanish paprika)

1/2 teaspoon pepper

2 teaspoons oregano

1/2 teaspoon cumin

Dice potatoes and onion. Place in a microwave-safe loaf pan. Add cloves and bay leaves. Pour 4 tablespoons oil over this and microwave on high for 5 minutes. Stir well and cook 5 more minutes. Stir again and cook 5 more minutes. Remove cloves and bay leaves. Meanwhile, stir together the eggs, not beaten, and remaining ingredients. Pour this over cooked potatoes and mix well. Pour this mixture into a 9-inch frying pan with remaining oil. Turn heat down to low, cover and fry for 9 to 10 minutes, or until browned. Remove lid and place a plate over pan to invert tortilla. Next, slide tortilla back into pan to brown second side. Fry 9 to 10 minutes with lid on. When done, invert tortilla onto a warm serving plate. Allow to set a few minutes before cutting.

Egg and Tortilla Casserole

Makes 12 to 16 servings

6 to 8 corn tortillas

2 tablespoons butter

2 dozen eggs

1 1/2 cups grated cheddar

1/2 cup green onions, chopped

1 to 2 cups sour cream

2 cups green chile salsa

1/2 to 1 cup green chiles, chopped

1/2 cup green chives, chopped

Preheat oven to 325 degrees. Sauté tortillas in butter until limp, then drain and cut into eighths. Scramble eggs with butter until soft, don't overcook. Layer in a 9 x 13-inch casserole dish: eggs, tortillas, cheese, onions, sour cream, salsa and chiles. Repeat layers. Bake covered for 45 minutes. Garnish with chives.

Red Hills with Pedernal, 1936, by Georgia O'Keeffe, oil on canvas, 20 x 30 inches, Museum of Fine Arts, bequest of Helen Miller Jones.

Italian Breakfast Bake

Makes 12 servings

1 long loaf day-old french bread,
    broken into small pieces
6 tablespoons unsalted butter,
    melted
3/4 pound Swiss cheese, shredded
1/2 pound Monterey Jack cheese,
    shredded
9 slices Genoa salami, chopped; or
    smoked salmon, vegetables or
    ham

16 eggs
3 1/4 cups milk
1/2 cup white wine
4 scallions, minced
1 tablespoon spice mustard
1/4 tablespoon fresh ground pepper
1/2 tablespoon cayenne pepper
1 1/2 cups sour cream
1 cup Parmesan cheese,
    freshly grated

Preheat oven to 350 degrees. Butter two 9 x 13-inch baking dishes. Spread bread over bottom and drizzle with butter. Sprinkle with cheeses and meat or vegetables. Beat together eggs, milk, wine, scallions, mustard and peppers. Pour over cheeses. Cover with foil. Refrigerate overnight. Remove from refrigerator 30 minutes before baking. Bake for 1 hour. Uncover and spread with sour cream and sprinkle with Parmesan. Return to oven until lightly brown, about 10 minutes.

Mex Benedict

Makes 1 serving

1 English muffin, split and toasted
2 slices tomato
2 pork sausage patties, grilled
2 poached eggs
4 tablespoons hollandaise sauce

2 tablespoons green salsa
2 tablespoons red salsa
4 servings hash browns, cooked with
    seasoning salt and green onions

Toast English muffin. On each half, place a slice of tomato, a slice of grilled pork sausage and a poached egg. Follow with hollandaise sauce and lace 1 side with green chile salsa and the other side with red chile salsa. Serve with a side of hash browns.

Bagelmania; Santa Fe, New Mexico—Mike Shirley, owner

Hyde Park Eggs

Makes 4 servings

1 (14-ounce) can condensed
  cream of mushroom soup
1/2 cup mayonnaise
1/2 cup milk

1 teaspoon chives, chopped
6 eggs, hard boiled
8 slices crisply cooked bacon,
  crumbled

Preheat oven to 350 degrees. Blend soup with mayonnaise and gradually add milk until well blended. Stir in chives. Slice eggs and layer with the mayo mixture in a 1-quart baking dish. Sprinkle bacon around edge of dish. Bake until bubbly, about 20 minutes.

K. C. Waffle House before it was Pasqual's, Santa Fe, New Mexico, ca. 1935. Photograph by T. Harmon Parkhurst, courtesy of the Palace of the Governors Photo Archives. Negative 50967.

Santa Fe Eggs

Makes 6 to 8 servings

1 pound sausage

1/4 pound mushrooms, chopped

1 medium onion, diced

6 to 8 eggs

3 tablespoons sour cream

5 ounces salsa

8 ounces cheddar, grated

8 ounces mozzarella, grated

8 ounces Velveeta, grated or cubed

Preheat oven to 400 degrees. Sauté sausage, mushrooms and onion. Drain on paper towel. Set aside. Combine eggs and sour cream in a blender and whip for 1 minute. Grease a 9 x 13-inch pan. Add blended eggs to the pan. Place eggs in preheated oven until eggs set, about 5 minutes. Watch carefully, as eggs set quickly. Remove dish from oven, and reduce oven to 350 degrees. Spoon salsa over eggs; then spread sausage mixture on top. Top with 3 layers of cheese. Bake at 350 degrees for 30 minutes, until cheese is melted and bubbly.

Cazuelitas

Makes 6 servings

4 eggs

1 1/2 cups thick cream

1/2 teaspoon salt

1 1/2 cups queso fresco, or Oaxacan cheese

2 large chile poblanos, roasted, seeded and diced

Preheat oven to 350 degrees. In a mixing bowl, beat eggs, cream and salt. Divide cheese evenly among 6 cazuelitas (ramekin soufflé cups). Top with chiles and fill with egg mixture. Place cazuelitas in a large, shallow pan filled halfway with hot water and bake for 45 minutes or until set, to create custard texture.

Los Poblanos Inn; Albuquerque, New Mexico—Penny and Armin Rembe, proprietors

Home of Sol and Marsha Wiener. Interior design by Robert L. Bowley. Photography: Daniel Nadelbach, photographic styling: Gilda Meyer-Niehof.

Canyon Road Breakfast

Makes 6 to 8 servings

1/4 cup butter
1/4 cup flour
1 cup cream
1 cup milk
1/4 teaspoon thyme
1/4 teaspoon marjoram
1/4 teaspoon basil

3/4 pound grated sharp
    cheddar cheese
1 dozen eggs, hard boiled, thinly
    sliced
1 pound bacon, cooked,
    drained and crumbled
1/4 cup parsley, finely chopped
1/4 cup buttered bread crumbs

Preheat oven to 350 degrees. Melt butter and add flour, cream and milk. Add herbs and cheese until melted in sauce. Place layer of sliced eggs in a 9 x 12-inch casserole dish; sprinkle bacon on eggs; sprinkle parsley over bacon. Add layer of cheese sauce. Repeat 2 more layers. Sprinkle top with buttered bread crumbs. Bake uncovered for 30 minutes.

Belgian Endive with Ham and Cheese

Makes 6 servings

12 leaves endive
12 slices broiled ham

SAUCE:
1 3/4 tablespoons butter
1 1/2 teaspoons flour
1 pint milk
1 3/4 cups aged cheddar, grated
Pepper, to taste
1/4 cup grated Parmesan

Preheat oven to 350 degrees. Remove bitter end of endive and cook in salted water until soft, about 15 minutes. Butter a casserole dish. Drain and arrange endive in dish after wrapping each in 1 slice of ham. Make cheese sauce: melt butter and add flour, stirring until bubbly. Add milk slowly and return to boiling. Remove from heat and mix in cheese. Add pepper, to taste. Sprinkle with Parmesan and bake about 20 minutes, until brown on top.

Green Chile Quiche

Makes 6 to 8 servings

1 (10-inch) pie shell
1 1/2 cups shredded sharp cheddar
1 1/2 cups shredded Monterey Jack
1 (4-ounce) can green chile, chopped
1 cup half-and-half

3 eggs, beaten
Dash of salt, to taste
1 teaspoon Santa Fe Seasons six
  seasonings (Whole Foods or
  Wild Oats)

Preheat oven to 325 degrees. Partially bake pie shell for 15 minutes. You may use a prepared or frozen pie shell. Sprinkle cheeses over bottom of pie shell. Distribute green chile over cheese. Beat half-and-half with eggs, salt and seasoning until well blended. Bake in oven for 45 minutes, or longer, until quiche is set. Insert toothpick to check. Let stand 15 minutes before cutting. May serve warm or cold. Slice into 1 to 1 1/2-inch slices as quiche is rich.

Egg Curry

Makes 5 to 6 servings

8 to 10 eggs, hard boiled
1/2 cup sliced scallions
1 to 2 cloves garlic
2 to 3 tablespoons butter
1/4 cup flour

1/2 cup chicken broth
1 1/2 cups coconut milk
2 tablespoons curry powder
1/2 teaspoon ginger
Salt and pepper, to taste

Boil eggs and leave in pan while preparing sauce. Sauté scallions and garlic in butter. Blend in flour and slowly add chicken broth. Cook until sauce begins to thicken. Add coconut milk and seasonings. Shell and halve eggs and add to curry sauce.

Three Musicians of the Baile, *ca. 1920–21 by Bert Geer Phillips, oil on canvas, Museum of Fine Arts, gift of Governor and Mrs. Arthur Seligman. Photo: Blair Clark.*

Hot Chicken Salad

Makes 6 to 8 servings

SALAD:

3 to 4 cups cooked chicken, diced
2 tablespoons lemon juice
1 cup celery, diced
1 cup mayonnaise
1 cup water chestnuts, sliced
1/2 cup onion, chopped
1/2 cup slivered almonds, toasted
2 cups cheddar, shredded
2 cups potato chips

DRESSING:

1 egg
1 tablespoon orange rind
2 tablespoons orange juice
1/2 cup sugar
2 teaspoons lemon rind
2 tablespoons lemon juice
1 cup whipping cream

Preheat oven to 350 degrees. Combine salad ingredients, except almonds, cheddar and potato chips. For dressing, cook first 6 ingredients over low heat until thickened, cool thoroughly. Then fold in whipping cream. Then lightly fold dressing in salad and place mixture in an 8 1/2 x 11 1/2-inch casserole dish and top with toasted almonds, 2 cups shredded sharp cheddar cheese, and 2 cups coarsely crushed potato chips. Bake for 30 minutes, until heated through and golden brown.

Chile Relleno Casserole

Makes 6 servings

2 pounds Monterey Jack and
    cheddar, grated
2 (7-ounce) cans whole green chiles,
    cut into strips
4 tablespoons flour

10 ounces milk
    (5 ounces evaporated + 5 ounces
    regular)
Salt and pepper, to taste
5 eggs, beaten
1/2 teaspoon oregano, optional

Preheat oven to 350 degrees. Spread half of grated cheese in greased 2-quart casserole dish. Lay chile strips over cheese. Top with remaining cheese. Blend flour, milk, salt, pepper and eggs together. Pour over cheese and chile. Bake for 45 minutes.

Caramelized Onion, Fig and Goat Cheese Tart

Makes 6 to 8 servings

2 medium onions, sliced
2 teaspoons olive oil
Salt and pepper, to taste
2 teaspoons herbs de Provence
1 package commercial frozen puff
    pastry, using 1 sheet

3/4 cup caramelized fresh
    figs or fig jam
3/4 cup fresh goat cheese, crumbled

Preheat oven to 350 degrees. Sauté onions slowly in olive oil, stirring frequently, until they are soft and brown. Add salt, pepper and herbs de Provence. Set aside. Roll out the puff pastry according to package directions. It helps to flour both sides. Place pastry on baking parchment on a baking sheet. Crimp edges. Keep in the refrigerator until you are ready to assemble the tart. Spread caramelized onion on pastry. Add dollops of fig jam or caramelized fresh figs evenly on top of onions. Add bits of fresh goat cheese evenly on top as well. Bake until pastry is puffed, crisp and browning, about 20 minutes.

Ham and Egg Soufflé

Makes 6 servings

8 slices white bread
1 cup Gouda, diced
1/4 cup melted butter
8 eggs
3/4 teaspoon dry mustard
2 cups milk

1/2 cup julienned
    sun-dried tomatoes, drained
1/3 cup snipped chives
2 cups ham or cooked spicy
    sausage, diced
1/2 teaspoon each, salt and pepper
1 cup grated cheddar

Preheat oven to 350 degrees. Trim off crust from bread slices and tear bread into 1-inch squares. Butter 9 x 12-inch baking dish. Then alternate bread and Gouda. Pour melted butter over top. Beat eggs well. Stir in mustard, milk, tomatoes, chives, meat, salt and pepper. Pour mixture in casserole dish. Cover and refrigerate for at least 4 hours, or overnight. Take casserole from refrigerator, sprinkle top with cheddar. Cover again and bake 30 minutes. Uncover and bake 20 minutes, or until puffed and golden brown.

Soups, Stews and Chilies

The Rabbit Hunter, *by Oscar Berninghaus, oil on canvas, 34 1/2 x 39 1/3 inches,*
Museum of Fine Arts.

Gazpacho

Makes 8 to 10 servings

6 large fresh tomatoes, peeled and
    chopped
1 onion chopped
1 or 2 bell peppers, chopped
1 bunch green onions, chopped
2 cucumbers, chopped
1 or 2 jalapenos, chopped
2 stalks celery, chopped
2 tablespoons concentrated beef
    broth
2 tablespoons olive oil
1/3 cup good balsamic vinegar

1 (28-ounce) can
    tomato juice
1/2 lemon, juiced
2 cloves garlic, minced
1 tablespoon sugar
1/4 cup chopped cilantro
    (or less, to taste)
10 to 15 basil leaves, chopped
1 tablespoon ground cumin
2 tablespoons Worcestershire sauce
Tabasco sauce, to taste
Salt and pepper

Mix all ingredients together in a large bowl. Serve cold with bowls of extra chopped tomatoes, croutons and diced avocado. Best if served the same day. Does not freeze well.

Think Spring Barley Soup

Makes 8 servings

3 cups chicken broth
3/4 cup medium pearl barley
1 1/2 cups minced sweet onion
1 cup minced carrot
1 cup white mushrooms, thinly sliced
1/2 cup diced celery

3 tablespoons butter
8 cups chicken broth
Salt and pepper, to taste
Light sour cream
1/4 cup pine nuts, toasted
Minced parsley

Combine chicken broth and barley in a large saucepan; bring to boil over medium heat and let simmer for 1 hour, or until all liquid is absorbed. In a soup kettle, sauté the onions, carrots, mushrooms and celery in butter until vegetables are softened, about 5 minutes. Add 8 cups of chicken broth and simmer for 30 minutes. Add the cooked barley and simmer for an additional 5 minutes. Add salt and pepper, to taste. Ladle into heated bowls; garnish with a dollop of light sour cream, toasted pine nuts and minced parsley.

Buttermilk-Yogurt Soup

Makes 4 servings

1 1/2 cups buttermilk
3/4 cup yogurt
1 (8-ounce) can whole red beets
1 large orange
2 hot-house cucumbers

1/2 cup fresh chives, reserve 4 whole
    pieces for garnish
1/4 cup fresh watercress; reserve
    some whole leaves for garnish
1/2 teaspoon pepper
1/4 teaspoon fine sea salt

In a medium-size glass bowl, strain buttermilk and add yogurt. Whisk together. Puree beets and their liquid in a blender. Add to buttermilk mixture. Cut orange in half, and then cut 2 thin slices from center; set them aside for garnish. Grate the orange peel and juice the orange. Add to above. Peel and seed cucumbers, and finely grate. Drain excess liquid. Cut chives into 1/4-inch pieces. Chop watercress. Add to above. Add pepper and salt. Mix well with rubber spatula. Serve chilled. Garnish with 1/2 slice of orange, watercress leaves and chives.

Cuisine Justine; Santa Fe, New Mexico—Justine Witlox-Becker

Andalusia Cold Soup

Makes 4 servings

1 quart tomato juice or stewed
    tomato pulp
1 tablespoon Worcestershire sauce
Juice of 1 lemon and 1 lime
2 tablespoons olive oil
Tabasco sauce, several dashes, or
    minced mild to medium green
    chile

2 extra-large hard-boiled eggs
1 medium cucumber, finely minced
1 shallot, very finely chopped
2 teaspoons dry mustard
1 lime, thinly sliced
1 clove garlic, well crushed
1 green pepper, finely chopped
Salt and pepper, to taste

Mix together all liquid ingredients. Then stir in rest of ingredients and chill. Serve garnished with small croutons.

Cold White Gazpacho

Makes 6 servings

3 cucumbers
3 cloves garlic
3 cups chicken broth

3 cups fat-free or regular sour cream
2 to 3 tablespoons white vinegar
Salt and pepper, to taste

Peel and core cucumbers, add cloves of garlic and puree in a blender. Then add chicken broth and sour cream. Add 2 to 3 tablespoons of white vinegar, plus salt and pepper, to taste. Chill. Serve with toasted sliced almonds, chopped chives or green onions.

Farmers Market Organic Vegetable Stew

Makes 8 to 10 servings

3 cubes beef bouillon

5 cups water

2 medium Yukon gold potatoes, peeled and cut into 1-inch pieces

3 Roma tomatoes, chopped

2 stalks celery, chopped

1 green sweet pepper, chopped

1 onion, chopped

2 cups shredded cabbage

4 ounces fresh green beans, trimmed and cut in half

1 small zucchini, chopped

1 (15-ounce) can red or black beans, rinsed and drained

8 to 10 fresh oregano sprigs, tied in a bunch

1/4 cup ketchup

1/4 teaspoon freshly ground black pepper

Dash or more bottled hot pepper sauce

Ground salt and pepper, to taste

In a Dutch oven, combine bouillon cubes and water; bring to a boil. Add potatoes, tomatoes, celery, green pepper and onion. Bring to a boil; reduce heat. Simmer uncovered 15 to 20 minutes. Add remaining ingredients, simmer uncovered 15 to 30 minutes, or until vegetables are tender. Remove and discard oregano, and season to taste with salt and pepper.

Mushroom Bisque

Makes 10 to 12 servings

1 (4-ounce) stick sweet butter

1 large onion, finely chopped

2 pounds mushrooms, finely chopped

Juice of 1 lemon

1/2 cup flour

2 quarts chicken stock

1/8 teaspoon cayenne pepper

1 tablespoon salt

3/4 tablespoon ground pepper

2 1/2 cups heavy cream

1 cup milk

1 cup dry sherry

1/2 cup finely chopped fresh chives

In a large skillet, melt butter and sauté onion, stirring constantly, 2 to 3 minutes. Add mushrooms and sauté for 4 minutes, stirring often. Reduce flame to medium low, add lemon juice, and stir. Cover and simmer for 2 minutes. Uncover and slowly add flour, stirring until completely blended. Still stirring, add chicken stock, cayenne, salt and pepper. Cover and simmer for 20 minutes. Remove from stove and puree in a food processor. In a large saucepan on low, slowly heat the cream and milk. Do not boil; stirring constantly. Slowly add the pureed mushroom mixture. When mixture is thoroughly blended, add sherry, stirring constantly. Cover and simmer on low for 4 minutes. Pour bisque into a heated tureen or individual bowls and garnish with chives.

Cauliflower Soup with Coriander

Makes 4 to 6 servings

3 tablespoons vegetable oil

2 onions, chopped

1 inch gingerroot, peeled, sliced into
thin strips

4 cloves garlic, chopped

1 teaspoon ground cumin

2 teaspoons ground coriander

1/4 teaspoon turmeric

1/8 teaspoon cayenne pepper, or to
taste

2 potatoes

2 heaping cups small
cauliflower florets

7 cups chicken broth

Salt, to taste

1 cup heavy cream

In a large, heavy saucepan, heat oil over moderate high heat until hot but not smoking. Add onions, gingerroot and garlic, and stir fry until onions are golden brown. Add cumin, coriander, turmeric and cayenne, stirring for 1 minute. Peel potatoes and cut into 1/2-inch cubes. Add potatoes, cauliflower, broth and salt, and stir into onion mix. Simmer until potatoes are tender, about 10 to 15 minutes. In a blender, puree soup in batches until smooth. Stir in cream and reheat soup over moderate heat.

Mimbres Pots, from the Collection of the Museum of Indian Arts and Culture/Laboratory of Anthropology.

Guinness Steak Chili

Makes 1 1/4 gallons

5 pounds cubed sirloin

Canola oil

4 cups diced onion

6 cloves garlic, crushed

6 tablespoons ancho chile powder

6 tablespoons chile powder

2 tablespoons ground cumin

5 tablespoons salt

4 bay leaves

1 pint Guinness Stout Beer

6 cups tomato puree

4 pounds canned pinto beans

8 cups beef stock, unsalted

Brown meat in oil. When most of liquid has evaporated, add onions and garlic cloves, until soft. Add dry spices and sauté for a few minutes. Deglaze with Guinness and add tomato puree, pinto beans and stock. Simmer for an hour or more, until meat is tender and sauce is thick.

Rooney's Tavern, Santa Fe, New Mexico—Jack Shaab, proprietor; Malik Hammond, chef

Sweet Potato and Pinto Bean Chile

Makes 6 servings

2 tablespoons vegetable oil

2 medium onions, chopped

1 to 2 tablespoons Chimayo red chile powder, medium to hot

1 teaspoon ground cumin

1 cup vegetable broth

2 medium sweet potatoes, peeled and cubed

1 (28-ounce) can diced tomatoes, undrained

2 (19-ounce) cans pinto beans, drained

1 teaspoon salt

1 teaspoon dried oregano

1/4 teaspoon cayenne pepper

1/2 teaspoon fresh cilantro, chopped

Heat vegetable oil in a large saucepan or Dutch oven. Add onions and cook, stirring over medium heat until onions are soft, about 5 minutes. Add chile powder and cumin and cook for another minute or so. Add vegetable broth and cubed sweet potatoes. Reduce heat to low and cook, covered, until potatoes are almost tender, about 10 minutes. Add tomatoes and their juice, beans, salt, oregano and cayenne pepper. Bring to a boil over medium heat, then let simmer until potatoes are tender, about 20 minutes. Remove from heat and stir in cilantro. Serve with corn bread.

Olive Soup

Makes 6 servings

2 cups green olives, soaked in water
    and drained, then sliced
1 small yellow onion, finely chopped
2 cloves garlic, minced
5 tablespoons olive oil, divided
4 cups chicken broth

4 tablespoons flour
1/2 cup heavy cream or 1 cup
    half-and-half
1/3 cup dry sherry
Tabasco, to taste

Sauté olives, onion and garlic in 2 tablespoons olive oil. Puree in a food processor with 1 cup chicken broth. Place in a large saucepan and add 3 more cups chicken broth. Stir in roux of 3 tablespoons olive oil and 4 tablespoons flour, to thicken. Let rest for 30 minutes, if possible. Add cream or half-and-half and heat. At the last minute, add sherry, and Tabasco, to taste.

Chilled Cantaloupe Soup

Makes 4 servings

1 large cantaloupe
Juice of 1 lime
2 tablespoons orange juice
1/2 cup sour cream

1/2 cup whipping cream
4 to 6 tablespoons honey
1/2 cup dry white wine, reduced to
    1/4 cup by boiling, then chill

Peel, seed, and coarsely chop the melon. Add remaining ingredients; put the whole thing in a food processor and puree. Taste for sweetness; add more honey, if needed, or if it's too sweet, add more lime juice. Chill and garnish with thin slices of lime when serving.

Corn Chowder

Makes 8 servings

4 cups corn
1/2 cup celery, diced
1 onion, diced
4 cloves garlic, chopped
3 poblano chiles, roasted and peeled

1/4 pound melted butter
1/4 cup all-purpose flour
1 quart vegetable stock
2 cups heavy cream
Salt and pepper, to taste

In a large saucepan, combine and sauté first 6 ingredients. Add flour and stir in. Then add vegetable stock, cream, and salt and pepper, to taste. Let simmer until soup is slightly thickened.

Las Campanas Country Club—Jeff Moses, executive chef

Navajo Serape, ca. 1875–1880. Made from handspun and commercial wool yarns. Museum of Indian Arts and Culture. Photo: Blair Clark.

Speedy Chicken Chile Soup

Makes 6 servings

2 whole large chicken breasts, skinned and boned

2 ears corn or 1 (15-ounce) can whole-kernel corn, drained

2 cups water

1 (14-ounce) can beef broth

1 (14-ounce) can chicken broth

1 (14 1/2-ounce) can tomatoes, chopped, undrained

1/2 cup onion, chopped

1 green pepper, chopped

2 chiles, roasted, peeled and sliced or 1 small can chopped green chile

1/2 teaspoon ground cumin

1/8 teaspoon black pepper

3 cups tortilla chips, coarsely crushed

1 cup grated cheese

1 avocado, diced

Cilantro, snipped

Lime wedges

Cut chicken into small cubes, set aside. Cut corn off the cob. In a large saucepan, combine water, broths, undrained tomatoes, onion and green pepper. Bring to a boil. Add chicken, reduce heat, cover and simmer for 10 minutes. Add corn, chile, cumin and pepper; simmer, covered, for 10 minutes. To serve, place crushed chips in bowls, ladle soup over chips. Sprinkle with cheese, avocado, cilantro and garnish with lime wedges.

Potato Green Chile Soup

Makes 6 servings

2 to 3 tablespoons vegetable oil

1 small onion, chopped

1 to 2 cloves garlic, chopped

1/2 teaspoon cumin

1/4 teaspoon pepper

Pinch oregano

3 medium potatoes, peeled and cut into small chunks

8 whole green chiles, chopped

5 cups chicken broth

Sour cream

Monterey Jack cheese

Heat oil in a 2-quart saucepan, add onion and garlic and cook over low heat, covered, for about 5 minutes. Uncover pan, raise heat and stir in cumin and pepper. Stir 2 to 3 minutes until onions show signs of browning. Add oregano, potatoes, green chiles and chicken broth. Bring to a boil and cook for 45 minutes to 1 hour. Serve with a dollop of sour cream and shredded Monterey Jack cheese.

Potato Poblano Chile Cream Soup

Makes 8 servings

6 medium red-skinned potatoes
1 white onion
6 ounces whole garlic
6 fresh poblano chiles

4 cups milk
4 cups heavy cream
4 tablespoons chicken base
1 bunch green onions
Pinch black pepper

Peel and cut potatoes into quarters. Peel and cut onion into quarters. Peel and slice garlic. Boil potatoes, onions and garlic together until potatoes are soft. While potatoes are boiling, grill or roast poblano chiles until soft. Wash and peel chiles and remove seeds. When potatoes, onions and garlic are cooked, drain water and add to a blender, and include the poblano chiles and milk, then puree. In a large soup stock pot, begin heating, at low, the heavy cream and chicken base. Chop the green onions including the green stems. Add all ingredients into the pot and bring to a boil over low heat. Add black pepper, to taste.

Mucho Gusto Authentic Mexican Food—Alex Castro, owner and chef

Fiesta Taco Soup

Makes 8 servings

1 pound ground meat
1 medium onion, chopped
1 (14 1/2-ounce) can hominy, with juice
1 (14 1/2-ounce) can corn, with juice
1 (14 1/2-ounce) can pinto beans
1 (14 1/2-ounce) can beef broth

1 (14 1/2-ounce) can Rotel tomatoes
1 (2 1/2-ounce) packet taco seasoning
Grated cheese
Cilantro
Sour cream
Avocados

Brown meat and onion together, drain liquid, and add the rest of ingredients. Simmer for 30 minutes. Serve with grated cheese, cilantro, and sour cream or avocados, thinly sliced.

Santa Fe Mountains
in October, *by Sheldon
Parsons, oil on plywood
panel, Museum of
Fine Arts.*

Cioppino

Makes 8 to 12 servings

2 onions, chopped

Crushed red pepper, to taste

2 stalks celery, chopped

5 cloves garlic, chopped

1 cup fresh parsley

3/4 cup extra-virgin olive oil

1 (46-ounce) can V-8 Juice

1 1/2 cups dry white wine

1 1/2 cups red wine

1 (8-ounce) bottle clam juice

1 (6-ounce) can
   tomato paste

4 large tomatoes, peeled and
   chopped

1 tablespoon Italian seasoning

1 teaspoon oregano

1 teaspoon thyme

4 bay leaves

Salt and pepper, to taste

1 pound firm white fish (cod or
   orange roughy), cut in pieces

1 pound shrimp, cleaned and shelled

2 pounds mussels and clams, cooked
   first and added at very end

1/2 pound scallops, small size

Make broth a day in advance. It can also be frozen. Sauté onions, red pepper, celery, garlic and parsley in olive oil until limp. Add rest of ingredients and blend well, bring to a simmer and cook uncovered for 30 minutes. Stir frequently, drain off extra olive oil. Shortly before serving, add the fish, or shellfish, or combination of all to the broth and cook for 5 minutes. Serve in large soup bowls.

Wild Rice Soup

Makes 4 to 5 servings

2 to 3 strips bacon, diced

1/2 cup onion, diced

1/2 cup celery, sliced

1/2 cup carrots, sliced

4 ounces wild rice, uncooked

4 1/2 cups chicken stock, divided

1 cup heavy cream

1 tablespoon butter

1 tablespoon flour

Sauté bacon in heavy saucepan or Dutch oven for approximately 3 minutes. Add vegetables and rice, and sauté until vegetables are tender-crisp, about 5 minutes. Stir in 4 cups of chicken stock and heat until boiling. Reduce heat and simmer, covered, approximately 1 hour, until rice is tender but not mushy. Rice should be splitting open but still maintain a bit of crunch. Stir in cream. Mix butter and flour well in a small bowl, whisk in 1/2 cup of the soup liquid until smooth, then add to the soup. If a thinner broth is desired, add an additional 1/2 cup of chicken broth. Season with salt and pepper, to taste.

Ski Time Cabbage Soup

Makes 4 quarts

2 pounds cabbage

1 large onion

1 pound lean pork roast or shoulder

1 (15-ounce) can sauerkraut

2 potatoes, white or red, with skins

2 carrots

3 quarts water or 12 cups vegetable
   or chicken broth

Salt and pepper

Coarsely chop cabbage, onion and pork and place in soup pot. Cover with water or broth. Simmer until pork is tender, about 2 hours. Cut or pull pork into bite-size pieces and return to pot. Add potatoes, diced with skins, and thinly sliced carrots. Simmer until potatoes are tender. Add sauerkraut. Season to taste with salt and pepper.

Taos Turkey Lentil Soup

Makes 12 servings

1 pound lentils

2 cloves garlic, minced

2 cups onion, finely chopped

3 1/2 quarts cold water or chicken
   broth

1 pound ground turkey, chicken or
   pork

2 ounces butter

2 teaspoons salt

1 tablespoon dill seed

1 teaspoon black pepper

2 cups homemade tomato sauce, or
   high-quality commercial tomato
   sauce

6 ounces spaghetti, broken and
   cooked

Place lentils, garlic and onion in a soup pot. Add cold water or chicken broth, cover and simmer for 2 hours. Sauté meat in butter for 10 minutes. After 2 hours of simmering, add meat, salt, dill, pepper and tomato sauce. Cook for 1 more hour. Add cooked spaghetti and serve.

Back Street Bistro—David Jacoby, proprietor and chef

Tortilla Soup

Makes 4 to 6 servings

8 cups chicken stock

1 (14 1/2-ounce) can whole peeled
    tomatoes

1 clove garlic, chopped

1 habanero pepper, seeded

Salt and pepper, to taste

1 dozen corn tortillas

1/4 cup olive oil

2 avocados

2 chicken breasts

12 shrimp, peeled and deveined,
    optional

3 red bell peppers, roasted

3 poblano peppers, roasted

1 cup caramelized onion

1 bunch cilantro, for garnish

2 limes, quartered

Bring chicken stock, whole peeled tomatoes, garlic and 1/4 of the habanero pepper to boil, simmer for 15 minutes. Puree and strain. Season with salt and pepper, to taste. This is the soup base. Cut tortillas into thin strips. Heat oil in sauté pan, cook strips until crispy; pull out of pan with tongs. Set strips on paper towels to remove excess oil. Cut avocados in half, remove pits, and cut in slices. In a sauté pan, with 1 tablespoon oil, sauté chicken, add shrimp, roasted red peppers, poblano peppers and caramelized onion. Once shrimp is fully cooked, remove ingredients from pan and place in center of soup bowl. Pour in soup base. Garnish with sliced avocado, tortilla strips, cilantro, and lime wedge.

Pueblo Green Chile Stew

Makes 4 servings

2 pounds boneless pork, cut
    into 1-inch cubes

3 tablespoons all-purpose flour

2 tablespoons butter, lard or bacon
    drippings

1 cup onion, chopped

2 cloves garlic, minced

6 tomatoes

1 teaspoon salt

1/2 teaspoon ground Mexican
    oregano

1/4 teaspoon ground cumin

20 fresh green chiles, roasted,
    peeled and chopped

Lightly coat pork cubes with flour. Melt butter in a large, heavy skillet or saucepan. Add pork cubes a few at a time, stirring to brown well. Push to the side of the pot. Add onion and garlic; cook until onion is soft. Stir in the browned meat. Add tomatoes, then salt, oregano and cumin. Cover and simmer 1 hour, stirring occasionally and adding water as needed. Add green chiles; simmer 30 minutes or longer, adding a little more water, if necessary, until flavors are well blended. Taste and adjust seasonings.

Jane Butel's Southwestern Kitchen—Jane Butel, proprietor, chef, author

New Mexico Senator Joe Montoya won the Capitol Chile Cook-off several times with this chile recipe!

The Last Supper, *by Domingas Goncalves*
Lima, called "Misterio" Barcelos. Braga, Portugal.
Painted earthenware, 11 inches high. ca. 1960.
Girard Collection. Museum of International Folk
Art. Photo by: Michel Monteau.

Buffalo Green Chili Stew

Makes 10 to 12 servings

2 pounds lean pork, cubed

1 pound ground buffalo, may substitute 1 pound ground beef

1 1/2 pounds red potatoes

1 pound green chiles, roasted, peeled and chopped

4 cloves garlic, minced

1/3 cup pork base or beef base

1/4 cup flour mixed in 1 cup cold water

1 gallon water

2 teaspoons salt and pepper (or to taste)

Brown meat in Dutch oven or heavy 2-gallon pot. When meat has browned, add water and scrape pan bottom to loosen tasty caramelized bits. Add remaining ingredients except flour, water, and salt and pepper. Cover and simmer until potatoes are soft. Mix flour and water together and add to mixture. Then add salt and pepper, simmer for 10 minutes, and serve with flour tortillas.

The Shed, Santa Fe, New Mexico—The Carswell Family, proprietors; Josh Carswell, chef

Red Chili Stew

Makes 8 servings

4 pounds ground beef

1 large onion, chopped

1 green pepper, chopped

1 (6-ounce) can tomato paste

1 (15-ounce) can stewed tomatoes

2 (8-ounce) cans tomato sauce

1 clove garlic, chopped

4 ounces green chile, chopped

8 ounces salsa

3 tablespoons pure red chile powder

1 tablespoon salt

Garlic salt, to taste

Cook ground beef and drain. Add remaining ingredients, cover and simmer for at least an hour to blend flavors. The amount of red chile powder can be adjusted according to how spicy you want the stew.

East-side Santa Fe home on East Place Avenue. Photography: Daniel Nadelbach, photographic styling: Gilda Meyer-Niehof.

Red Chile Posole

Makes 6 servings

1 pound frozen posole
1 onion, chopped
2 pounds boneless pork roast, cubed
1 clove garlic, minced
1 cup Red Chile Sauce
1/2 teaspoon oregano
Salt and pepper, to taste

RED CHILE SAUCE:
2 tablespoons lard
2 tablespoons flour
1/4 cup red chile powder
2 cups cold water
3/4 teaspoon salt
1/2 teaspoon garlic salt
Oregano, optional

Rinse posole several times to wash off lime. Place onion in large Crock-Pot. Fill Crock-Pot with water, leaving enough room to add posole. Cook over medium heat for 30 minutes, and then add posole and cubed pork. Cook posole and cubed pork in water on high heat in Crock-Pot for several hours until posole has blossomed and until pork begins to fall apart and is tender. Add water as necessary to keep from scorching. Add Red Chile Sauce, oregano, salt and pepper. Cook for another 10 to 15 minutes. Serve garnished with chopped green onions, chopped cilantro and quartered limes. May be served with fresh tortillas or corn bread.

RED CHILE SAUCE:
Heat lard in medium saucepan on medium heat. Stir in flour and cook until golden brown. Add chile powder and cook for an additional minute. Gradually add water and stir constantly, making sure no lumps form. Add seasonings to sauce and simmer at low heat for 10 to 15 minutes.

Governor Bill Richardson, Santa Fe, New Mexico

Roasted Squash Soup with Apple Brie

Makes 8 servings

1 large butternut squash
1 carrot
1 medium onion
1 leek, white part only
2 tablespoons butter
8 cups chicken stock

1 apple, peeled and chopped
1 bay leaf
1 teaspoon sugar
Salt and pepper
8 ounces Brie
Chives, snipped

Preheat oven to 350 degrees. Cut squash lengthwise and remove seeds. Place cut side down on pan and bake until tender, about 45 minutes. Chop carrot, onion and leek into 1-inch pieces and place in a large pot. Gently sauté in butter. Do not brown. Scrape flesh from cooked squash and add to vegetables. Add stock and bring to a boil. Add apple, bay leaf and sugar to mixture. Simmer uncovered for 40 to 45 minutes. Remove bay leaf and puree soup in batches. Season with salt and pepper. Slice off outer skin of Brie and cut in 1/2-inch pieces. Place cheese in bottom of bowl and fill with hot soup. Garnish with chives.

Superbowl Chili

2 tablespoons olive oil

3 pounds ground chuck

1 pound Italian sausages, Hot Johnsonville brand, simmer 5 minutes, then remove from casing and break up with fork

3 medium onions, chopped

1 large green pepper, chopped

2 tablespoons minced garlic

1 large jalapeno chile, seeded and chopped, or small can chopped green chiles

1/3 cup chile powder, Tex-Mex type

1 (28-ounce) can Italian plum tomatoes, chopped, with liquid

1 (14 1/2-ounce) can Mexican-style stewed tomatoes

1/2 cup tomato sauce or half 6-ounce can tomato paste

1 (12-ounce) can beef stock

1 tablespoon kosher salt

2 teaspoons freshly ground pepper

1 teaspoon cayenne pepper

1/3 cup cumin seeds

1/2 teaspoon cumin

1/4 teaspoon hot sauce, Jardine's Texas Champagne Pepper Sauce or Tabasco

3 tablespoons red wine vinegar

2 teaspoons paprika

1 tablespoon dried oregano

1 small bay leaf

1 (12-ounce) can beer

1/3 cup light brown sugar

1 or 2 (15 1/2 -ounce) cans S & W kidney beans, drained

1 or 2 (15 1/2-ounce) cans S & W kidney beans, in zesty sauce, not drained, or 3 (15 1/2-ounce) cans ranch-style pinto beans

Garnishes: cheddar or Monterey Jack cheeses, sour cream, chopped white onion, chopped green pepper, cubed or sliced avocado, chopped cilantro or fresh salsa.

Heat oil in a large skillet. Add beef and sausage and stir until lightly browned, about 10 minutes. Drain and reserve 3 tablespoons fat. Set aside. Return reserved fat to skillet, add onions and green peppers and cook over medium heat until lightly browned. Add garlic and cook 1 minute. In a large casserole dish, or stock pot, combine beef, sausage, onions and garlic. Add chile, chile powder, tomatoes with liquid, tomato sauce or paste, stock, salt, pepper, cayenne, cumin, hot sauce, vinegar, paprika, oregano, bay leaf and beer, and simmer for 35 minutes, stirring frequently. Add brown sugar and beans and cook another 10 minutes. Remove bay leaf. Remove from heat and cool. Refrigerate overnight. Reheat and serve with shredded white cheddar or Monterey Jack, sour cream, chopped white onion, chopped green pepper, chopped avocado, fresh salsa with cilantro, and your favorite corn bread. Freezes well.

Salads

Valario, *by James Stovall Morris, oil on canvas board panel, 18 x 24 inches,*
Museum of Fine Arts.

Fruit Salad with Honey Ricotta Dressing

Makes 6 servings

DRESSING (MAKES
  1 CUP):

4 ounces Ricotta, well drained

1 tablespoon honey

1/3 cup freshly squeezed orange juice

1/2 teaspoon freshly grated orange
  zest

1/2 tablespoon chopped fresh mint

1 tablespoon Gran Marnier (optional)

SALAD:

1/2 pineapple

1 pint strawberries

2 kiwifruits

1 small bunch red grapes

1 medium apple or pear

Juice of 1/2 lemon

Confectioners' sugar, for garnish

Place Ricotta, honey and orange juice in a blender. Puree until light and smooth, about 2 to 3 minutes. Add orange zest and mint, and puree briefly. Transfer dressing to a bowl and stir in Gran Marnier, if desired. Set aside and refrigerate.

Peel, slice and cut fruits, as desired. Brush apple and pear with lemon juice to keep from discoloring. This salad may be served in several ways: one way is to toss all bite-size pieces of fruit with dressing and serve in a martini or stemmed glass, or another way is to layer fruits in a clear glass bowl or parfait glasses, alternating layers of fruits with dressing. Top final layer with a sprinkling of powdered sugar and a dollop of remaining dressing. A third way to serve salad is to arrange fruit on a platter, either in slices or whole, and serve dressing on the side. A final dusting of confectioners' sugar enhances the sweetness of fruit.

The Cheese Lover's Cookbook and Guide *by Paula Lambert,*
© 2000, *all rights reserved.*

Red Pepper and Black Bean Salad

Makes 4 to 6 servings

2 large red peppers, chopped

1 (15 to 16-ounce) can
  black beans, rinsed and drained

1/2 cup yellow bell pepper, chopped

1/2 cup red onion, finely chopped

1/4 cup fresh Italian parsley, chopped

1/4 cup fresh basil, chopped

1 1/2 tablespoons red wine vinegar

1 tablespoon olive oil

1 teaspoon minced garlic

1 teaspoon grated orange peel

Salt and pepper, to taste

Combine all ingredients in a large bowl, toss to blend. Season to taste with salt and pepper. Serve chilled or let stand 30 minutes at room temperature before serving.

Asparagus and Goat Cheese Salad

Makes 4 to 6 servings

3 whole lemons, unpeeled

1/2 cup olive oil

1 pound asparagus, trimmed and cleaned

1/4 cup white balsamic vinegar

1 teaspoon Dijon mustard

Kosher salt and pepper, to taste

12 ounces seasonal greens, such as baby romaine or baby spinach

4 ounces goat cheese, crumbled

2 tablespoons slivered almonds, toasted

Prepare grill. Slice lemons 1/2 inch thick. Brush lightly with olive oil and grill each side until lightly caramelized, about 3 minutes. Place asparagus spears on a parchment-lined pan and roast in a 400-degree oven until spears are bright green, about 7 to 9 minutes, depending on their thickness. Remove from pan immediately to prevent over-cooking. To make vinaigrette, place vinegar, mustard and juice from 2 slices of grilled lemon in a small bowl. While whisking, drizzle in olive oil until mixture is emulsified. Adjust seasonings to taste. Place greens on a serving dish and top with asparagus. Sprinkle with goat cheese and almonds. Drizzle with grilled lemon vinaigrette. Garnish with remaining grilled lemon slices.

Beef Salad

Makes 12 servings

SALAD:

3 pounds cooked roast beef, thinly sliced

10 new potatoes

2 cups baby carrots

3 (6-ounce) packages snow peas, defrosted

4 cups mushrooms, sliced in half

1 red onion, coarsely chopped

1 head red leaf lettuce

1 (7-ounce) package baby spinach leaves

DRESSING:

2/3 cup mayonnaise

1/3 cup plain yogurt

2 tablespoons horseradish

1 teaspoon paprika

In a large bowl, place beef slices cut or torn into 2-inch squares. Boil new potatoes for 1/2 hour, cool, and quarter. Boil baby carrots for 20 minutes and cool. Add snow peas, mushrooms and onion. Add dressing, a little at a time to desired amount. In a large bowl, place torn red leaf lettuce and baby spinach. Top with meat mixture just before serving. Garnish with thinly sliced red onion, if desired.

Sour Cream Fruit Salad

Makes 8 to 10 servings

1 (14 1/2-ounce) can mandarin oranges, drained
1 cup sour cream
1 cup coconut
1 cup pecans

2 cups small marshmallows
1 cup white grapes
1 (7-ounce) can pineapple tidbits, drained

Mix all ingredients together well. Will keep for 4 to 5 days in refrigerator. Garnish with maraschino cherries.

Molded Beet Salad

Makes 6 servings

1 (3-ounce) package lemon gelatin
3/4 cup juice from canned beets
2 tablespoons vinegar
1 tablespoon prepared horseradish
Onion salt, to taste
Garlic salt, to taste

Freshly ground pepper, to taste
1 cup beets, chopped
3/4 cup finely diced celery
Shredded romaine lettuce or red leaf lettuce leaves
Mayonnaise or sour cream for topping, optional

Dissolve gelatin in 1 cup hot water. Add beet juice, vinegar and horseradish. Season with onion and garlic salts and pepper, to taste. When gelatin is slightly thickened, add beets and celery. Pour into large greased mold or 6 individual molds. Chill until firm. Serve on lettuce, with or without mayonnaise or sour cream topping.

Thai Carrot Salad

Makes 6 to 8 servings

1 1/2 pounds carrots, peeled, cut into 2 x 1/4-inch strips
2 tablespoons extra-virgin olive oil
2 tablespoons fresh lime juice
1 tablespoon fresh ginger, minced
2 tablespoons nam plah (Thai fish sauce)

1 teaspoon honey
1 teaspoon garlic, minced
Freshly ground black pepper, to taste
1/3 cup finely chopped cilantro

In a large bowl, toss together all ingredients except cilantro. Let stand at room temperature for 2 hours. Just before serving, add cilantro and toss.

Chicken, *1948, by Milton Avery, oil on canvas board, Museum of Fine Arts, gift of the Lannan Foundation.*

Chutney and Chicken Salad

Makes 6 servings

SALAD:

4 skinless, boneless chicken breast
   halves, cooked and cut into 1-inch
   chunks
2 to 3 red bell peppers, cut into
   1-inch chunks
1 bunch broccoli florets
2 cups red seedless grapes

DRESSING:

1/2 cup mayonnaise
1 to 2 tablespoons curry powder
1/2 cup lavender chutney or substitute Major Grey's Chutney

Toss salad ingredients together. Stir salad dressing ingredients together (thin with cream, optional). Add salad dressing to salad right before serving and toss lightly. To serve, place salad on top of red butter lettuce and sprinkle with toasted slivered almonds.

Southern Corn Bread Salad

Makes 8 servings

1 package corn bread mix, prepared
   according to directions
1 pound bacon, cooked crisp
1 green bell pepper, chopped or
   fresh, chopped green chile
1 red (or orange or yellow) sweet
   pepper, chopped

1 large onion, chopped
4 medium tomatoes, chopped
1/2 cup sweet pickles, chopped
1/2 cup pickle juice
1/2 to 1 cup mayonnaise

Arrange chunks of cooked corn bread in a large 2-quart casserole dish. Top with a layer of crumbled bacon. Add in layers peppers, onion, tomatoes, pickles, pickle juice and mayonnaise. Do not stir. Cover and refrigerate overnight.

Dixon Apple Cider Salad

Makes 10 servings

1 quart apple cider
2 (3-ounce) packages
   lemon gelatin
3 cups chopped, unpeeled apples
1 cup chopped celery
1/2 cup coarsely chopped pecans or
   walnuts

FRUIT MAYONNAISE:
1 (3-ounce) package soft cream
   cheese
3 tablespoons powdered sugar

Mix together
and stir in:
3/4 cup mayonnaise
1/2 cup sour cream
3 tablespoons orange juice
2 teaspoons orange rind, grated

Bring 2 cups cider to boil. Pour over gelatin and stir until dissolved. Let cool and stir in rest of cider. Chill until partially set and mix in apples, celery and nuts. Pour into a 2-quart mold and chill overnight. Unmold over serving plate. Top with Fruit Mayonnaise at last minute.

Sumi Cabbage Salad

Makes 10 to 12 servings

1 pound bag shredded cabbage
1/4 cup sliced almonds, browned
1/4 cup sesame seeds, browned
8 green onions, finely chopped
2 packages ramen noodles, crushed
   in package, no flavor package

DRESSING:
1/3 cup sugar
1/2 cup Canola oil
9 tablespoons rice vinegar
1 tablespoon black pepper

Brown almonds and sesame seeds in a skillet (no oil or water). Combine first 5 ingredients a in bowl. Add dressing ingredients and toss well. Cover with plastic wrap. Refrigerate for 1 day, toss periodically to soften noodles. Keeps well in refrigerator for several days.

Chinese Cold Noodle Salad with Sesame Peanut Butter Sauce

Makes 4 servings

1 pound fresh Asian-style noodles

2 tablespoons sesame or corn oil

DRESSING:

1/4 cup peanut butter, preferably chunky

1/4 cup warm water

1/2 teaspoon salt

2 teaspoons sugar

2 tablespoons soy sauce

1 tablespoon red wine vinegar

2 tablespoons sesame oil

1/2 teaspoon cayenne pepper

2 cloves garlic, finely chopped

3 tablespoons scallions, finely chopped

To prepare sauce, blend peanut butter with warm water to make a thin sauce. Add remaining ingredients except for garlic and scallions. Mix well. This can be prepared in advance and kept tightly covered in refrigerator for several weeks. Before serving, stir well. To prepare noodles, bring 4 quarts of water to a rolling boil over heat. Add noodles and bring to a boil again. Cook for 1 to 2 minutes. Drain and rinse immediately under cold water, drain thoroughly. Put into a large bowl and toss with 2 tablespoons oil. Use immediately, or cover and chill in refrigerator for up to 2 hours. Toss noodles with sauce. Garnish with garlic and scallions. Noodles can also be prepared with meats and vegetables such as chicken, pork, ham, shredded lettuce, cucumbers or bean sprouts.

Paula's Mozzarella and Tomato Salad

Makes 8 servings

2 large ripe tomatoes, peeled and sliced 1/4 inch thick

8 ounces fresh mozzarella, sliced 1/4 inch thick

1/4 teaspoon salt

1/4 teaspoon freshly ground black pepper

2 tablespoons extra-virgin olive oil

8 leaves fresh basil

Arrange tomato and mozzarella slices on a platter or individual salad plates, overlapping slices and fanning them out like a deck of cards. Sprinkle with salt and pepper. Drizzle with oil. Garnish with basil, cut into very thin slices or tear into bits and sprinkle on top or take whole basil leaves and tuck them here and there, peeking out between mozzarella and tomato slices. Serve immediately.

Variation: add 1/4-inch slices of avocado, brushed with lemon juice to prevent darkening.

The Cheese Lover's Cookbook and Guide *by Paula Lambert, © 2000, all rights reserved.*

Wild Rice, Pine Nut, and Dried Cranberry Salad with Orange Vinaigrette

Makes 8 servings

6 1/2 cups water
1/2 cup canned chicken broth
2 1/2 cups wild rice, uncooked
1 cup dried cranberries
1 cup golden raisins
3/4 cup pine nuts
1 cup chopped green onions
1/2 cup chopped parsley

2 tablespoons freshly
    grated orange zest
1/4 cup frozen orange
    juice concentrate
1/4 cup rice vinegar
1/2 cup olive oil
Salt and pepper, to taste

Bring water and broth to boil, add rice and simmer until rice is tender, about 40 minutes. Transfer cooked rice to a large bowl until cool. Mix cranberries, raisins, pine nuts, green onions, parsley and orange zest into cooled rice. In a small bowl, whisk together orange concentrate, vinegar and olive oil to make vinaigrette. Add vinaigrette to rice salad and toss to coat salad ingredients. Season to taste with salt and pepper. Best if made a day ahead, then cover and refrigerate. Bring to room temperature before serving.

Dilled Chicken Salad

Makes 4 servings

12 ounces linguini, cooked al dente
1 whole chicken breast
Salt, to taste
1 small onion
2 cloves garlic
4 peppercorns
4 medium chopped dill pickles
4 stalks celery, diced
6 green onions, chopped
2 tablespoons capers,
    rinsed and drained
12 small pimento-stuffed
    olives for garnish
2 hard-boiled eggs,
    chopped, for garnish

DRESSING:
1/2 cup sour cream
1/2 cup mayonnaise
Juice of 1 lemon
1/2 teaspoon diced dill weed
1 teaspoon salt
1/2 teaspoon ground pepper

Cook and cool pasta. Simmer chicken with salt, onion, garlic and peppercorns. Cool and chop. Mix dressing and toss remaining ingredients with dressing, to taste. Garnish with chopped hard-boiled eggs.

New Potato and Sweet Potato Salad

Makes 8 servings

2 sweet potatoes, peeled and sliced

6 to 8 red-skinned new potatoes, sliced

1 bunch watercress, washed and dried

3 tablespoons scallions, chopped

Salt and fresh cracked pepper

BASIL AND SPINACH DRESSING:

2 tablespoons minced shallots

2 teaspoons minced garlic

1 tablespoon raspberry vinegar

1 tablespoon Dijon mustard

1/2 cup chopped fresh spinach

1/4 cup minced fresh basil

2 tablespoons minced fresh mint

1/4 cup vegetable oil

2 tablespoons extra-virgin olive oil

1 teaspoon salt

1 tablespoon hot water

Boil potatoes separately until done and drain very well. Mix together gently with scallions and 1/2 of dressing. Cool. Just before serving, place potatoes on a bed of watercress leaves. Drizzle with rest of dressing and garnish with 1/2 cup halved white or red seedless grapes and 1/2 pint fresh raspberries.

DRESSING:

In the bowl of a food processor, combine shallots, garlic, vinegar, mustard, spinach, basil and mint. With the processor running, slowly add oils, salt and hot water.

Mediterranean Salad

Makes 8 servings

1/2 loaf french bread

8 ripe tomatoes (plum tomatoes preferred)

1 red onion, halved and thinly sliced

1 red pepper, roasted, peeled and julienned

3/4 pound fresh mozzarella or feta cheese, cubed

1 cup Greek-style black olives, drained

1/3 cup capers, rinsed and drained

1 bunch parsley, roughly chopped

1 bunch basil, roughly chopped

Salt and pepper, to taste

1/4 cup olive oil

1/8 cup fresh lemon juice

1/8 cup red wine vinegar

Fresh oregano, to taste

Cube bread and toast in oven on baking sheet. Set aside to cool. In a large bowl, place tomatoes, onion, red pepper, cheese, olives, capers, parsley, basil and bread. Add salt, pepper, oil, lemon juice and vinegar. Toss gently and let sit at room temperature for 1 hour. It can then be refrigerated for a few hours but it is best served at room temperature. Garnish with fresh oregano.

Curried Chicken Salad

Make 4 cups

4 boneless, skinless, fresh chicken breasts, approximately 2 pounds

1/4 cup virgin olive oil

1 cup safflower mayonnaise

2 teaspoons reduced-sodium tamari or other soy sauce

2 teaspoons curry powder

1/4 teaspoon turmeric

1/2 cup Brazil nuts

1/2 cup Kalamata olives

1/3 cup parsley

Preheat oven to 350 degrees. Clean chicken breasts, remove tendons and dry with paper towels. Rub both sides with olive oil. Place in oblong glass baking dish. Bake uncovered in center of oven for approximately 30 minutes, turning over once halfway through cooking time. Test for doneness on thickest part before removal. Place on plate, cover with vented plastic wrap and refrigerate while preparing rest of ingredients. In a medium-size glass bowl, whisk together dressing: mayonnaise, olive oil, tamari, curry powder and turmeric. Place in refrigerator. Cut chicken in 1/2-inch or smaller cubes. Using rubber spatula, mix with dressing. Place back in refrigerator. Chop Brazil nuts medium-fine. Coarsely chop olives and parsley and add to chicken mixture.

Cuisine Justine—Justine Witlox-Becker, chef

Latir Ranch, home of Tom and Odetie Worrell. Photography: Daniel Nadelbach, photographic styling: Gilda Meyer-Niehof.

Chinese Chicken Salad

Makes 12 servings

9 cups cooked and shredded chicken
(about 6 whole breasts)
1 cup scallions, chopped
3 heads iceberg lettuce, chopped
1 1/2 cups toasted slivered almonds
6 tablespoons toasted sesame seeds
2 cups julienned snow peas
1 1/2cups sliced water chestnuts
Chow mein noodles

DRESSING:
1 1/2 teaspoons dry mustard
6 tablespoons honey
6 tablespoons sugar
3 tablespoons soy sauce
6 tablespoons sesame oil
1 1/2 cups salad oil
3/4 cup rice vinegar

To make salad, in a large bowl, combine all ingredients except chow mein noodles. You can blanch snow peas, if preferred. Combine all ingredients for dressing and shake to blend. Add dressing to salad and top with chow mein noodles.

Thai Shrimp Salad

Makes 4 servings

DRESSING:
2 tablespoons finely grated fresh
    ginger
2 serrano chiles, seeded and minced
2 cloves garlic, minced
2 shallots, minced
3/4 cup sweet rice wine vinegar
1/2 cup chicken stock
1 teaspoon sesame oil
2 teaspoons soy sauce
1/4 cup fresh lime juice
1/2 teaspoon red chile pepper flakes
    (or to taste)

SHRIMP:
20 medium shrimp, peeled
2 tablespoons sesame oil
Salt, to taste

SALAD:
1/2 head each romaine lettuce and
    cabbage
1/2 each red and yellow bell pepper,
    slivered
1 small red onion, sliced very thinly
1/2 cup fresh mint and cilantro,
    chopped

Mix dressing ingredients in a glass bowl and set aside. Heat sesame oil over medium heat and add lightly-salted shrimp. Stir until cooked. Don't overcook. Remove and keep warm. Assemble fresh cold greens, add shrimp, pour dressing over and toss lightly. Optional: thin strips of beef tenderloin can be substituted for shrimp.

Festive Salad with Cranberries and Blue Cheese

Makes 10 servings

1/2 cup cranberries
1/2 cup pecans, chopped
1/2 cup blue cheese or goat cheese
1 (7-ounce) package spring mix salad
    greens

DRESSING:
1 cup sweetened rice vinegar
1/3 cup extra-virgin olive oil
1/2 teaspoon salt
1/4 teaspoon cracked pepper
1 tablespoon Gran Marnier or
    Chambord liqueur
1 teaspoon lemon juice

Mix first 3 ingredients. Mix dressing ingredients. When ready to serve, toss all with spring salad mix.

Arugula, Orange and Fennel Salad

Makes 6 to 8 servings

1/4 cup minced shallots
3 tablespoons extra-virgin olive oil
1 1/2 tablespoons fresh lemon juice
Salt and pepper, to taste
2 large oranges

7 cups arugula
1 large fennel bulb,
    cored and sliced thinly crosswise
1 small red onion, thinly sliced

Whisk minced shallots, olive oil and lemon juice in a medium bowl to blend. Add salt and pepper, to taste. Peel oranges and, using a small sharp knife, cut between membranes to extract orange segments. Combine arugula, fennel and onion in bowl. Toss with enough dressing to coat. Add orange segments and toss. Season with additional salt and pepper, if needed.

Salad Surprise

Makes 10 to 12 servings

1 head lettuce, broken
1 (7-ounce) package fresh spinach
1 (10 1/2-ounce) package
    frozen peas, thawed
6 hard-boiled eggs
1 bunch green onions, cut up,
    greens and all
1 pound bacon, fried and crumbled
Grated Swiss cheese

DRESSING:
1 cup mayonnaise
1 cup sour cream
1 package Hidden Valley Ranch
    dressing mix

Combine dressing ingredients.

Put all ingredients into a salad bowl, mix and then spread salad with mixed dressing. Cover with a thin layer of grated Swiss cheese. Let stand in refrigerator overnight.

Blue Cheese Dressing

Makes 3 cups

2 cups mayonnaise

1/2 cup sour cream

4 teaspoons sugar

1/2 teaspoon dry mustard

1/2 teaspoon granulated garlic

1/2 teaspoon onion powder

1/4 cup white wine vinegar

4 ounces blue cheese

Combine mayonnaise and sour cream. Dissolve sugar, mustard, garlic and onion in vinegar. Add to mayonnaise mixture. Crumble in blue cheese and stir. Cover and chill for 2 hours.

Pomegranate and Feta Salad

Makes 6 servings

1 head romaine lettuce,
   washed and torn

1 bunch spinach, stems removed

Seeds of 1 pomegranate

1/4 cup roasted pine nuts

1/2 cup crumbled feta

DRESSING:

1/3 cup olive oil

1 tablespoon red wine vinegar

2 tablespoons maple syrup

1 teaspoon Dijon mustard

1/2 teaspoon oregano

Salt and pepper

Toss lettuce and spinach together in a large salad bowl. Add pomegranate seeds, pine nuts and feta. Whisk dressing ingredients together and store in refrigerator. Toss with salad ingredients just before serving.

Parmesan Dressing

Makes 2 1/2 cups

1 pint mayonnaise

1 teaspoon anchovy paste

1 teaspoon garlic powder or 1 fresh
   clove of garlic, crushed

1 cup grated or shredded Parmesan

Mix all ingredients together and let set overnight. Thin a bit with milk, if necessary. Great over lettuce wedges with croutons or a mixed green salad.

Cowboy Camp, *New Mexico, ca. 1885. Photograph by Dona B. Chase, courtesy of the Palace of the Governors Photo Archives. Negative 56990.*

Red Chile Caesar Salad

Makes 6 servings

Inner leaves of 3 to 4 heads of red
or green romaine lettuce, or
combination of both
Chile-Garlic Croutons (see below)
1/3 cup shaved Parmesan cheese

DRESSING:
1 tablespoon roasted garlic
1 teaspoon salt
1 1/2 teaspoons dry mustard
6 fillets anchovy
1 teaspoon Worcestershire sauce
2 coddled eggs
2 tablespoons freshly squeezed
    lemon juice
1/4 cup grated Parmesan cheese
1/3 cup red wine vinegar
2 to 3 tablespoons medium Chimayo
    ground red chile powder
1 cup olive oil

Place romaine leaves in a large bowl and add dressing. Toss well and then serve on individual plates with Chile-Garlic Croutons (see below) on top and shaved Parmesan cheese. To make dressing, place all dressing ingredients except for vinegar, chile and oil in a food processor. Place vinegar and chile in an enamel or stainless-steel saucepan and simmer for 3 minutes. While food processor is running, pour vinegar mixture into ingredients and slowly add all oil. Refrigerate until ready to use.

Chile-Garlic Croutons

Makes 4 cups

1 loaf italian or french bread
4 garlic cloves, sliced
1/3 cup olive oil
2 tablespoons New Mexican Red
    Chile powder

Preheat oven to 325 degrees. Remove crust from bread with a serrated knife and cut bread into 3/4-inch cubes. On a shallow baking pan, arrange bread cubes in 1 layer, bake them in the middle of the oven, stirring occasionally, for 10 to 15 minutes, or until they are golden, and transfer the croutons to a large bowl. In a skillet, cook garlic with red chile in oil over moderately low heat, stirring, until it is golden. Remove garlic with a slotted spoon and discard. Drizzle oil and red chile over croutons and then toss to coat them well. Sprinkle croutons with salt to taste and toss again.

Spring Salad with Sage-Pine Nut Vinaigrette

Makes 6 to 8 servings

1 pound spring mix salad greens
1 large red onion
1/2 cup sliced radishes

DRESSING:
1/4 cup pine nuts, roasted
1/4 cup fresh sage leaves
1/4 cup balsamic vinegar
3/4 cup olive oil
1 tablespoon minced garlic
1/2 teaspoon salt

Mix all dressing ingredients in a blender. Serve on salad of greens, onion and radishes. Top with additional pine nuts, if desired.

Spinach Pear Salad

Makes 6 servings

12 cups spinach leaves
6 cups Bibb lettuce
1 red onion, thinly sliced
3 small pears, cored and sliced
1/2 pound bacon, cooked and
    broken into bite-size pieces
Toasted macadamia nuts,
    roughly chopped

DRESSING:
3 tablespoons white wine vinegar
3 tablespoons Dijon mustard
2 tablespoons honey
3 tablespoons sesame seeds, toasted
1 teaspoon minced garlic
Salt and pepper, to taste
1/2 cup vegetable oil

In a large bowl, combine spinach, lettuce, red onion and pears. In a separate bowl, whisk all ingredients for dressing. Toss with salad. Divide salad among 6 plates and sprinkle each with bacon and nuts.

Navajo Blanket, ca. 1880–1900. Phase III chief's style. Made from Germantown commercial wool yarns, Museum of Indian Arts and Culture. Photo: Blair Clark.

Romaine Salad with Berries and Mandarin Oranges

Makes 4 servings

1 or more bunches romaine or
    1 bag mixed greens
1 cup thinly sliced celery
1 onion, thinly sliced
1 can mandarin oranges, drained
1/2 cup sliced strawberries
    or raspberries
1/2 cup toasted slivered almonds,
    pecans or walnuts, optional

DRESSING:
3/4 cup white balsamic vinegar
1 tablespoon water
1/4 teaspoon dry mustard
1 to 2 cloves garlic, minced
1 teaspoon sugar
1 teaspoon dry basil, tarragon or
    herb, to taste
Salt and pepper, to taste
1 cup olive oil

Mix all dressing ingredients, except oil, in a blender. Add oil slowly into blender and blend until thick and smooth. Toss together with salad.

Mixed Greens with Honey Lime Dressing

Makes 8 servings

2 (8-ounce) bags butter lettuce
    with radicchio
1 1/2 cups raisins
1/2 to 3/4 cup dry-roasted
    sunflower seeds

DRESSING:
1 cup light olive oil
1/2 cup and 3 to 4 tablespoons
    fresh lime juice
2 to 3 teaspoons grated lime zest
4 to 5 teaspoons honey
Dash white pepper

Toss lettuce with dressing that has been whisked together. Dressing can be refrigerated but needs to be at room temperature before tossing with salad. Divide among salad plates. Sprinkle each plate with raisins and sunflower seeds.

Lime Dressing

Makes 1 cup

1/4 cup virgin olive oil
2 tablespoons peanut oil
1/2 cup fresh lime juice
1 tablespoon minced fresh cilantro

1/4 teaspoon dried oregano
Dash cayenne pepper
Freshly ground pepper
Salt

Combine all ingredients in a 12-ounce jar with tight-fitting lid. Shake vigorously until well blended. Serve immediately or refrigerate until ready to use.

Taco Salad

Makes 6 servings

1 1/2 pounds ground beef
3/4 cup water
1/4 teaspoon oregano
1/2 teaspoon cumin
1/2 teaspoon red chile powder
1/2 teaspoon minced garlic
Salt and pepper, to taste
1 (15-ounce) can pinto or ranch-style
    beans, chilled and drained
1 head iceberg lettuce, chopped
1 pound cheddar or Monterey Jack
    cheese, grated
1 onion, diced
1 (4-ounce) can green chile, chopped
2 tomatoes, diced
1/2 cup olives, chopped
2 cups small corn chips

DRESSING:
1 avocado
1 lime, juiced
1 (8-ounce) bottle french or italian
    dressing
1/4 teaspoon red chile powder

Combine all dressing ingredients in a food processor, process for 2 minutes and then cover and refrigerate.

Brown beef, adding water and spices. Add beans and simmer. Pour into bowl and chill. In a bowl, combine lettuce, cheese, onion, green chile, tomatoes and olives. Chill. Just before serving, toss salad ingredients with dressing, to taste. Place in a serving bowl, and top with beef-and-bean mixture and corn chips.

Deluxe Thousand Island Dressing

Makes 2 cups

1 1/4 cup mayonnaise
1/3 cup Heinz chili sauce
1/4 cup buttermilk
1 teaspoon sugar
1/2 teaspoon MSG
1/8 teaspoon white pepper
1/2 teaspoon celery salt
1 clove garlic, crushed
1/4 teaspoon garlic powder
1 small onion

ADD IN:
1 peeled hard-boiled egg
1 sprig fresh parsley
1 medium bell pepper
1 small sweet pickle or bread and
    butter pickle
1/2 stalk celery with a few inner
    leaves

ADD IN:
1 teaspoon minced onion
3 tablespoons Parmesan cheese

Combine first list of ingredients in a blender until smooth and then add in the second group of ingredients a little at a time, turning blender off and on until ingredients are finely chopped (do not over process).

Pour dressing in a bowl and add 2 remaining ingredients.

Cover and put in refrigerator. Let sit overnight before using.

Herbed Garlic and Parmesan Croutons

Makes 24 servings

2 large cloves garlic, sliced thin
    lengthwise

1 teaspoon dried oregano, crumbled

1 teaspoon dried basil, crumbled

1 teaspoon dried thyme, crumbled

1/2 teaspoon salt plus additional,
    to taste

1/2 teaspoon pepper

1/2 cup olive oil

1 loaf Italian bread, cut into 3/4-inch
    cubes (about 7 cups)

1/4 cup finely grated fresh Parmesan

Preheat oven to 350 degrees. In a small saucepan, combine garlic, oregano, basil, thyme, salt, pepper and oil, and simmer the mixture for 5 minutes. Discard garlic. Toss bread cubes with oil mixture, spread them in a jelly roll pan, and bake in middle of oven for 8 minutes. Sprinkle with Parmesan and bake for 7 minutes more, or until golden. Sprinkle croutons with additional salt and let cool. Croutons will keep in an airtight container for 1 week. Serve croutons as topping for tossed green salad.

Pasta Fiesta Salad

Makes 8 servings

1 (11 to 12-ounce) package vermicelli
    pasta

6 ounces Gerard's Original French
    Dressing

1/2 cup water

2 teaspoons white sugar

2 cloves garlic, minced

3 fresh jalapenos, finely chopped

Salt, to taste

1 tablespoon poppy seed

1 teaspoon celery seed

1/2 teaspoon caraway seed

1 cup hearts of celery leaves, finely
    chopped

1 bunch green onions and tops, finely
    chopped

6 to 8 large sprigs parsley, finely
    chopped

Cook vermicelli in boiling water according to package directions. Rinse and drain. Put in a large bowl and coat well with french dressing. Mix water and sugar together. Add water-sugar mixture, garlic, jalapenos, salt, poppy seed, celery seed and caraway seed. Up to this point, the salad may be made the day before and kept refrigerated. One hour before serving, add hearts of celery, onions and parsley. Serve cold.

Home of Tom and Sue Pahlman. Photography: Daniel Nadelbach, photographic styling: Gilda Meyer-Niehof.

Pepper Croutons

Makes 10 servings

4 cups 1-inch cubes italian or
   french bread

2 tablespoons olive oil

1/2 teaspoon freshly ground pepper

1/2 teaspoon salt

Preheat oven to 350 degrees. In a baking pan, toss bread cubes with oil, pepper and salt, and toast them in middle of oven, tossing occasionally, for 15 minutes, or until golden. The croutons may be made 2 days in advance, cooled and kept in an airtight container.

Mango and Rum Dressing

Makes 1 cup

1 very ripe mango, peeled and pitted

2 tablespoons rum

2 tablespoons fresh lime juice

2 tablespoons fresh lemon juice

1 1/2 teaspoons dried mint,
   powdered

1 teaspoon lime zest

1/2 teaspoon vanilla extract

1 small clove garlic, mashed with
   side of knife

1/8 teaspoon cayenne pepper

1/2 cup virgin olive oil

Salt, to taste

Place mango pulp in a blender or food processor with all ingredients except olive oil and salt. Blend until smooth. With the machine running, slowly pour in oil. Add salt, to taste. Refrigerate dressing for 1 hour before serving. Because mango can ferment with the slightest heat, keep refrigerated until ready to use.

Tarragon Buttermilk Dressing

Makes 3/4 cup

1/3 cup buttermilk

1/3 cup sour cream

1/4 cup minced parsley

1 tablespoon mayonnaise

4 teaspoons fresh or 2 teaspoons
   dried tarragon

1 teaspoon drained capers

1/4 teaspoon minced rosemary

1/8 teaspoon ground
   green peppercorns

Dash white pepper

Whisk all ingredients together in a small bowl. Cover and refrigerate for 1 hour to allow flavors to blend.

Hot Seafood Salad

Makes 8 servings

1 pound cooked medium shrimp

1 medium onion, chopped

1 medium green pepper, chopped

1 cup finely chopped celery

8 ounces sautéed fresh sliced
mushrooms

2 (4 1/2-ounce) cans water chestnuts,
drained and sliced

4 hard-boiled eggs, chopped

1 cup toasted, slivered or sliced
almonds

1 cup mayonnaise

1 cup sour cream

1 teaspoon salt or seasoned salt

2 teaspoons Worcestershire sauce

2 teaspoons each grated lemon rind
and lemon juice

1 pound lump crabmeat

2 cups buttered bread crumbs

Paprika

Preheat oven to 350 degrees. Mix all ingredients together, adding crab last. Place in a buttered 3-quart casserole dish. Cover with 2 cups buttered bread crumbs and dust top with paprika. Bake for 30 to 35 minutes.

Entrees

Old Santa Fe, *ca. 1950s, by Gustave Baumann, color woodcut, 6 x 7 1/2 inches, Museum of Fine Arts,* © *1989 Ann Baumann.*

Sandia Peak Stuffed Tenderloin

Makes 12 servings

1 1/4 pounds fresh spinach, rinsed
    and stemmed
1/2 pound exotic or domestic
    mushrooms, chopped
2 tablespoons butter
1 1/2 cups shredded Swiss cheese
2 eggs, beaten
2 1/2 teaspoons fennel seeds
1 teaspoon sage

Salt and pepper, to taste
1 (8-pound) whole beef tenderloin,
    trimmed
6 to 8 cloves garlic, minced
1 1/2 teaspoons coarse
    ground pepper
1/2 cup beef broth
1/2 cup Madeira or dry sherry

Preheat oven to 500 degrees. Cook spinach until it wilts. Cool, drain, squeeze and chop. Sauté mushrooms in butter until juices evaporate. Cool and mix with spinach, cheese, eggs, 1 teaspoon fennel seeds, sage, salt and pepper. Split filet lengthwise to within 1/2 inch of each end, to form a pocket. Spoon spinach filling in and pat down carefully. Blend garlic, 1 1/2 teaspoons fennel seeds, and pepper and pat on outside of filet. Place meat in oven. Reduce heat to 350 degrees and roast for 18 minutes per pound or an internal temperature of 135 to 140 degrees. Remove from oven and pour drippings into saucepan. Add broth and Madeira. Simmer until reduced. Serve with meat.

The Broadmoor's Chutney Pepper Steak

Makes 4 servings

4 (6-ounce) filets beef steak
2 tablespoons unsalted butter
1/4 cup Major Grey's Mango Chutney
2 teaspoons cracked black pepper
3 ounces Armagnac or other brandy

In a large skillet, sauté filets in melted butter over medium-high heat. Cook for 3 to 4 minutes per side for medium rare. Top with chutney and black pepper. Pour Armagnac into skillet, let warm and carefully flambé. Serve steaks with sauce spooned over.

Seven-Bar Brisket

Makes 8 servings

6 pounds brisket

MARINADE:

2 ounces liquid smoke
1/4 cup Worcestershire sauce
1/2 teaspoon red chile powder
1 teaspoon salt
1 tablespoon pepper
1 tablespoon onion salt
1 tablespoon garlic salt
1 tablespoon celery salt

BASTING SAUCE:

2 tablespoons garlic, minced
2 medium onions, sliced
1/4 cup Worcestershire sauce
1 (12-ounce) can beer
16 ounces beef broth
1 tablespoon fresh lime juice
1 teaspoon cumin
1/2 teaspoon red chile powder
1/2 teaspoon red chile flakes
Salt and pepper, to taste

Place meat fat side up in a large pan with heavy foil. Add marinade, seal tightly with foil and refrigerate for 24 hours. Preheat oven to 275 degrees. Cook for 2 hours, then remove from oven. Open foil and pour off any marinade.

Pour basting sauce over meat, reseal and continue cooking for 2 more hours. Remove from oven, open foil and turn meat, fat side down. Cover with favorite barbeque sauce, seal and return to oven for another hour. Remove from oven to platter and serve. If you don't want to cover with barbeque sauce, you can add 6 to 8 celery stalks, whole carrots and quartered (lengthwise) potatoes. Cook for last hour.

Brisket can be cooked on a low-heat grill. Put brisket on grill over a pan of water (more water may have to be added as meat cooks). Close lid and smoke meat 5 to 6 hours, or until meat temperature is 190 to 225 degrees.

Filet of Beef with Gorgonzola Sauce

Makes 6 servings

1 (4 to 5 pounds) whole beef filet, trimmed and tied
4 cups heavy cream
3 to 4 ounces crumbly Gorgonzola

3 tablespoons freshly grated Parmesan
3/4 teaspoon kosher salt
3/4 teaspoon ground black pepper
3 tablespoons minced fresh parsley

Preheat oven to 500 degrees.

GORGONZOLA SAUCE:

Bring heavy cream to full boil over medium-high heat. Boil rapidly for 45 to 50 minutes until thickened, stirring occasionally. Remove from heat and add Gorgonzola, Parmesan, salt, pepper and parsley. Whisk until cheese melts and it's now ready to serve over beef.

BEEF:

Spread butter with fingers on baking sheet. Place beef on baking sheet. Sprinkle with salt and pepper, roast for exactly 22 minutes for rare, 25 minutes for medium rare. Remove from oven. Cover tightly with foil. Allow to rest for 20 minutes. Remove strings, slice thickly and serve with sauce.

My Favorite Meatloaf

Makes 8 servings

3 tablespoons olive oil
1 cup minced onion
1/2 cup each minced green onion, celery and carrot
1/2 cup minced green bell pepper and red bell pepper
3 cloves garlic, minced
1 teaspoon salt
1 teaspoon freshly ground pepper
1/4 teaspoon cayenne pepper

1/2 teaspoon each white pepper, ground cumin and ground nutmeg
1/2 cup half-and-half
1/2 cup ketchup
1 1/2 pounds lean ground beef
1/2 pound ground pork
3 eggs, beaten
3/4 cup dry bread crumbs
Favorite bottled barbeque sauce

Preheat oven to 350 degrees. Sauté first 4 ingredients in olive oil until softened. Cool. Combine all other ingredients (except bread crumbs and barbeque sauce) to cooled vegetables. Soak bread crumbs in half-and-half for a few minutes before adding. Mix and form into 8 individual loaves. Place on baking sheet. Bake 40 minutes. Cover loaves with barbeque sauce and bake 5 to 10 minutes more.

Jinja Asia Cafe, Santa Fe, New Mexico—Lesley Allin, owner and chef

Green Chile Meatloaf

Makes 8 servings

2 1/2 pounds ground beef
1 yellow onion, diced
5 cloves garlic, minced
8 Hatch green chiles roasted, peeled and chopped
1/4 cup Dijon mustard
1/2 cup ketchup

2 tablespoons fresh thyme leaves
4 eggs
2 cups panko bread crumbs
Salt and freshly ground pepper, to taste
4 slices apple-wood-smoked bacon

Preheat oven to 375 degrees. Combine ground beef, onion, garlic, chiles, mustard, 1/4 cup ketchup, thyme, eggs, panko and season liberally with salt and pepper. Mix by hand until mixture is homogenous. Form mixture into loaf on lightly oiled shallow baking pan. Brush outside of loaf with remaining ketchup and top with slices of raw bacon. Bake in oven until just cooked through. Remove and let rest for 10 minutes before cutting.

At Santacafe, we serve this meatloaf as a sandwich with chipotle aioli and Gorgonzola cheese on house-made semolina bread.

Santacafe—David Seller, executive chef; Judith F. Ebbinghaus, owner

Winter Scene, *Museum of Fine Arts, Santa Fe, New Mexico, December 22, 1918. Photograph by Wesley Bradfield, Palace of the Governors Photo Archives. Negative 28858.*

Meatballs–Danish Frikadeller

Makes 6 to 8 servings

1 pound ground beef
2 tablespoons chopped onion
1/4 cup bread crumbs
1 egg, beaten
1/2 cup milk
1 teaspoon dry mustard
1 teaspoon salt
1/2 teaspoon pepper
Flour
2 tablespoons Crisco or butter

SAUCE:
1 tablespoon butter
1 tablespoon flour
1 cup milk
1 (14-ounce) can
    cream of mushroom soup

Preheat oven to 350 degrees. In a bowl, blend together first 8 ingredients by hand. Shape mixture into 1-inch balls, roll in flour and brown in Crisco or butter.

SAUCE:
Melt butter, blend in flour, add milk and soup, and mix until smooth. Place meatballs in a casserole dish, cover with sauce and bake for 45 minutes. Or you can place meatballs in sauce in a saucepan and simmer over very low heat for 45 minutes–stir frequently.

French Meat Pie

Makes 2 (8-inch) pies

2 large sweet onions, finely chopped
2 tablespoons olive oil
Splash vermouth (optional)
1 3/4 pounds lean ground beef
1/2 pound ground pork
1/2 pound ground veal

2 small to medium boiled potatoes,
    mashed, save cooking water
Beef broth (optional)
Salt and pepper, to taste
1 teaspoon ground cloves
1 teaspoon cinnamon
Flour, as needed

Preheat oven to 325 degrees. Sauté onions in olive oil until softened, add vermouth. Add meats to brown. Add mashed potatoes and liquid (potato water or beef broth). Simmer 1 hour. Adjust liquid as needed. Add salt and pepper to taste, and cloves and cinnamon. Add flour if there is too much liquid, to thicken consistency. Make 2 double pie crusts. Sprinkle dusting of flour on bottom crust before putting meat mixture into pie tin. Bake for 30 minutes, then bake an additional 30 minutes at 350 degrees.

Marinated Flank Steak

Makes 4 servings

1/2 cup oil

1/4 cup lemon juice

1 tablespoon grated onion

2 tablespoons chopped parsley

1 teaspoon marjoram

1 teaspoon thyme

1/2 teaspoon salt

1 clove garlic, minced

1/2 teaspoon Tabasco sauce

1/4 cup butter

2 tablespoons chopped chives

2 tablespoons blue cheese

1 1/2 pounds flank steak,
   trimmed of all fat

Combine first 9 ingredients in sealable container and shake. Pour over flank steak in a shallow glass dish, cover and marinate 2 hours each side. Cream butter with chives and blue cheese. Remove steak from marinade and grill 2 to 3 inches above hot coals for 5 minutes per side. Remove steak to a carving board, spread with butter–blue cheese mixture and slice thinly on the diagonal.

Kefta Tagine (Morocco)

Makes 4 servings

1 pound ground beef

1/2 teaspoon cinnamon

1/2 teaspoon turmeric

1/4 teaspoon cayenne pepper

1 teaspoon salt

1/2 teaspoon pepper

1 tablespoon paprika

1 small to medium onion, minced

3 tablespoons chopped parsley

3 tablespoons chopped cilantro

1 large tomato, diced

2 tablespoons olive oil

4 eggs

Mix ground beef with all spices, 1/4 cup of minced onion, parsley and cilantro. Form tiny meatballs (1/2 to 3/4 inch in diameter). Dice tomato. Heat oil, and gently brown meatballs in large frying pan, shaking pan to brown meatballs evenly. Add remaining onion, tomato and a little salt. Cover and cook over low flame, shaking pan occasionally, for 20 minutes. Once keftas are cooked, transfer to a warm tagine, or round, shallow serving casserole dish. Return to stove. Break 1 egg for each guest on top of keftas. While sauce is simmering, break eggs on top, salt them lightly and cook until eggs are softly poached. Serve with crusty bread, which guests will break into pieces and use to scoop up meatballs.

Wild Horses, *1937, by Gerald Nailor (Toh Yah), Navajo, tempera on board, 12 3/4 x 14 inches, Museum of Fine Arts.*

Soft Tacos

Makes 4 to 6 servings

1 1/2 pounds lean ground beef

2 cups red chile sauce

12 tortillas (blue corn, if possible)

Canola oil

1 pound longhorn cheese, grated

1/2 head lettuce, chopped

3/4 cup onion, diced

1 cup tomatoes, chopped

Preheat oven to 375 degrees. Brown meat and drain any grease. Mix in 1 cup chile sauce. Fry tortillas quickly in hot oil until limp. Drain on paper towel. Using oven-safe plates, put 2 to 3 tacos per person. Place 3 tablespoons of meat on each tortilla and an extra 2 tablespoons of red sauce on each. Add some cheese, lettuce, onion and tomatoes. Fold over and sprinkle with extra cheese. Place plates in oven and heat until cheese melts.

Tacos

Makes 6 servings

1 pound ground chuck

1 cup potato, cooked and diced

12 corn tortillas, folded

1 cup grated longhorn cheese

1 small head lettuce, chopped

1 small onion, diced

2 small tomatoes, diced

1 1/2 cups chile sauce or salsa

Oil

Boil meat and potatoes separately until cooked. Drain each and mix. On a baking sheet, place tortillas and sprinkle with cheese. Warm in oven or on grill until cheese melts to tortillas. Remove from oven. Put 2 tablespoons of meat-potato mixture on each taco. Add some chopped lettuce, onion and tomatoes. Sprinkle with cheese and serve immediately with sauce or salsa.

Note: Filling can be beef, chicken or fish.

Salpicon

Makes 12 servings

3 pounds brisket

2 onions, 1 halved and 1 chopped

1 large carrot, quartered

1 stalk celery, quartered

2 to 4 cloves garlic

1 cup chopped cilantro

1 (12-ounce) can chopped tomatoes

Salt and pepper, to taste

1 large tomato, chopped

2 (4-ounce) cans chopped green
chiles

1/4 cup light olive oil

1/4 cup vinegar

1/2 pound Monterey Jack cheese, cut
in 1/4-inch cubes

2 large avocados, sliced lengthwise

Mango slices

Preheat oven to 325 degrees. Cover brisket with water in a heavy pot. Add halved onion, carrot, celery, garlic, 1/2 cup chopped cilantro, canned tomatoes, salt and pepper. Cover and cook in oven approximately 4 hours until very tender. Remove from liquid, cool slightly and shred with fork. In a large bowl, combine beef, chopped onion, chopped tomato, remaining cilantro, green chiles, oil, vinegar, salt and pepper. Let cool in refrigerator at least 6 hours. Before serving, toss with cheese and turn into a decorative bowl. Garnish with sliced avocado, mango and more cilantro. Serve with warm corn or flour tortillas, pinto beans, guacamole and green salad. For spicier flavor, add chile chipotle or pickled jalapenos. This is actually a cold meat salad that makes a great entree.

Carne Guisada in Crock-Pot

Makes 9 to 10 servings

3 pounds lean roast (such as rump)

1 onion, chopped

2 large cloves garlic, chopped

1 (5-ounce) can green chiles

1 (14 1/2-ounce) can diced tomatoes
with green chiles

1 (14 1/2-ounce) can diced tomatoes
without green chiles

1 tablespoon cumin

1 tablespoon chile powder

1 teaspoon salt

Flour tortillas

Sour cream, salsa and garnishes,
such as avocado

Place roast in Crock-Pot. Mix other ingredients and pour on top. Cook for 8 to 10 hours on low. When done, take roast out and shred, then put back in juices. Serve on warm tortillas with sour cream and garnishes. Can also be served over rice.

Hungarian Goulash

Makes 8 servings

1 1/4 to 1 1/2 pounds stew meat,
    cut into bite-size pieces

1 tablespoon olive oil

2 to 3 medium onions, peeled
    and chopped

2 tablespoons Hungarian sweet
    paprika (do not use
    Spanish paprika)

2 to 3 carrots, washed and cubed

2 to 3 stalks celery, washed and
    sliced into bite-size pieces

1 (32-ounce) can peeled whole
    tomatoes, sliced

2 tablespoons caraway seeds

2 to 3 cubes beef bouillon

1 large bay leaf

2 medium to large potatoes, peeled
    and cut in chunks

Salt, if needed

Brown meat in oil in a large saucepan on stove. As it is browning, add onions and cook until they are transparent and meat is completely browned. Stir in paprika (be careful not to burn) and add water to cover meat. Cover and cook on low heat until meat is practically tender, 1 to 1 1/2 hours. Add carrots and celery and cook for about 10 minutes. Add tomatoes, caraway seeds, beef bouillon, bay leaf and potatoes. Add water, as needed. Simmer covered until meat and vegetables (cooked but not mushy) are done. Add salt to taste, if needed.

Italian-Style Roast

Makes 12 to 16 servings

10 pounds beef rump (pot roast)

2 1/2 quarts water

3 to 4 cloves garlic, crushed

1 tablespoon oregano

1 tablespoon fennel seed

2 teaspoons red chile powder

1 tablespoon anise seed

2 teaspoons rosemary leaves

2 1/4 teaspoons black pepper

2 1/4 teaspoons paprika

Salt, to taste

SAUCE:

1 (6-8 ounce) can tomato soup

Italian seasoning, to taste

Preheat oven to 350 degrees. Mix water and all seasonings in a large roasting pan and stir thoroughly. Brown meat in skillet with a bit of olive oil, then add to seasoned water. Put roast in oven for 1 hour. Reduce heat to 300 degrees and cook for about 4 to 5 more hours. Once roast is cooked, slice thinly, and reheat in sauce to serve.

SUMMER CLOUDS

118

Gustave Baumann

Santa Fe Beef Fajitas

Makes 6 servings

3 pounds round or skirt steak

MARINADE:
1/8 cup red chile powder
1/2 cup lime juice
1 teaspoon cumin
1 tablespoon minced garlic
1 cup tequila
2 tablespoons Worcestershire sauce

PICO DE GALLO:
4 green onions, diced, tops included
1 small red onion, diced
1 seeded, unpeeled cucumber,
   minced
12 serrano chiles, seeded and minced
1/3 cup cilantro, chopped

5 Roma tomatoes, diced
3 tablespoons lime juice

VEGETABLES:
2 each red and green bell peppers,
   cut into thin strips
2 onions, sliced
1 teaspoon cumin
1 teaspoon oregano
1 teaspoon coriander
1 tablespoon red chile powder
Flour tortillas
Sour cream
Shredded cheese
Picante sauce

Trim meat. Slice in long strips 1 x 5 inches long.

MARINADE:
Whisk all ingredients and pour over meat. Cover with plastic wrap and refrigerate overnight. Prepare Pico de Gallo and refrigerate. Toss vegetables with seasonings. Sauté in skillet with lard or bacon drippings. While cooking vegetables, grill meat, about 3 minutes on each side. Mix meat and vegetables on platter. Place some on each flour tortilla. Add Pico de Gallo, a dab of sour cream and shredded cheddar cheese. May also serve with picante sauce.

Santa Cruz Short Ribs

Makes 4 servings

3 pounds short ribs, 3 inches long
1 cup water
1 cup ketchup
1/4 cup apple cider vinegar
1 tablespoon Worcestershire sauce
1 tablespoon sugar
2 onions, thinly sliced

1/4 cup prepared horseradish
1/2 teaspoon dry mustard
1 bay leaf
12 peppercorns
1/2 teaspoon salt
8 whole cloves

Preheat oven to 350 degrees. In a large pot, cover ribs with water and place over high heat, bringing water to boil. Reduce heat to low and simmer for 2 hours. Remove from heat and place ribs in a baking dish. Add rest of ingredients to ribs, cover, and bake in oven for another 1 1/2 hours. Remove ribs to a hot platter. Spoon some sauce over and serve.

Summer Clouds, *by Gustave Baumann, color woodcut, Museum of Fine Arts,* © *1989 Ann Baumann.*

Pecos Ranch Pepper Steaks with Onions

Makes 4 servings

4 New York or rib-eye steaks,
1 1/2 inches thick
Salt
1/2 cup fresh cracked peppercorns
1 tablespoon butter
2 tablespoons olive oil

ONIONS:
1 tablespoon butter
2 tablespoons olive oil
3 onions, sliced
1/2 teaspoon salt
1/2 teaspoon sugar
1 teaspoon thyme

Preheat oven to 375 degrees. Rinse and pat dry steaks. Sprinkle both sides with salt then coat both sides with peppercorns. In a large skillet that will hold 4 steaks, put in butter and olive oil and add steaks. Brown over medium-high heat for 4 to 5 minutes. Turn steaks and brown other side for 2 to 3 minutes. Place pan in oven and bake until cooked to taste. For medium rare, bake 6 to 8 minutes. Put steaks on plates and top with onions.

ONIONS:
Put butter and oil in a 12-inch skillet over medium heat. Add onions and salt. Cover and cook until limp. Uncover, add sugar and thyme, and stir until onions begin to brown (may have to increase heat).

Marinated and Grilled Butterflied Leg of Lamb

Makes 6 servings

6 1/2 pounds lamb
1 1/4 cups olive oil
3/4 cup soy sauce
1/4 cup Worcestershire sauce
2 tablespoons dry mustard
2 1/4 teaspoon salt

1 teaspoon ground pepper
1/4 cup red wine vinegar
1 1/2 teaspoons dried parsley flakes
1/3 cup fresh lemon juice
2 cloves garlic, crushed

Have butcher butterfly lamb. Mix rest of ingredients together. Marinate lamb in mixture overnight in roasting pan. Cook lamb on gas grill at medium heat, covered, for about 1 hour, basting occasionally.

Pinchos Morunos

Makes 6 servings

2 pounds lamb (top round is best)
1 small onion, diced
3 tablespoons olive oil
4 cloves garlic, chopped
1 1/2 teaspoons ground cumin
1 tablespoon parsley, chopped

1 tablespoon paprika
1 teaspoon oregano, chopped
1/2 teaspoon flake chile pequins
Salt and pepper, to taste
Small pinch saffron

Trim lamb well and cut into 2-inch cubes. Set aside. Place all other ingredients in processor fitted with metal blade. (You can use mortar and pestle, adding onion last). Process until smooth. Do not overprocess or marinade will be runny. Marinate lamb overnight before using. Prepare lamb on skewers. Grill or broil to medium rare. A great addition to a summer's night grill event.

El Meson Kitchen

Rosemary and Garlic Roasted Leg of Lamb

Makes 6 to 8 servings

1 (5 1/2 to 6-pound) leg lamb, bone removed
8 cloves garlic

3 tablespoons fresh rosemary, chopped
3 tablespoons olive oil
Salt and pepper, to taste

Preheat oven to 325 degrees. Trim and discard fat from lamb. Thinly slice 4 cloves of garlic, and make small, shallow cuts in surface of lamb and insert a garlic slice in each. Combine rosemary, oil and remaining 4 cloves of garlic (minced or pressed). Coat lamb and refrigerate for at least 4 hours or until next day. Remove lamb from marinade, reserve marinade. Place lamb on rack and insert meat thermometer in thickest part. Roast, uncovered, in oven until thermometer registers 110 to 120 degrees for medium rare (about 1 1/2 hours). Transfer leg of lamb to serving platter and keep warm. Salt and pepper, to taste. Thinly slice lamb and garnish with rosemary sprigs. Suggestions: Serve with roasted potatoes and sautéed haricot verts.

Las Campanas Country Club—Brad Gallegos, chef

Sates Kambling

Makes 10 sates

1/2 cup minced onion

1 clove garlic, minced

1 teaspoon fresh coriander or
 cilantro, chopped

1 teaspoon minced, peeled fresh
 gingerroot

1 tablespoon rice wine vinegar

1 tablespoon vegetable oil

1 teaspoon chile paste

2 pounds boneless lamb shoulder,
 trimmed and cut into 3/4-inch
 cubes

SAUCE:

1 tablespoon vegetable oil

1/2 cup crushed, unsalted,
 dry-roasted peanuts

2 tablespoons chopped shallots

1 clove garlic, finely minced

1/2 cup shrimp paste

1 tablespoon fresh lemon juice

1/2 tablespoon chile paste

2 cups water

Use 10 (10-inch) wooden skewers soaked in water for 30 minutes. In a shallow dish, combine onion, garlic, coriander, gingerroot, vinegar, oil and chile paste. Add lamb, and coat with marinade. Cover and chill overnight.

SAUCE:

In a saucepan, heat oil over a medium heat until it is hot but not smoking. Add peanuts, shallots, garlic and shrimp paste, stirring for 1 minute, until mixture is thickened. Add lemon juice, chile paste and water. Simmer sauce, stirring occasionally, for 5 to 7 minutes, or until it is thickened. Season sauce to taste with salt and pepper. Thread lamb onto skewers and grill on oiled rack set, 5 to 6 inches over hot coals, turning and cooking for 8 minutes on each side. Transfer lamb to a serving plate and pour the sauce over it.

Lamb Shanks with Chile Wine Sauce

Makes 4 to 6 servings

3 tablespoons olive oil

4 to 6 lamb shanks

Salt and pepper

3 cups chopped onions

1 generous cup chopped carrots

1/4 cup tomato paste

1 3/4 cups dry red wine

2 cups beef broth

3 large poblano chiles, chopped

1 (14 1/2-ounce) can
 chopped tomatoes with juice

1 large red bell pepper, chopped

1 cup chopped celery

3 cloves garlic, chopped

1 bay leaf

1/2 cup chopped parsley

Preheat oven to 325 degrees. Heat 1 tablespoon oil in Dutch oven over medium to high heat. Season shanks with salt and pepper, then brown on all sides for 20 minutes. Transfer to bowl. Heat remaining oil in Dutch oven, add onions and carrots. Sauté until tender, about 10 minutes, and add tomato paste. Stir, add wine and bring to boil, scraping off brown bits in pan. Reduce to half, about 5 minutes. Return shanks to pot. Add stock and all remaining ingredients except parsley. Cover and bake 2 1/2 to 3 hours. Transfer shanks to a deep platter and cover. Discard bay leaf. Puree sauce and thicken at a simmer, approximately 15 minutes. Sauce shanks, sprinkle with parsley and serve.

Dijon Crusted Rack of Lamb

Makes 6 servings

4 (6 to 8 chops per rack)
New Zealand racks of lamb
Salt and pepper
Olive oil
Dijon mustard
1/4 cup fresh thyme, finely chopped
1/4 cup fresh oregano, finely chopped

1/4 cup fresh rosemary, finely chopped
1/4 cup fresh parsley, finely chopped
1 cup panko bread crumbs

Preheat oven to 375 degrees. Trim and discard any excess fat from lamb. Season lamb racks with salt and pepper. In a large skillet, sauté lamb racks in olive oil on both sides, to sear. In a shallow pan, roast in oven for 10 minutes, then remove from oven and cool. Coat lamb racks with Dijon mustard. In a medium-size bowl, combine thyme, oregano, rosemary, parsley and panko. Pat mixture over lamb (this gives crust effect).

Las Campanas Country Club—Brad Gallegos, chef

Marinated Leg of Lamb

Makes 4 to 6 servings

3/4 cup olive oil
1/4 cup red wine vinegar
Juice of 1 lemon
1 onion, roughly chopped
1 tablespoon sea salt
1 tablespoon pepper

3 bay leaves
4 cloves garlic, peeled and cut in half
4 sprigs rosemary
1 (4 to 6-pound) boneless leg lamb, cut into 2 to 3-inch cubes

Mix all ingredients except lamb in a bowl. Put cubed lamb in a big storage bag and pour marinade over. Let rest overnight in refrigerator, massaging bag periodically. Bring lamb to room temperature and grill outside over charcoal to desired doneness, brushing often with marinade. This recipe is also great with pork.

Nedra Matteucci Galleries—Nedra and Richard Matteucci

Red Chile-Piñon-Crusted Lamb Chops

Makes 6 servings

2 full racks (16 to 18 chops) lamb

2 1/4 cups red chile sauce (from powder)

1 tablespoon olive oil

1 cup bread crumbs

1 cup pine nuts

1 tablespoon unsalted butter (softened)

1 teaspoon salt

1/2 teaspoon black pepper

RED CHILE SAUCE:

36 medium dried red New Mexico or Anaheim chiles

2 tablespoons chopped fresh garlic

1 tablespoon olive oil

Salt, to taste

Preheat oven to 400 degrees. Cut fat off back end of bones of lamb rack. Rub 3/4 cup red chile sauce over meat on both sides of lamb rack, cover, and let marinate in refrigerator overnight. Next day, remove lamb rack from refrigerator. In a medium-size skillet over medium high heat, add oil and sear lamb rack in pan for approximately 2 minutes on each side. Remove meat from skillet.

In a food processor, pulse bread until finely ground into small crumbs, measuring 1 cup. Add pine nuts and pulse again for 30 seconds, until nuts are coarsely ground. Add softened butter, salt, black pepper and pulse an additional 15 seconds. Remove crust from food processor and place into bowl. Press crumbs onto backside of rib rack, covering each lamb chop all the way up to exposed bone, until meat on lamb rack is completely covered. Crust should be approximately 1/4 inch thick.

In a roasting pan, place crusted lamb rack with crust side up and bake for 12 minutes for medium-rare chops or longer for more well-done chops. Remove from oven and place rack on wood cutting board. Place remaining Red Chile Sauce in saucepan and heat over medium heat until warm. Slice each chop from rack and serve 2 to 3 chops per person, with approximately 1/4 cup of Red Chile Sauce.

RED CHILE SAUCE:

Rinse, stem and seed chiles (about 6 cups) and place them in a pot filled with water. Cover, bring to a boil, reduce heat and simmer 20 to 30 minutes, until the chiles are tender (soft and pliable). Drain. Heat chopped fresh garlic in olive oil for approximately 2 minutes, until golden brown. Place the cooked chiles, along with sautéed garlic and salt, into a blender or food processor. Blend to a thick puree. Add 2 to 3 cups of chicken stock and blend, until desired consistency of sauce. Blend for another minute. Press sauce through fine sieve and serve. This sauce can be made ahead of time.

Home of Terry Brewer on Old Santa Fe Trail. Photography: Daniel Nadelbach,
photographic styling: Gilda Meyer-Niehof.

Lamb Loin en Croute

Makes 4 servings

2 loins spring lamb, trimmed
Salt and pepper
2 tablespoons butter
1/2 pound wild mushrooms, chopped
1 medium onion, chopped
1 tablespoon fresh rosemary,
   finely chopped

1 tablespoon thyme
Splash brandy or cognac
1 tablespoon fresh parsley
2 puff pastry sheets
1 egg, beaten

Preheat oven to 325 degrees. Salt and pepper lamb loin and sear on all sides in skillet on high heat until brown. Refrigerate until cold. Melt butter over medium heat and sauté mushrooms, onion, rosemary, thyme, salt and pepper until fully cooked. Stir often. Remove from heat, deglaze with brandy and parsley. Let cool. When loins and mushroom mixture are cool, spread each loin with 1/2 of mushrooms. Set aside.

Lay out 1 sheet of puff pastry at a time, keeping others covered with damp towel. Put 1 lamb loin on puff pastry sheet. Fold in ends over ends of loin and roll up. Brush ends of puff pastry with egg to seal before rolling. Repeat with remaining lamb and sheets of puff pastry. If you wish, cut remaining puff pastry sheet into 4 crosswise strips, brush with egg and coil around to form a flower shape. Place one on top of each loin and brush with more egg. Loins can be prepared a few hours ahead of time, covered lightly and refrigerated.

Note: Loins should be brought to room temperature for at least 30 minutes before baking to ensure proper cooking. Bake uncovered for 10 to 15 minutes or until just golden brown, do not overcook. This recipe is also great with pork.

Las Campanas Country Club—Brad Gallegos, chef

San Juan Pork Tenderloin

Makes 2 servings

2 teaspoons sugar
1 1/2 teaspoons coarsely
   ground pepper
1 teaspoon sea salt

1/2 teaspoon ground coriander
1/2 teaspoon ground cumin
1 pound pork tenderloin
1 tablespoon balsamic vinegar

In a small bowl, mix sugar, pepper, sea salt, coriander and cumin. Rub pork with mixture on all sides and wrap in plastic wrap. Refrigerate for 4 hours or overnight. Remove pork from plastic wrap, and tie every 2 inches with butcher string, tucking tail under for uniform thickness. Brush tenderloin with balsamic vinegar. Cook on low on preheated barbeque grill for 25 minutes. Turn halfway through. Center should be pink. Internal temperature should be 155 degrees. Cut pork into 1/2-inch slices.

Nuevo Carne Adobada

Makes 4 to 6 servings

RED CHILE:
1 pound red chile pods, dried
 and seeded
3 quarts water
3 cloves garlic
Salt, to taste
Dash oregano and cumin
1 medium onion, chopped (optional)

PORK
TENDERLOIN:
2 pounds pork tenderloin
Salt, to taste

RED CHILE SAUCE:
Remove stems and seeds. Wash pods in colander with running water to remove dust that may have accumulated from ristra while drying outdoors. Soak pods in water and simmer on stove for about 45 minutes, until pods are quite soft. Place chile in batches in blender with enough of remaining water in pot and puree chile. Add garlic, salt, oregano, cumin and onion. Remove chile from blender and pour into a food mill (this will remove skin from pods completely and creates a very silky finish). Process chile in food mill and pour contents in a sauce pot. Set aside 2 cups of uncooked red chile for pork marinade. The remaining chile may now be simmered for 30 to 45 minutes over medium to low heat.

PORK TENDERLOIN:
Pour 2 cups of red chile over raw pork as a marinade and set aside in refrigerator for about 4 hours or overnight. Grill tenderloins over high heat and turn them until seared. Remove and place tenderloins in heavy-duty aluminum foil with remaining marinade and cook over medium heat on grill until done (usually 12 to 18 minutes, depending on heat and size of tenderloins). Use thermometer to check temperature of pork. Normally it should read 170 degrees. Alternate cooking method: cook in oven at 300 degrees until pork is tender and thermometer reads 170 degrees.

Blend and serve. Great over pork, ham and beef.

Pork Ribs with Barbeque Sauce

Makes 4 servings

1 (8-ounce) can tomato paste
1 cup ketchup
1/2 cup water
1/2 onion, minced
1/4 cup each lemon juice
    and sherry
1 cup brown sugar
2 tablespoons each white wine
    vinegar, tarragon and molasses
1 tablespoon each vegetable oil and
    Worcestershire sauce

2 teaspoons dry mustard
1/2 teaspoon garlic salt
1 teaspoon salt
1/8 teaspoon each allspice and
    cayenne pepper
1/8 to 2 teaspoons chile powder,
    according to preference
3 drops Tabasco sauce, or to taste
5 pounds baby back spareribs

Combine all ingredients in heavy, high-sided saucepan and simmer at least 30 minutes. Can be stored in refrigerator when cooled. Broil ribs at 550 degrees to brown, 7 minutes per side. Cover with 2 cups of sauce. Broil at 400 degrees for 15 to 20 minutes, watching distance from flame carefully, so as not to burn. Spoon in another cup of sauce and broil another 15 to 20 minutes. Spoon on rest of sauce and broil at 300 degrees for 15 minutes. If desired, turn broiler to 550 degrees to char top just before serving.

Kathryn Huelster, professional cooking instructor

Peanut and Spice Crusted Pork Tenderloin

Makes 4 servings

1 1/2 to 2 tablespoons extra-virgin
    olive oil
1 to 1 1/2 pounds pork tenderloin
1 teaspoon kosher salt
1 teaspoon ground ginger

1 teaspoon ground coriander
4 tablespoons finely chopped
    peanuts
2 teaspoons Dijon mustard
2 teaspoons honey

Preheat oven to 350 degrees. In a large ovenproof sauté pan, heat oil on medium heat. Add pork tenderloin and sear on all sides, turning to prevent burning. Remove from heat and set aside. In a small bowl, mix together salt, ginger, coriander and peanuts. Spread out on baking sheet and set aside.

In a small bowl, combine Dijon mustard and honey, then whisk and spread honey mixture over pork tenderloin. Next, roll pork tenderloin in nut mixture. Press firmly to adhere. Return pork tenderloin to sauté pan. Transfer pan to oven and cook 25 to 30 minutes or until internal temperature registers 155 degrees.

*Ten Miles to Saturday Night, 1975, by Robert Lougheed, oil on canvas,
Museum of Fine Arts.*

Stuffed Chiles in Nut Sauce

Makes 8 servings

NOGADA SAUCE:
5 slices firm white bread, crusts
    removed
Cold milk
4 cups heavy cream
4 1/2 cups shelled pecans or walnuts
Salt, to taste

STUFFED CHILES:
16 poblano chiles
3 1/2 pounds tomatoes, chopped
1 medium onion, chopped
Chopped parsley, to taste
1 stick cinnamon
3 1/2 cups raisins
1 1/2 cups shelled almonds, peeled
Pinch sugar
1/2 cup green olives, pitted and
    halved (optional)
Pomegranate seeds or
    canned cherries, chopped
    for garnish
Parsley sprigs, for garnish

NOGADA SAUCE:
Soak bread in small amount of cold milk. Liquefy cream, nuts, salt and milk-soaked bread in blender. The sauce should be quite thick, so more cream may be added, if needed. Refrigerate until well chilled.

CHILES:
Peel chiles. Place them directly over gas flame or under broiler until they char and blister, turning from time to time. Put them in a plastic bag and seal it for 10 to 20 minutes to loosen the skins. Slit each peeled chile along one side and carefully remove seed and veins; leave stem end intact. In a large, heavy saucepan, fry tomatoes, onion, parsley and cinnamon stick in oil until onions are soft. Add raisins, almonds, sugar and olives. Cook, stirring occasionally, for 20 minutes or until browned. Remove cinnamon stick.

Stuff chiles with stuffing mixture until they are well filled. Arrange warm chiles on serving platter and pour chilled Nogada Sauce on top. Garnish with pomegranate seeds and parsley sprigs. Serve right away.

Ham Loaf

Makes 6 to 8 servings

2 eggs, well beaten
1 pound ground ham
2 teaspoons baking powder
1 teaspoon Worcestershire sauce
1 cup light cream (half-and-half)
1 cup bread crumbs
1 pound ground lean pork
1/2 cup onion, chopped
1 teaspoon parsley, chopped
1/2 teaspoon salt

GLAZE:
1/3 cup brown sugar
1 teaspoon dry mustard
1/4 cup vinegar

HORSERADISH
SAUCE:
1/4 cup mayonnaise
1/4 cup sour cream
2 tablespoons prepared mustard
1 tablespoon minced chives
1/3 cup prepared horseradish
1 teaspoon lemon juice

Preheat oven to 375 degrees. Beat eggs, add ham and rest of ingredients, and mix thoroughly. Butter a 2-quart loaf pan, line with waxed paper and fill.

GLAZE:
Combine glaze ingredients and boil 2 minutes. Pour over meat after 30 minutes. Set pan in hot water and bake for about 1 to 1 1/2 hours. Serve with Horseradish Sauce.

HORSERADISH SAUCE:
Blend and serve. Great over pork, ham and beef.

Veal Chops with Rosemary Sauce

Makes 4 servings

SAUCE:
2 tablespoons butter
1 tablespoon finely minced shallots
1 1/2 teaspoons finely
   minced rosemary
2 tablespoons dry vermouth
1/2 cup veal stock (beef broth)
1/2 cup whipping cream
Salt and pepper

VEAL:
4 (8-ounce) veal chops, 1 inch thick
Salt and pepper
1/4 cup butter
3 medium zucchinis
2 tablespoons butter
1 medium tomato peeled, seeded and
   diced
4 sprigs fresh rosemary

SAUCE:
Melt butter in skillet, over medium heat, add shallots and rosemary, and cook 3 minutes. Add vermouth and boil until almost no liquid remains (2 minutes). Add stock and boil until liquid is reduced by half (4 minutes). Add cream until slightly thickened, and add salt and pepper.

VEAL:
Season veal with salt and pepper. Melt 1/4 cup butter and cook 3 minutes per side for medium rare. Transfer to platter. Tent with foil to keep warm. Slice zucchini into 1/4-inch slices. Melt 2 tablespoons butter and sauté zucchini until crisp (1 minute). Divide among 4 plates. Top with veal chop. Reheat sauce and pour over veal. Sprinkle diced tomato with rosemary over dish and serve.

Buffaloaf with Hatch Green Chile

Makes 8 servings

5 or more ounces Hatch green chile
  (or use frozen chopped)
1 onion
Butter
Olive oil
2 pounds ground buffalo meat
2 eggs
1 dash Worcestershire sauce
  (or more)

1 dash Tabasco sauce (or more)
3 cloves garlic, minced, or 1 tablespoon powdered garlic
1 tablespoon mustard powder
2 tablespoons bread crumbs
Dash paprika
Dash black pepper
1/2 to 3/4 cup ketchup

Preheat oven to 365 degrees. First prepare chile: remove stems, seeds and skin, then dice, assuming already roasted; or use a frozen brand like Bueno, saving all the work. If using Bueno, there may be excess fluids to drain after defrosting. Chop and sauté onion with a little butter and olive oil (olive oil helps prevent butter from burning). Except for ketchup, thoroughly mix all ingredients, adding onion last if it is still warm. Shape into an oval loaf, about 8 inches long and 5 inches wide. Place on slotted surface of broiling pan. Pour some ketchup on top of loaf, and spread and pattern it with a fork. Cook in oven for 1 1/2 hours at 7,000 feet or 350 degrees for 1 1/2 hours at sea level.

Sandia Rabbit in Wine Sauce

Makes 4 servings

2 tablespoons butter
Salt and pepper
1 rabbit, cut into servings
1 medium onion, finely chopped
Sprigs rosemary

1 clove garlic, minced
2 bay leaves
2 (8-ounce) cans tomato sauce
4 cups water
2 cups dry red wine

Melt butter in cooking pan. Salt and pepper rabbit. Sauté rabbit for 1/2 hour slowly. Add onion, rosemary, garlic and bay leaves, and cook for 10 minutes so rabbit can absorb flavors. Add tomato sauce, water and red wine. Simmer for 1 to 1 1/2 hours, covered. Remove bay leaves.

Optional: sprinkle with grated Parmesan.

Note: Serve with polenta as a bed. Place 2 pieces of rabbit on polenta and cover with sauce.

Saint Francis Cathedral, *East San Francisco Street, Santa Fe, New Mexico.*
Courtesy of the Palace of the Governors Photo Archives. Negative 10012.

Roast Loin of Venison

Makes 4 servings

2 loins venison

2 cups red wine

2 medium onions, thinly sliced

6 sprigs parsley

2 bay leaves

12 peppercorns

2 cloves garlic

Dash thyme

1/2 cup melted butter

Salt and pepper, to taste

ANCHO CHILE AND HONEY SAUCE:

8 whole cumin seeds

1 teaspoon whole coriander seeds

2 tablespoons oil

4 to 6 dried ancho chiles, seeded

1 small onion, diced

4 cloves garlic, diced

8 Roma tomatoes, quartered

3 cups chicken broth

8 whole sprigs cilantro

1/3 cup honey

1/3 cup fresh lime juice

Salt and pepper, to taste

Place venison in baking dish. Add wine, onions, parsley, bay leaves, peppercorns, garlic and thyme. Cover and refrigerate at least 24 hours. Preheat oven to 400 degrees. Pour off marinade, saving 1/2 cup of liquid. Mix melted butter with marinade. Salt and pepper meat and bake in oven for 25 minutes. Reduce heat to 325 degrees and bake until meat thermometer says venison is medium rare, basting entire time with marinade mixture. Serve with Ancho Chile and Honey Sauce.

ANCHO CHILE AND HONEY SAUCE:

Combine cumin and coriander seeds in pan over medium heat and toss until toasted. Do not burn. In a skillet, heat oil over medium heat. Add chiles, onion, garlic and tomatoes. Cook until all are limp. Add broth and seeds. Continue cooking another 30 minutes until liquid is reduced. Remove to blender and add cilantro. Blend. Strain into a small saucepan. Add honey, lime juice, salt and pepper. Continue simmering for 15 to 25 minutes until smooth. Ladle over each serving of venison. You can also add 1 cup jalapeno pepper jelly to sauce, if desired.

Tequila Seared Mahi-Mahi

Makes 4 servings

2 tablespoons olive oil

2 cloves garlic, minced

6 slices thick bacon, cut in 1-inch pieces

Salt and pepper, to taste

4 fillets mahi-mahi, 1 inch thick

2 cups peeled, seeded and chopped tomatoes

1/4 cup tequila

1 tablespoon chopped fresh cilantro

Hot red pepper, optional

In an ovenproof sauté pan, heat oil over medium heat. Sauté garlic and bacon until brown. Salt and pepper both sides of fish. Add fish to sauté pan and sear until lightly browned. Add tomatoes. Once heated, put mixture on top of fish and add tequila and cilantro. Scrape browned sauce from bottom of pan. Reduce to low heat, cover and cook 15 minutes.

Gingered Salmon

Makes 4 servings

3/4 cup freshly peeled and grated
    ginger
1 cup sugar
1 teaspoon cayenne pepper
Salt, to taste
4 (6-ounce) fillets salmon
3/4 cup sesame seeds

1 cup rice vinegar
1/2 cup fresh lime juice
1/4 cup fish sauce
1/4 cup brown sugar
3 tablespoons grated lemon zest
3 tablespoons olive oil
Fresh cilantro, for garnish

In a glass bowl, mix ginger, half the sugar, cayenne pepper and salt. Coat each side of fish with mixture, then press into sesame seeds on a flat plate. Set aside. In a saucepan, blend vinegar, lime juice, fish sauce, remaining sugar, brown sugar, lemon zest and salt. Set aside. In a large sauté pan over medium heat, add olive oil. Add fish and sauté until golden on both sides. Reduce heat and cook for a few minutes. At the same time over low heat, warm vinegar mixture until hot. Transfer fish to plates and drizzle with vinegar sauce. Serve while hot.

Salmon a la Greque

Makes 10 servings

1 side fresh salmon, skin on
Salt and pepper, to taste
2 fresh lemons, sliced
4 Roma tomatoes, sliced

2 cups sliced artichoke hearts, canned
1 cup sliced Kalamata olives
1/2 cup olive oil
3 ounces fresh basil leaves

Preheat oven to 350 degrees. Place side of salmon, skin side down, on well-oiled baking sheet and sprinkle with salt and pepper. Arrange sliced lemons and tomatoes on top, not overlapping each other. Sprinkle the artichoke hearts and olives all over top. Drizzle with olive oil. Place in oven and cook until the thickest part of salmon is medium (use knife to separate and check). Remove from oven and sprinkle on basil leaves. Allow to cool if served alfresco, or serve hot.

Peas in a Pod Catering—Catherine O'Brien and Glenda Griswold, proprietors

Escalopes of Salmon with Sauce Moutarde

Makes 2 servings

1 (12-ounce) fillet fresh salmon

1 cup flour

2 tablespoons cooking oil

4 slices lemon

4 sprigs parsley

SAUCE
MOUTARDE:

Dash oil

1 tablespoon minced shallots

1 1/2 cups dry white wine

1 1/2 cups heavy cream

1 rounded tablespoon Dijon mustard

1/8 pound butter

Salt and pepper, to taste

Slice salmon on the bias, across the fillet, in 1/4-inch slices. Dredge lightly in flour and place in a skillet preheated with cooking oil. Sauté 15 to 20 seconds on each side and remove to a preheated platter. Top with hot Sauce Moutarde and garnish with lemon and parsley.

FOR THE SAUCE:

Sauté shallots in oil in a 1- to 2-quart saucepan. Do not brown. Add white wine and bring to a boil. Reduce the liquid until there is only a trace left. Stir in cream and mustard. Reduce heat and let sauce simmer, stirring frequently. Continue cooking until sauce is thick and bubbly. Remove from heat. Cut butter into wedges and drop into sauce, one at a time, stirring until smooth. Do not let it boil once butter is added as it will separate.

Santa Ana Sea Bass

Makes 4 servings

1/2 cup unsalted butter

4 fillets sea bass, about 6 to 8 ounces each

1/2 cup lemon juice

1/3 cup capers

2 tablespoons parsley, finely chopped

3 tablespoons olive oil

1 pound small cherry tomatoes (red and yellow, if possible)

Over medium heat, warm a large sauté pan. Add half the butter. When melted, add bass and cook until white. Turn and cook until meat starts to separate. Remove to hot platter. Wipe sauté pan clean with paper towels. Melt remaining butter until brown. Add lemon juice, capers and parsley. Stir and blend. Pour over bass and serve.

At the same time as sautéing fish, in a small sauté pan, heat olive oil over medium heat, add tomatoes and cook gently until warmed through. Add as a dressing around fish.

Seared Halibut with Butternut Squash and Spinach

Makes 4 servings

1 large butternut squash, peeled,
seeded and diced into 1/2-inch
squares
1/4 cup olive oil
Salt, pepper and corn oil, as needed
2 fresh shallots, peeled and diced
small

1 cup orange juice
1/2 cup sugar
1 (12-ounce) bag cranberries
4 (6-ounce) portions fresh halibut
2 (8-ounce) bunches spinach

For the squash: Drizzle squash with olive oil and season with salt and pepper, to taste. Place in oven and bake until firm yet tender, approximately 20 to 30 minutes. (Before cooking halibut or spinach, make sure the squash is cooked.)

For the cranberry compote: Place shallots into a 4-quart saucepan with orange juice. Bring orange juice to boil, add sugar and cranberries. Turn heat down to simmer and cook until all berries are popped. Take off heat and let cool. (Can be made 1 day ahead. Refrigerate if doing so. Bring to room temperature before serving.)

For the halibut: Place corn oil in a hot sauté pan and sear halibut until golden brown on top. Turn halibut over and place into oven 5 to 7 minutes.

For the spinach: Place corn oil in a hot sauté pan. Gently add spinach and mix until just hot, not cooked. Season with salt and pepper; immediately place on serving plates. Place squash on top of spinach. Put halibut on squash and ladle cranberry sauce on halibut.

Las Campanas Country Club—Brad Gallegos, chef

Crusted Halibut

Makes 4 servings

4 (6 to 8-ounce) fillets halibut
3 tablespoons finely grated
horseradish
2 cloves garlic, minced
Salt, to taste
2 tablespoons finely grated
orange peel

1 cup bread crumbs
2 tablespoons olive oil
2 tablespoons peanut oil
1 teaspoon sesame oil
Dash red chile powder, optional

Preheat oven to 375 degrees. In a glass bowl, combine horseradish, garlic, salt, orange peel, and bread crumbs. Spread mixture on flat plate. Press each fillet into crumbs, making sure both sides are covered. In oven-safe sauté pan heat oils over medium heat. Place fillets in sauté pan. Don't knock off crumbs. Brown crust until golden brown. Turn uncooked side down and bake in preheated oven until fillets are firm in the middle, about 4 minutes. (Before placing in oven, you can sprinkle with red chile powder.)

Calamari a la Mannie

Makes 4 to 6 servings

1 pound calamari pieces
2 cups flour
2 quarts oil
1/4 cup extra-virgin olive oil
2 teaspoons garlic powder

Juice of 2 lemons
1/2 cup parsley, chopped
White pepper, to taste
Salt, to taste

Dredge calamari in flour and deep fry in oil, drain. Coat bottom of sauté pan with olive oil and add enough of fried calamari to fit comfortably in bottom of pan. Sprinkle with garlic powder. Squeeze lemons over calamari, sprinkle parsley, and a dash of white pepper. Salt, to taste. Serve hot. Continue with rest of calamari as above until complete.

Piquant Tilapia

Makes 2 to 3 servings

1 (1-pound) fillet tilapia
1 teaspoon butter
1 cup red pepper, diced
1 teaspoon grated orange rind
1 teaspoon fresh ginger, minced

1/2 teaspoon Dijon mustard
   (coarsely grained)
1/4 cup sushi vinegar
1/4 cup fresh cilantro, chopped
2 tablespoons chicken broth

Set aside fish, butter and red pepper. Mix rest of ingredients in a small bowl. In a large skillet, sauté fish in butter for 2 to 3 minutes. Add rest of ingredients, including red pepper. Cover skillet and cook for 3 to 5 minutes or until fish is done. Serve immediately.

Trout with Bacon

Makes 6 to 8 servings

6 to 8 fillets whole freshwater trout,
   cleaned
Salt and pepper, to taste
1 strip uncooked bacon, per trout
3/4 cup salad oil
2 tablespoons Worcestershire sauce

1 tablespoon dry mustard
1 teaspoon ground pepper
1/4 cup wine vinegar
3/4 teaspoon dried parsley
1 clove garlic, crushed
2 tablespoons lemon juice

Season inside of trout with salt and pepper, to taste. Put bacon slice inside fish. Combine all remaining ingredients and brush inside and outside well with mixture. Wrap fish in foil and broil under heat for 5 to 8 minutes on each side, depending on thickness of fish.

Swordfish Tomatillo

Makes 4 servings

1 tablespoon olive oil

2 tablespoons molasses

1 teaspoon hot pepper

1/4 cup lime juice

4 fillets swordfish steaks or
   red snapper, quartered

TOMATILLO
   SAUCE:

3 tablespoons Canola oil

1 small onion, diced

3 cloves garlic, minced

1/2 pound tomatillos, husked
   and quartered

2 serrano chiles, minced

1/2 teaspoon cumin

1 cup chicken broth

2 tablespoons chopped fresh cilantro

2 tablespoons chopped parsley

3/4 cup hulled pumpkin seeds,
   toasted

Salt and pepper, to taste

4 leaves spinach, for garnish

In a glass bowl, whisk olive oil, molasses, hot pepper and lime juice. Add fish to the marinade, turn, and marinate for 10 minutes. Grill fish over hot heat, turning once, until browned (about 5 minutes). Serve at once with Tomatillo Sauce on side.

TOMATILLO SAUCE:
In a deep sauté pan, heat oil over medium heat. Add onion and garlic until soft. Reduce heat and add tomatillos, chiles and cumin. Stir, cover and cook until tomatillos are soft (stirring occasionally). Transfer to blender. Add broth, cilantro, parsley, and pumpkin seeds and blend. Salt and pepper, to taste. Divide between 4 small bowls at each serving. Garnish with spinach leaves.

Sicilian Swordfish

Makes 6 servings

1 1/2 pounds fresh swordfish (should
   be white or pink in color, never
   brownish), cut into 1/4-inch slices

1 large white onion, diced

2 stalks celery, diced

2 tablespoons extra-virgin olive oil

2 cups fresh tomatoes, diced

1/2 cup pine nuts

1 cup raisins

1 tablespoon salted capers

1 bay leaf

1 tablespoon flat-leaf parsley,
   chopped

Pinch of oregano

1 cup pecorino cheese (or Romano)

Fresh bread crumbs

Flour

Olive oil

Marsala wine

Preheat oven to 350 degrees. Buy a single center-cut piece of swordfish. Very gently pound the slices until thin, taking care to not break them. Set aside. Prepare stuffing by sautéing onion and celery in olive oil until soft. Add tomatoes, pine nuts, raisins, capers, bay leaf, parsley and oregano. Sauté for 10 minutes. Set aside to cool. Use 2/3 of stuffing; once cooled, add pecorino and bread crumbs. Mix thoroughly. Reserve the other 1/3. Place just a little over 1 tablespoon of stuffing onto each slice of fish, roll gently and secure with toothpick. Dredge in flour and cook in skillet with hot olive oil, browning all sides. Glaze with a splash of Marsala. Sprinkle remaining stuffing over top and bake in oven for about 10 minutes. Serve with remaining sauce.

Osteria d'Assisi—Ling Pertusini, owner; F. Ventricini, chef

Music in the Plaza, *1920, by John Sloan, oil on canvas, Museum of Fine Arts. Gift of*
Mrs. Cyrus McCormick. Photo: Blair Brown.

Three-Mustard Crabcakes

Makes 4 to 6 servings

1 pound lump crabmeat, all shell and
    cartilage removed

1 medium chopped onion, sautéed in
    2 tablespoons butter

2 eggs, divided

1 1/3 cup panko bread crumbs,
    divided

2 tablespoons mayonnaise

2 tablespoons whipping cream

1 tablespoon Dijon mustard

1 tablespoon dry mustard

1 tablespoon yellow mustard

2 scallions, diced

1/4 cup roasted red peppers, finely
    diced

2 tablespoons capers, drained

Dash white pepper

Dash curry dill

1/4 teaspoon grated lemon rind

Juice of 1 lemon

1/4 cup butter

1/4 cup olive oil

Lightly mix together crab, onion, 1 egg, 1/3 cup panko bread crumbs, mayonnaise, whipping cream, mustards, scallions, red peppers, capers, pepper, dill, lemon rind and lemon juice. Lightly form into 4 to 6 patties and dip into reserved beaten egg and panko. Chill again. Sauté in combination of 1/4 cup butter and 1/4 cup olive oil. Drain and serve with remoulade, cocktail or hollandaise sauce.

Baked Crab and Rice

Makes 4 servings

8 ounces fresh lump crabmeat, all
    shell and cartilage removed

4 hard-boiled eggs, chopped

1 (8-ounce) can evaporated milk

1/2 teaspoon salt

1 cup slightly undercooked rice

1 cup mayonnaise

1/2 cup sour cream

1/4 teaspoon tarragon

1 tablespoon fresh parsley, chopped

1/2 cup onion, chopped

1/4 teaspoon cayenne pepper

1 1/2 cups grated cheddar cheese

1 cup buttered bread crumbs

Preheat oven 350 degrees. Mix all ingredients together except for cheese and bread crumbs. Put in a small casserole dish and top with cheese and bread crumbs. Cover lightly with aluminum foil and bake for 35 to 40 minutes, removing foil after 20 minutes. Let cool a few minutes before serving.

Grilled Tuna with Cannellini Beans and Garlic Mayonnaise

Makes 4 servings

4 tuna steaks, 1 inch thick
1/2 teaspoon thyme
2 cloves garlic
1 tablespoon fennel seeds
1/2 teaspoon dried red chile pepper flakes
3 cups olive oil
Salt and coarse pepper, to taste
3 tablespoons pine nuts
2 cups cooked cannellini beans
2 onions, grilled
Garlic Mayonnaise

GARLIC MAYONNAISE:

8 fillets salt-packed anchovy, chopped
2 shallots, finely diced
2 tablespoons lemon juice
3 tablespoons extra-virgin olive oil
Salt and pepper, to taste

TUNA:

Mix all spice ingredients in a deep dish. Salt and pepper both sides of tuna and put in dish. Cover with olive oil and marinate overnight. Using a heavy sauté pan, heat 2 tablespoons olive oil over medium heat. Add tuna and cook for 10 minutes, turning once. Lower heat, add pine nuts, and cook. Tuna is done when it is still slightly pink in center. Serve with hot cannellini beans and grilled onions. Drizzle with Garlic Mayonnaise.

GARLIC MAYONNAISE:

Combine ingredients in a bowl and stir together until blended. Add more lemon juice, if needed.

Lib's Shrimp Santa Fe

Makes 4 to 6 servings

2 1/2 pounds shrimp, peeled and deveined
1 teaspoon rosemary leaves
1 medium onion
6 green onions, with tops

1 stick (1/2 cup) butter
8 ounces olive oil
1 clove garlic
Salt and pepper, to taste
3 jars mild picante sauce

Preheat oven to 325 degrees. Mix all ingredients except shrimp and picante sauce. Bake in oven for 30 minutes. Stir in shrimp and continue to bake for 30 minutes. Add picante sauce. Continue to bake for 30 minutes more. Serve with rice and crusty french bread.

Elizabeth and Randy Travis

Shrimp Creole

Makes 8 servings

1/4 cup flour
1/4 cup butter
2 cups onions, chopped
1/2 cup green onions, chopped
2 cloves garlic, minced
1 cup green peppers, chopped
1 cup celery, chopped
1 teaspoon thyme
2 bay leaves
3 teaspoons salt

1/2 teaspoon pepper
6 ounces tomato paste
1 (16-ounce) can tomatoes with liquid
8 ounces tomato sauce
1 cup water
4 pounds raw shrimp, peeled
1 teaspoon Tabasco sauce
1/2 cup parsley, chopped
1 tablespoon lemon juice
2 cups cooked rice

In a Dutch oven, make a dark brown roux of flour and butter. Add onions, green onions, garlic, green peppers, celery, thyme, bay leaves, salt, and pepper and sauté uncovered, over medium heat until onions are transparent and soft, about 30 minutes. Add tomato paste and sauté 3 minutes. Add tomatoes, tomato sauce, and water and simmer slowly, partly covered for 1 hour, stirring occasionally. Add shrimp and cook until just done, about 5 minutes. Add Tabasco, parsley and lemon juice. Stir, cover and remove from heat. Serve over rice. Best when refrigerated overnight. Also freezes well. Heat quickly, without boiling and serve immediately.

Grilled and Curried Shrimp

Makes 4 servings

20 large shrimp, raw
1 stick (1/2 cup) butter
1 tablespoon Worcestershire sauce

2 tablespoons curry powder
2 tablespoons seasoned salt
Dash Chimayo red chile, optional

Preheat oven to 400 degrees. Split shrimp and keep shells intact. Prepare sauce by melting butter in saucepan and adding Worcestershire sauce and curry. Place shrimp on baking pan and bake until they turn pink (5 to 10 minutes). Add salt and red chile to the sauce at the last minute. Cover shrimp with sauce and cook under broiler until tails turn up (5 to 10 minutes).

South-of-the-Border Shrimp

Makes 6 to 8 servings

2 pounds large shrimp, shelled and
   deveined, with tails left intact

3/4 cup olive oil

1/4 cup white wine vinegar

2 to 3 tablespoons fresh lemon juice

2 large garlic cloves, minced

1/2 teaspoon crushed red pepper
   flakes

Salt and ground black pepper,
   to taste

1/2 cup finely chopped cilantro

2 jalapeno peppers, seeded and
   minced

1 large lemon, sliced

1 large red onion, sliced

Bring a large pot of water to a boil. Add shrimp and cook until pink, about 3 minutes. Drain and transfer to a large bowl of ice water until shrimp are cooled. Drain and place shrimp in a large bowl. In a medium-size bowl, whisk together oil, vinegar, lemon juice, garlic, red pepper flakes, salt and black pepper. Stir in cilantro, tossing to coat. In a large, shallow dish, layer shrimp, minced jalapenos, lemon slices and onion. Pour remaining marinade over shrimp. Cover and refrigerate at least 6 hours.

Baked Seafood Supreme

Makes 8 to 10 servings

8 ounces scallops, poached until
   slightly underdone

8 ounces shrimp, cooked until
   slightly underdone

4 lobster tails, chopped into chunks
   and sautéed

4 to 8 ounces crabmeat, canned or
   purchased cooked

2 cups minute rice, cooked slightly
   and drained

2 tablespoons sherry

2 teaspoons salt

1/4 teaspoon pepper

8 ounces fresh mushrooms, sliced

1 pint heavy cream or half-and-half

1 green pepper, diced

Preheat oven to 350 degrees. Mix all ingredients well. Put in a 2 1/2-quart casserole dish. Bake for 45 minutes.

Lobster and Saffron Risotto

Makes 6 servings

3 tablespoons unsalted butter

2 tablespoons minced shallots

2 medium tomatoes, peeled and
chopped, or 3/4 can chopped
Italian tomatoes

1/2 teaspoon saffron threads, crushed

1 cup dry white wine

1/2 cup cream

2 (12-ounce) lobster tails, cubed

Salt and pepper, to taste

5 cups lobster broth

2 tablespoons chopped fresh parsley

2 tablespoons olive oil

2 tablespoons each chopped carrots,
celery, onion

2 cups arborio rice

Melt 1 tablespoon of butter in a small sauté pan over medium-low heat. Add shallots, tomatoes, saffron and 1/2 cup of dry white wine. Bring to a simmer and reduce liquid by 1/3. Add cream and continue to simmer for 3 minutes. Remove from heat and stir in lobster meat, salt and pepper.

Bring lobster broth to a simmer on top of stove. Heat 2 tablespoons butter and olive oil in a 4- to 6-quart heavy casserole dish over medium heat. Add carrots, celery, and onion and sauté for 2 to 3 minutes or until softened, do not brown. Add rice and sauté, stirring constantly using a wooden spoon, for 1 minute, making sure all of rice is coated. Add remaining 1/2 cup of dry white wine and continue to stir until it is completely absorbed. Add the simmering lobster broth, 1/2 cup at a time, stirring constantly, making sure rice does not stick and broth is absorbed before adding next 1/2 cup.

After stirring and adding broth for approximately 20 minutes, rice should be firm to the bite. Add lobster-tomato mixture with parsley and stir thoroughly to combine. Adjust seasoning and serve immediately in warmed bowls.

Note: To prepare lobster meat and broth, place 2 lobster tails into a large pot with 2 quarts of water and bring to a boil over high heat. Cook for approximately 10 minutes or until meat is opaque. Remove tails and, when cool enough to handle, remove meat and cube. Return shells to water and add 1 onion quartered, 1 carrot cut into 4 pieces, 2 celery stalks cut into 4 pieces and 3 sprigs of fresh parsley.

Dan Ostermiller, artist
Represented by Nedra Matteuci Galleries

Miniature dresser, Mexico. Wood, earthenware, basketry, 13 1/2 inches high, c. 1950, Girard Collection. Museum of International Folk Art, Santa Fe, New Mexcio. Photo by: Michel Monteau.

Razorhead Oysters

Makes 8 servings

16 large shucked oysters
5 slices bacon, crisp
3 leeks, finely chopped
1 stalk celery, finely chopped

2 tablespoons white wine
1/2 teaspoon cayenne pepper
1 cup whipping cream
Panko bread crumbs
8 ramekins

Preheat oven to 500 degrees. Crisp bacon, reserving 2 tablespoons of bacon fat. Sauté leeks and celery in bacon fat until soft. Add white wine and cayenne pepper. Simmer until reduced. Add whipping cream; simmer until thickened. Crumble bacon and add to sauce. Place 2 oysters in each ramekin. Top with leek mixture. Sprinkle with panko bread crumbs. Place ramekins on baking sheet. Place in oven for 10 minutes until bubbly. Can be made up to 2 hours before cooking (refrigerate).

Scalloped Oysters

Makes 6 to 8 servings

1 cup fresh bread crumbs
1 cup fresh cracker crumbs
1/2 cup unsalted butter
1/4 cup minced parsley
1/4 cup snipped dill
3 minced shallots

20 to 24 fresh oysters
3 tablespoons oyster juice
1/2 cup fish stock
1/2 cup heavy cream
Dash Tabasco sauce
1/2 cup white wine
Salt and pepper, to taste

Preheat oven to 425 degrees. Mix together bread and cracker crumbs, butter, parsley, dill and shallots. Spread half in bottom of 8 1/2 x 11 1/2-inch baking dish. Layer oysters over crumbs. Mix together oyster juice, fish stock, cream, Tabasco, wine, salt, and pepper and drizzle over oysters. Cover oysters with rest of crumb mixture. Bake for 25 to 30 minutes, or until golden and bubbly.

Macarrones Verde

Makes 4 servings

2 medium onions, thinly sliced

2 cloves garlic, minced

1/4 teaspoon black pepper

1 teaspoon Spanish smoked paprika

1/2 teaspoon oregano

1/2 teaspoon sweet basil

3 bay leaves

1 tablespoon olive oil

2 pounds boneless cooked chicken, skinless and diced

1 (14 1/2-ounce) can golden mushroom soup

1 (14 1/2-ounce) can green chile enchilada sauce (hot)

1/4 cup green chiles, diced (fresh or 4-ounce can)

4 ounces sliced mushrooms

8 ounces macaroni

4 ounces Spanish olives, sliced

10 ounces grated white cheddar or Monterey Jack

Preheat oven to 375 degrees. Sauté onions, garlic and spices in oil until onions are limp. Add cooked chicken, soup, enchilada sauce, chiles and mushrooms. Simmer 10 minutes. Meanwhile, cook macaroni al dente. Layer chicken mixture, then macaroni, olives and 1/3 cheese in a 9 x 13-inch glass casserole dish in 2 layers. Top with 2/3 cheese and bake uncovered for 30 minutes. Serve with green salad. Freezes well.

Chicken Sour Cream Enchiladas

Makes 6 servings

5 cups cooked and shredded chicken

3 cups grated cheese (cheddar or Monterey Jack)

1 onion, diced

3 cups green chile, chopped

8 ounces green tomatoes, diced

1 clove garlic, diced

Salt and pepper

1 pint sour cream

12 (6-inch) tortillas

Preheat oven to 400 degrees. In a pot, mix chicken, 1 cup cheese, onion, green chile, tomatoes, garlic, salt and pepper. Cook over low heat until mixture is hot, stirring occasionally. Remove from stove. In a 9 x 13-inch baking dish, place 1 cup sour cream in bottom of dish. Fry tortillas in oil until soft, not crisp, and drain on paper towels. Fill each tortilla with chicken mixture, then roll up and place in a baking dish (seam side down). Repeat with all 12 tortillas. Pour remaining chicken mixture over top, cover with sour cream and sprinkle with remaining cheese. Bake for 30 minutes or until hot and cheese is melted.

Chicken Pepperika Olé

Makes 4 servings

1 large onion, sliced
2 teaspoons hot Hungarian paprika
1/4 pound butter
8 fresh green chiles, peeled and
    seeded
8 sticks mozzarella
8 chicken breast halves, boned,
    skinned, butterflied and
    pounded thin
Flour mixed with salt and paprika
12 ounces cooked pasta
1 tablespoon poppy seeds

SAUCE:
2 (14-ounce) cans cream of
    chicken soup
1 cup sour cream
Sauce will be thick.

Sauté onion and paprika in butter until transparent, remove onion with slotted spoon. Stuff each chile with cheese and wrap in chicken breast, folding over to seal. Tie with string in little packages. Dredge chicken in flour mixed with salt and paprika and fry on all sides in butter until golden brown. Return onion to pan and cook covered for 30 minutes on low heat. Remove chicken from pan and add sauce, stir to simmer, add chicken and cook until hot. Toss pasta with 1/2 stick of butter and poppy seeds. Pour chicken over pasta and serve.

Betty Sabo, artist

Chicken Spaghetti

Makes 10 servings

1 large hen
2 or 3 chicken breasts
1/3 cup chicken fat
1 onion, chopped
1 bell pepper, chopped
1/3 cup butter
1 (28-ounce) can tomatoes
1 (8-ounce) can mushrooms
1 (14-ounce) can cream of
    mushroom soup

1 (14-ounce) can cream of
    chicken or celery soup
1 pound cheddar, grated
Salt and pepper, to taste
2 (8-ounce) packages spaghetti

OPTIONAL:
1 (4-ounce) can green chile, chopped
1 (4-ounce) can pimento
1 (4-ounce) can black olives, sliced

Preheat oven to 350 degrees. Boil hen and chicken breasts, bone and cut into bite-size pieces. Skim off 1/3 cup fat. Sauté onion and bell pepper in chicken fat and butter. Add rest of ingredients. Boil spaghetti in chicken broth, undercook slightly. Mix all ingredients together and bake for 1 hour.

*Spring in Santa Fe, ca. 1950, by Randall Davey, oil on canvas,
Museum of Fine Arts.*

Chicken and Brown Rice Primavera

Makes 4 servings

1 tablespoon oil

3/4 pound boneless, skinless chicken breasts, cut into strips

2 cloves garlic, minced

1 1/2 cups chicken broth

1 cup broccoli florets

1/2 cup medium red pepper, cut into strips

1/2 cup carrots, sliced

1/2 cup yellow squash, sliced

1/2 teaspoon ground pepper

1 1/2 cups instant whole-grain brown rice, uncooked

1/2 cup Parmesan, grated

Heat oil in a large skillet on medium heat. Add chicken and garlic, cook and stir until chicken is browned. Stir in broth, vegetables and ground pepper. Bring to a boil. Stir in rice. Return to a boil. Reduce heat to low. Cover and simmer 5 minutes. Remove from heat and stir. Cover and let stand 5 minutes. Stir in cheese and serve.

Chicken India

Makes 4 servings

2 whole boneless, skinless chicken
breasts, cut in half
1 cup fat-free plain yogurt
1 tablespoon lemon juice
1/2 teaspoon ginger
1/2 teaspoon curry powder
1/4 teaspoon cloves
4 teaspoons grated lemon zest
1 teaspoon salt
1/2 teaspoon cumin
1/4 teaspoon ground red pepper
1/4 teaspoon pepper

COUSCOUS OR
JASMINE RICE:
2 cups chicken broth
1 1/2 cups couscous
4 tablespoons currants
2 tablespoons sliced green onion tops
1/2 teaspoon pepper

Preheat broiler. Combine yogurt, lemon juice and spices in a zip-lock plastic bag. Add chicken and marinate 24 to 48 hours. Turn occasionally. Remove chicken and discard marinade. Spray skillet with nonstick spray. Broil 4 to 8 minutes, turning once, until done. Can also be grilled. Serve over Couscous or Jasmine Rice. Serve with vegetable and fruit salad. May be frozen.

COUSCOUS OR JASMINE RICE:
Bring broth to a boil. Stir in couscous or rice. Remove from heat, cover and let stand for 5 minutes. Stir in currants, onion and pepper.

Lemon Dijon Chicken in Crème Sauce

Makes 2 servings

1 pound chicken breast, boneless,
    skinless, cut into bite-size pieces
3 teaspoons olive oil
3 cloves garlic, minced
6 dried morel mushrooms soaked in
    1/4 cup white wine

3 tablespoons Dijon mustard
Juice of 1 large lemon
1/2 cup fresh heavy cream
Salt, to taste

Sauté chicken in olive oil in a heavy pan over high heat until almost done. Reduce heat. Add minced garlic cloves. Slice mushrooms and add wine and mushrooms to chicken. Add mustard and lemon juice. Let mixture cool down. Add cream and salt, to taste. Serve alone or over couscous or pasta and with salad greens.

Chicken Wrap

Makes 4 servings

4 skinless chicken breasts
2 ounces vegetable oil
3 tablespoons red chile powder
1/2 teaspoon garlic powder
Pinch of salt and pepper
4 (10-inch) flour tortillas

1 cup mayonnaise
2 cups grated cheddar
2 cups chopped romaine lettuce
2 tomatoes, coarsely chopped
2 whole avocados (sliced or cubed)

FOR THE CHICKEN:
Mix vegetable oil, red chile powder, garlic powder, salt and pepper with chicken. Allow to marinate for at least 6 hours. Then grill chicken breast until cooked. Slice chicken into thin slices and set aside to cool.

FOR THE WRAP:
Place tortillas on flat work surface. Spread on mayonnaise and evenly place grated cheese, romaine lettuce, chopped tomatoes, avocados and sliced chicken on all 4 tortillas. Fold both ends of tortilla and roll. Serve warm or cold.

Las Campanas Country Club—Brad Gallegos, chef

Chicken Florentine

Makes 16 servings
(may be halved or doubled)

20 medium or 24 small halves
   boneless, skinless chicken breasts
Herb bouquet of 1 bay leaf
3 cups good dry white wine
6 cups chicken stock
Salt, to taste
1 teaspoon dried thyme
4 sprigs parsley

ROUX:
1/3 cup butter
1/3 cup flour
2 teaspoons Dijon mustard
1/2 cup heavy cream (optional)
1/4 teaspoon white pepper
1 1/2 cups grated Gruyère
4 bunches fresh spinach
1/3 cup freshly grated Parmesan

Preheat oven to 450 degrees. Flatten chicken pieces slightly with a mallet. Arrange chicken in a large flame-proof pot. Bury herb bouquet in center. Mix wine and stock, salt lightly, and pour over chicken. Add thyme and parsley. Cover and gradually bring to a simmer. Poach very gently for 25 to 30 minutes (may take less time at sea level). Skim surface, discard bouquet and drain chicken, reserving 5 cups of liquid. Over medium heat, make roux. Combine poaching liquid with roux and stir until thick. Stir in cream and white pepper. Remove from heat and stir in Gruyère. Wash and dry spinach. Remove stems and chop coarsely. Butter a large, shallow baking dish. Spread spinach over bottom and place chicken pieces on spinach so they touch but don't overlap. Pour sauce generously over chicken, covering each piece completely. Sprinkle with Parmesan. Bake about 10 minutes if ingredients are warm, 15 to 20 minutes if cold. Sauce should be bubbly and slightly brown on top.

Rosemary-Lemon Chicken

Makes 4 servings

1 large onion, quartered

2 carrots, cut in 2-inch pieces

1 large fennel bulb

1 cup green olives

2 large sprigs rosemary

Salt and pepper, to taste

8 chicken thighs with skin

1/4 cup olive oil

Juice of 2 lemons

Preheat oven to 400 degrees. Spray a 9 x 13-inch glass casserole dish with cooking spray. Put onion, carrots and fennel in bottom of dish. Next add olives, rosemary, salt and pepper. Next, layer in chicken thighs. Make sure chicken covers olives and rosemary or they will burn. Drizzle with olive oil and lemon juice. Salt and pepper, to taste. Bake for approximately 1 hour until chicken skin is brown and crispy. Serve with couscous. Spoon lemon broth over chicken. So easy and yummy. Can be assembled ahead of time.

Chicken Tangine

Makes 4 to 6 servings

Chicken breasts (bone in or out) or
   parts of your choice, skinned and
   equal to 1 whole chicken

1/2 bunch parsley, chopped

1/2 bunch cilantro, chopped

Grated rind of 1 lemon

Juice of 2 lemons

6 to 8 whole cloves garlic

3 heaping tablespoons fancy hot
   crushed paprika

1/2 teaspoon cumin

Generous pinch saffron

1/2 teaspoon cayenne pepper

1/4 cup oil

2 red onions, coarsely chopped

1 cup Kalamata olives, pitted

Salt and pepper, to taste

Preheat oven to 350 degrees. Mix all ingredients and marinate at least 6 hours. Add 1/2 cup water and bake for 1 hour. Do not overcook. Serve with rice and plain yogurt.

Chicken Santa Fe

Makes 2 servings

2 boneless, skinless chicken breasts

Salt and pepper, to taste

1/2 cup flour

1 tablespoon olive oil

1 jar picante sauce

4 slices jalapeno Jack cheese

Preheat oven to 325 degrees. Salt, pepper and flour the chicken. Pound to 1/2 inch thick. Brown in skillet with olive oil. Transfer to a baking dish and pour picante sauce over to cover. Bake uncovered for 35 minutes. Add a slice of cheese to each chicken breast for last 5 minutes. Easy to prepare, low in fat, and very good with black beans and a green salad.

Chicken Artichoke Casserole

Makes 6 servings

2 whole chicken breasts

1 cup sherry

1 bay leaf

Salt and pepper, to taste

8 ounces sliced mushrooms

1/2 cup sliced green onions

2 tablespoons butter

Garlic salt, to taste

2 (7 1/2-ounce) cans artichoke hearts, drained and quartered

3/4 cup mayonnaise

1/2 cup sour cream

1 cup grated Parmesan

Preheat oven to 350 degrees. Cook chicken in water with 1/2 cup sherry, bay leaf, salt and pepper. Sauté mushrooms and green onions in butter and garlic salt. Remove skin and bones from chicken breasts and cut into 1-inch pieces. Place cooked chicken pieces and artichoke hearts in a 2-quart casserole dish. Add mushrooms and onions. Fold in mayonnaise, sour cream, 1/2 cup sherry and 1/2 cup Parmesan. Top with remaining cheese. Bake uncovered for 25 minutes or until cheese begins to brown. May be frozen.

Chicken Breasts with Wild Rice and Mushrooms

Makes 4 servings

4 chicken breast halves, skinned, boned, pounded thin

1/4 cup onion, minced

1/4 cup fresh parsley, minced

1/4 cup celery leaves, minced

1/2 cup fresh mushrooms, chopped

4 tablespoons butter plus more for basting

1 cup wild rice, cooked

1/2 cup fine bread crumbs

Salt and pepper, to taste

1 teaspoon sage

1 teaspoon poultry seasoning

1 teaspoon chicken granules

1/4 cup sherry, or to taste

Preheat oven to 375 degrees. Put onion, parsley, celery and mushrooms in a food processor to chop. Sauté onions, parsley, celery and mushrooms in 4 tablespoons butter. Mix in wild rice, bread crumbs, salt, pepper, sage, poultry seasoning, chicken granules and sherry. Place pounded chicken breasts on waxed paper. Divide stuffing mixture into 4 equal portions. Put 1/4 mixture in center of boned chicken. Wrap 4 sides over stuffing, tucking in edges. Place into shallow pan, overlapped ends down. Brush liberally with butter. Roast uncovered 1 hour or until golden brown and cooked through. Brush often with melted butter. It may be necessary to cover loosely with foil to prevent over browning. Let stand for 5 minutes before serving. Make early in the day and refrigerate, remove to room temperature and bake just before serving.

Whole Roast Asian Duck

Makes 4 servings

1 (3 to 5-pound) duck

BRINE:
1 cup soy sauce
1/4 cup salt
1/2 cup sugar
1 gallon water

HOISIN SAUCE:
2 cups soy sauce
3 tablespoons garlic
4 cups orange juice
2 tablespoons ginger
2 cups brown sugar
1 cup molasses

SUSHI RICE:
3 1/3 cups short-grain rice
4 cups water
5 tablespoons sugar
2 teaspoons salt
5 tablespoons rice wine vinegar
3-inch kombu sheet, optional

BRINE:
Combine all ingredients.

HOISIN SAUCE:
Mix all ingredients and bring to a boil. Simmer slowly until desired thickness.

METHOD:
Tie duck legs together. Drop in boiling water for 3 minutes. Then marinate in brine for 24 hours in refrigerator. Once marinated, lacquer with Hoisin Sauce and place in oven at 300 degrees for 3 hours. Meat should be tender and easily fall off bone. Serve with Sushi Rice or noodles.

SUSHI RICE:
Thoroughly rinse rice until water runs clear. Put in pot, cover with water and bring to a boil. Once boiling, reduce to low heat for 15 minutes. While rice is cooking, dissolve sugar, salt and vinegar together. Turn rice into wooden bowl. Using a spatula, turn vinegar mixture into rice a little at a time. Do not refrigerate. Should be eaten same day.

Las Campanas Country Club—Jeff Moses, executive chef

Breast of Duck

Makes 6 servings

4 tablespoons Canola oil
2 pounds duck breast
2 apples, peeled, thinly sliced
4 green onions, including tops, minced
1 clove garlic, minced

1 teaspoon thyme
1 bay leaf
Salt and pepper, to taste
1/2 cup apple cider vinegar
1 1/2 cups chicken stock
1/4 cup maple syrup

Heat oil in deep skillet over medium-high heat (don't let it smoke). Quickly add breast halves and brown both sides. Remove breasts and set aside. Lower heat and stir in apples, onions, garlic, thyme, bay leaf, salt and pepper until lightly brown. Stir in vinegar and cook 3 more minutes. Add chicken stock and syrup. Stir. Reduce heat to low and add duck breasts. Simmer meat slowly for 10 to 15 minutes, turning only once. Remove from heat when medium rare.

For Chalupas: dice meat and set aside while making chalupas and relish (see recipe on page 154).

Adobe home in Nambé. Photography: Daniel Nadelbach, photographic styling: Gilda Meyer-Niehof.

Duck Chalupas with Mango Relish

Makes 6 servings

MANGO RELISH:

2 ripe mangos, peeled, pitted and
   chopped

1/2 cup sweet onion, diced

1/3 cup green bell pepper, diced

1/3 cup jicama, diced

1/2 teaspoon dried red chile flakes

Juice of 2 limes

Salt and pepper, to taste

2 tablespoons cilantro, chopped

OTHER FIXINGS:

Vegetable oil

6 large corn tortillas

Cooked black beans

Duck (see Breast of Duck recipe on
   page 153)

1 large ripe avocado, pitted, peeled
   and sliced

CHIPOTLE AIOLI:

3 tablespoons mayonnaise

1 teaspoon chopped Hatch green
   chile

1 tablespoon chopped cilantro

1/2 teaspoon minced garlic

2 teaspoons fresh lime juice

1/2 jigger tequila

Salt and pepper, to taste

For relish: Combine all ingredients in a bowl and refrigerate until needed.

In a deep skillet, pour oil to 1/2 inch deep and heat over medium heat. Fry 1 tortilla at a time. Hold down tortilla with wooden spoon in center so tortilla becomes cup-shaped. Drain on paper towel. To assemble Chalupas: layer black beans, chopped duck and Mango Relish. Garnish with slices of avocado. Drizzle with Chipotle Aioli.

CHIPOTLE AIOLI:

Blend all ingredients together in a blender.

Duck Leg and Marinated Duck Breast

Makes 4 servings

FOR THE BREAST:
Zest of 1 orange
Zest of 1 lemon
Zest of 1 lime
2 tablespoons molasses
2 tablespoons olive oil
1/4 cup plum sauce
4 duck breasts

FOR THE BRAISED DUCK LEGS:
4 duck legs
1/4 cup plum sauce
Salt and pepper, to taste
1/4 bunch celery, chopped
2 carrots, chopped
1 yellow onion, chopped

2 cloves garlic, chopped
2 shallots, chopped
2 sprigs thyme and sage
2 cups red wine
4 cups chicken stock

FOR THE SAUCE:
1 shallot, chopped
1 clove garlic, chopped
1/4 cup prunes, chopped
2 sprigs thyme
2 sprigs basil
2 tablespoons honey
2 tablespoons plum sauce
1 cup port wine
2 cups veal stock
1 cup chicken stock

FOR THE BREAST:
Mix all ingredients together and let sit overnight.

FOR THE BRAISED DUCK LEGS:
Preheat oven to 350 degrees. Marinate duck legs in plum sauce overnight. Season with salt and pepper. Sear duck legs on griddle until dark brown. Sear breasts until dark brown. Combine duck with sauce in a deep pan, then cover with foil. Bake for 1 1/2 hours until tender.

FOR THE SAUCE:
Sauté first 5 ingredients until fully cooked, then add 2 tablespoons honey and 2 tablespoons plum sauce. Cook for 3 minutes on high, then add wine and reduce by half. Add veal stock and chicken stock. Reduce to sauce consistency.

Amaya, Hotel Santa Fe—Patrick Kline, executive chef

Special City Mounted Police,
DeVargas Pageant, Palace of the
Governors courtyard, Santa Fe, 1911.
Photograph by Jesse L. Nusbaum,
courtesy of the Palace of the Governors
Photo Archives. Negative 10805.

Turkey Loaf

Makes 8 servings

2 pounds ground turkey

1 1/2 cups bread crumbs

1/2 package onion soup mix

2 eggs, lightly beaten

1/2 cup minced celery

1/2 cup minced carrot

3/4 cup ketchup

1/2 cup warm water, if needed

4 strips bacon

8 ounces tomato sauce

Preheat oven to 350 degrees. In a large bowl, combine turkey, bread crumbs, soup mix, eggs, celery, carrot and ketchup. Mix by hand (add water, if dry). Shape into loaf and place in greased loaf pan. Drape bacon lengthwise over turkey loaf, and then pour tomato sauce on top. Bake for 1 hour.

Pasta a la Caprese

Makes 4 servings

4 large fresh tomatoes, peeled and diced

2 cloves garlic, crushed

1 sweet red pepper, diced

20 leaves fresh basil or 1 tablespoon crushed dry basil

1/2 cup olive oil

1 teaspoon salt

1/2 teaspoon fresh black pepper

1 pound pasta (rotelli or rigatoni)

8 ounces mozzarella, cubed

Fresh ground Parmesan

At least 2 to 4 hours before serving, mix first 7 ingredients in a large bowl. Let stand at room temperature 30 minutes before serving. Cook pasta, drain and rinse in hot water. Add mozzarella to hot pasta. Add sauce and top with Parmesan. Serve immediately.

Most Popular Penne

Makes 4 to 6 servings

6 ounces dried penne or other small-style pasta

1/2 cup red onion, chopped

3 cloves garlic, diced

Olive oil

1 cup Mascarpone

5 ounces fontina, shredded

2 tablespoons shredded Parmesan

1 tablespoon whole-grain mustard

1/4 teaspoon black pepper

1/2 teaspoon salt

1 tablespoon dried parsley

2 tablespoons half-and-half

Preheat oven to 400 degrees. Cook pasta in boiling water according to package directions. Drain well. While pasta is cooking, sauté onion and garlic in olive oil until barely done. Return pasta to mixing bowl, and stir in 3 cheeses, sautéed onion and garlic, mustard, and seasonings. Stir in half-and-half for creaminess. Transfer to baking dish and place in oven for 25 to 30 minutes, until golden and bubbly. Serve with salad and crusty bread.

Egyptian Rice and Lentils

Makes 6 servings

1 cup brown lentils

5 cups water

1 1/2 cups rice

1 medium onion, finely diced

1/2 cup olive oil

2 tablespoons butter

2 teaspoons salt

1 to 2 teaspoons pepper

EASTERN SALAD:

4 tomatoes, chopped

2 cucumbers, chopped

1 cup dried fresh parsley

TAHINA SAUCE:

Sesame butter mixed with juice of 1 lemon and 2 to 3 tablespoons water

Rinse lentils in cold water, allow to soak 10 to 15 minutes, strain. Put in pot with 5 cups water. Bring to a boil. Partly cover, reduce heat to low and simmer until barely tender. In the meantime, put rice in a bowl, rinse and soak in cold water. Fry onion in olive oil until lightly brown, stirring frequently. Drain and set aside. Add rice and butter to cooked lentils, cover and bring to a boil. Cook on low heat until liquid is absorbed, about 35 minutes. Remove from heat and let rest in pan about 20 minutes. Invert onto a large plate. Top with olive oil and onions. Add salt and pepper. Serve with pita bread and Eastern Salad.

EASTERN SALAD:

Combine ingredients and toss with 5 tablespoons Tahina Sauce.

Southwest Pasta

Makes 4 servings

2 tablespoons olive oil

2 (10 to 12-ounce) boneless, skinless chicken breasts, diced

1/2 cup pine nuts

1/2 cup pesto

1/4 cup sun-dried tomatoes

1/4 cup marinated artichoke hearts

Black pepper, to taste

6 ounces linguine

1/4 cup grated Parmesan

Heat olive oil at medium-high heat in a large, heavy skillet. Add chicken and cook through, about 20 minutes. Drain excess liquid and return to heat. Add pine nuts and cook until lightly brown. Reduce heat to low and add pesto, tomatoes, artichoke hearts and pepper. Cook linguine until al dente. Drain. Combine chicken-pesto mixture with linguine. Sprinkle with Parmesan and serve. Great with crusty italian loaf.

Ravioli with Tomato Cream Sauce

Makes 8 servings

RAVIOLI:

1 package frozen wonton wrappers

1 small container Ricotta

2 eggs

1 teaspoon parsley

Salt and pepper, to taste

Cornmeal

TOMATO CREAM SAUCE:

2 teaspoons olive oil

2 cloves garlic, chopped

1 (28-ounce) can peeled tomatoes, chopped

Salt and pepper, to taste

5 to 8 fresh basil leaves, chopped

1 cup heavy cream

1/4 cup toasted pine nuts

RAVIOLI:

Sprinkle baking sheet with cornmeal (this will keep prepared ravioli from sticking). Combine Ricotta, 1 egg, parsley, salt and pepper. Prepare egg wash with 1 egg mixed with 2 tablespoons water. Place one wonton wrapper on work surface. Drop 1 heaping teaspoon of cheese mixture onto center of wonton. Brush egg wash on edges of wrapper and fold in half to form a triangle. Press edges together; place on cornmeal-prepared baking sheet. Repeat. Drop ravioli into boiling water. Cook about 2 minutes. Remove with slotted spoon and place in sauce.

TOMATO CREAM SAUCE:

Pour olive oil into a large skillet over low heat. Sauté garlic and then add tomatoes. Increase heat to medium. Add salt and pepper. Cook sauce for 30 minutes. Add basil. Reduce heat to medium low. Just before you are going to boil ravioli, reduce heat to low and stir in cream. Place ravioli in sauce to coat. Remove and arrange in circular fan on plate. Sprinkle with pine nuts and basil leaves to garnish. These delicate ravioli are made with wonton wrappers and should be served with a sauce that is not too robust.

Butternut Pasta

Makes 4 servings

1 medium butternut squash

2 to 3 tablespoons butter

3 tablespoons Dijon mustard

Salt and pepper, to taste

1/2 cup craisins

1/4 to 1/2 cup pine nuts, toasted

1/2 cup amaretto cookies, crushed

Rigatoni

1 cup fresh Parmesan, grated

Peel and cube squash. Melt butter and simmer squash until soft. Mash squash, adding mustard, salt and pepper. Mix squash, craisins, pine nuts and amaretto cookies. Serve over rigatoni. Top with Parmesan and serve.

Paella Valenciana

Makes 4 to 6 servings

1 to 2 pounds frying chicken, cut up

1 chorizo, sliced (1 per pound of chicken)

2 to 4 tablespoons olive oil

1 onion, diced

1 clove garlic, diced

1 (8-ounce) can peeled tomatoes or 3 fresh tomatoes (blanched, peeled, seeded, chopped and drained)

1 large red pepper, seeded and chopped or 1 can pimentos

1 teaspoon each of salt and pepper

1 teaspoon paprika

12 ounces (2 cups) long-grain rice (washed and soaked in cold water for 30 minutes, then drained)

1 to 2 (14-ounce) cans chicken broth

Juice of 1 lemon

1/8 teaspoon powdered saffron soaked in 1/2 cup hot water for about 20 minutes

1 (10-ounce) box frozen peas (or use fresh, shelled peas)

1 (10-ounce) box frozen artichokes (optional)

1 (10-ounce) box frozen asparagus (optional)

1 to 1 1/2 pounds cooked lobster

6 ounces large prawns or shrimp

1 quart mussels, scrubbed and steamed (optional)

1 quart clams, scrubbed and steamed (optional)

1 teaspoon parsley

In a large ovenproof pan, preferably with handles on sides, fry chicken pieces and chorizo slices over medium heat in olive oil with onion and garlic. When cooked, remove chicken and chorizo from pan and set aside. Add tomatoes, red pepper or pimentos, salt, pepper and paprika to pan. Cook, stirring occasionally until mixture is thick. Add rice and broth to mixture, then lemon juice and saffron. Bring to a boil. Reduce heat to low and stir in all vegetables. Return chicken pieces and chorizo to pan, then add seafood. After cooking liquid has been absorbed, remove pan from heat. Sprinkle with parsley and serve immediately.

Enchilada con Espinacas

Makes 12 servings

2 pounds ground chuck

1 large onion, finely chopped

1 (10-ounce) can tomatoes and green chiles (or 2 cups salsa)

1 (12-ounce) package frozen spinach, thawed, blanched and squeezed dry

Salt and freshly ground pepper, to taste

1 (10-ounce) can cream of mushroom soup

1 (8-ounce) carton sour cream

1/4 cup milk

1/4 teaspoon garlic powder

1/2 cup butter

12 to 16 tortillas, blue corn, if possible

2 (4-ounce) cans green chile, chopped

1/2 pound longhorn or mild cheddar, grated

Place meat in a heavy skillet, cook over medium heat until it loses all its color. Drain off any fat or liquid. Stir in the next 5 ingredients. In a bowl, combine the next 4 ingredients and mix well. Dip half the tortillas in melted butter. Arrange on bottom and sides of large, shallow casserole dish. Spoon in meat mixture. Do not disarrange tortillas. Spread chopped chiles over mixture with all but 1/2 cup of cheese. Cover with remaining tortillas dipped in butter; add sauce, smoothing over whole surface. Cover with plastic wrap. Refrigerate overnight. Preheat oven to 325 degrees. Sprinkle casserole with reserved cheese before placing in oven. Bake for 35 to 45 minutes.

Governor Carruthers' Baked Steak with Butter Crumb Dumplings

Makes 8 to 10 servings

CASEROLE:

2 pounds round steak

1/3 cup flour

1 teaspoon paprika

1/4 cup salad oil

1/2 teaspoon salt

1/8 teaspoon pepper

2 (10-ounce) cans cream of chicken soup

1 (15-ounce) can onions

1 cup sour cream

BUTTER CRUMB DUMPLINGS:

2 cups flour

4 teaspoons baking powder

1/2 teaspoon salt

1 teaspoon poultry seasoning

1 teaspoon celery seed

1 teaspoon instant minced onions

1/4 cup salad oil

1 cup milk

1/4 cup melted butter

1 cup dried bread crumbs

Sift flour with 4 teaspoons double-acting baking powder, salt and poultry seasoning. Add celery seeds and instant minced onions. Stir in salad oil and cup of milk until the dough is moist. Drop by rounded tablespoon in melted butter, then roll in bread crumbs to coat. Lay dumplings on top of casserole and bake.

Preheat oven to 425 degrees. Coat round steak, cut into 2-inch pieces, with flour and paprika, brown in salad oil in skillet. Add salt, pepper and 1 cup water. Cover and simmer 30 minutes, transfer to a 3-quart casserole dish. In the same skillet, heat 1 can cream of chicken soup, undiluted. Stir in liquid drained from can of onions, plus water to make 2 cups. Bring to a boil, pour over meat. Toss in onions and top with dumplings. Bake uncovered for 25 to 30 minutes. Serve, topped with sauce—heat 1 can cream of chicken soup with 1 cup sour cream until hot. Serve with broccoli and green salad.

Katherine Carruthers, former first lady of New Mexico

Casa Fettuccine with Italian Sausage

Makes 4 to 6 servings

3/4 pound Italian sausage

1/4 pound ground smoked prosciutto

1/2 teaspoon garlic

2 cups cream

2 ounces grated Gruyère

2 ounces grated mozzarella

2 ounces grated Parmesan

2 ounces grated fontina

1 pound fettuccine

Fresh cracked pepper

Over medium heat, sauté sausage, breaking it apart as it cooks. When almost done, add prosciutto and garlic, continue cooking about 5 minutes. Add cream and bring to a boil. Add cheeses and stir. Cook fettuccine as directed on package. Drain and add to cream sauce, mix and serve. Top with cracked pepper.

Duck and Venison Gumbo

Makes 10 servings

3 to 4 double skinless duck breasts

2 1/2 pounds venison, cut into bite-size pieces

3 quarts water

ROUX:

1/2 cup salad oil

1/2 cup flour

1 bunch green onions, finely chopped

2 medium onions, finely chopped

4 to 5 ribs celery, finely chopped

1 tablespoon salt

Red pepper, to taste

Green onion, chopped

Parsley, chopped

1 to 2 teaspoons filé powder

*Santa Fe home of Bill and Kelly Smythe.
Architect and builder of the kitchen: Sharon
Woods. Photography: Daniel Nadelbach,
photographic styling: Gilda Meyer-Niehof.*

Start duck breasts and venison to boil in a large pot. Make a roux, and when it is mahogany colored, remove from heat, add green onions, onions and celery to sauté. Return to heat until they are tender. Add roux and vegetables to pot or add 3 to 4 ladles of boiling duck and venison stock to skillet and stir until smooth. Then add back to pot. Cook for 3 to 4 hours until meat is tender. Add salt and red pepper. Fifteen minutes before serving, add other ingredients. Serve over white rice.

ROUX:

The secret to gumbo is the roux. Have patience and 45 minutes to spare to make a good roux. The iron skillet is extremely slow (one notch off the lowest) and you must stir it constantly. If the phone rings, don't answer it! For dark roux, the end color is mahogany and it will be grainy. Take roux off burner before adding the vegetables to sauté them and then return skillet to burner. If you are not used to making roux, you may sauté vegetables in a separate skillet. Enjoy the experience–the end product is definitely worth the work.

Baked Sauerkraut with Pork Sausage

Makes 8 servings

3 tablespoons bacon fat or
    cooking oil
1/2 cup onions, chopped
1 pound ground pork
1 clove garlic, crushed or finely
    chopped
1 teaspoon salt
1 teaspoon paprika
Ground black pepper

1/4 pound smoked bacon,
    cut in 1/4-inch pieces
1/2 pound Hungarian or other
    smoked sausage, cut in 1/4-inch
    slices
1/4 cup white rice
2 pounds fresh or canned sauerkraut
1 cup sour cream
Additional sour cream for serving

Preheat oven to 325 degrees. Sauté onions in bacon fat until they begin to wilt. Add pork and brown it thoroughly. Stir in garlic, salt, paprika and pepper. Cover and simmer 10 minutes. In another frying pan, cook bacon until it starts to render fat. Add sausage slices and cook 5 minutes or until bacon starts to brown. Parboil rice for 10 minutes.

Grease deep 2- or 3-quart dish. Rinse sauerkraut and squeeze dry. Spread 1/3 of it on bottom of dish. Put in bacon and sausage mixture, including pan fat. Spread another 1/3 of sauerkraut over this and dot with 2 tablespoons sour cream. Sprinkle with rice. Add pork mixture with all its juices. Cover with remaining sauerkraut. Pour 1 cup of water into pork skillet, swish it around, and pour it over sauerkraut. Then spread rest of sour cream on top. Place in center of oven and bake, uncovered for 1 1/2 hours or until food shrinks away from sides of dish and sour cream topping turns golden brown. Remove from oven and let stand 20 minutes. Serve with extra sour cream. Serve with tossed green salad and solid red wine. Tastes great reheated.

Spaghetti a la Carbonara

Makes 4 servings

1 pound spaghetti
1/2 cup chicken broth
1/4 cup dry white wine
3 cloves garlic, minced
8 tablespoons butter
6 slices bacon, cooked and crumbled
    or country ham, diced
Salt and pepper, to taste
3/4 cup freshly grated Parmesan
1/4 cup grated Romano

OPTIONAL:
2 tablespoons parsley
1 cup frozen peas
1 to 2 teaspoons crushed chile
    pequins, to taste

Cook the spaghetti in a large pot of boiling salted water until it is tender but still firm. Drain and keep warm (do not rinse spaghetti). In a large skillet, combine chicken broth, wine, garlic, butter and bacon. Bring mixture to a boil. Season with salt and pepper. Add warm spaghetti and toss well. Finally, add Parmesan and Romano, toss again and serve on warm plates.

Four-Cheese Lasagne

Makes 8 servings

1 (20-ounce) bag frozen spinach, rinsed and squeezed dry

5 tablespoons unsalted butter, divided

1/2 cup chopped white onion

2 teaspoons minced garlic

3/4 pound portobello mushrooms, stems removed and sliced (about 3 large) or packaged baby portobello mushrooms, crumbled

3/4 teaspoon salt

1/2 teaspoon freshly ground black pepper

4 tablespoons flour

2 cups whole milk

1/8 teaspoon freshly grated nutmeg

2 1/2 cups grated Parmesan

15 ounces fresh Ricotta

1 1/2 cups grated fontina or provolone

1 1/2 cups grated mozzarella

1 pound lasagna noodles, cooked to al dente

For meat lovers, add 1/2 pound ground beef and 1/2 pound Italian sausage

Preheat oven to 350 degrees. Bring a large pot of salted water to a boil. Add spinach and cook for 2 minutes. Drain in fine mesh strainer, pressing with large spoon to release as much water as possible. Finely chop and set aside. In a large skillet, melt 1 tablespoon of butter over medium-high heat. Add onions and garlic and cook, stirring for 1 minute. Add mushrooms, 1/4 teaspoon each of salt and black pepper and cook, stirring until the mushrooms are tender and have given off their liquid, about 5 minutes. Remove from heat and let cool.

To make the béchamel sauce, in a large saucepan, melt the remaining 4 tablespoons of butter over medium heat. Add flour and cook, stirring, to make a light roux, about 2 minutes. Whisking constantly, slowly add the milk and continue to cook, stirring occasionally until thickened, 2 to 3 minutes. Add remaining salt, black pepper, nutmeg and 1 cup of Parmesan and cook, stirring until thickened, about 2 minutes. Remove from heat. In a bowl, combine Ricotta, fontina and mozzarella cheeses. Fold in 1/4 cup of the béchamel sauce. Across the bottom of a deep-dish 9 x 13-inch lasagne pan, spoon enough béchamel sauce to cover (about 1/2 cup). Then add 1/4 of mushrooms and sprinkle 1/4 of spinach across. Arrange layer of cooked noodles side-by-side across the sauce. Spread another layer of béchamel over noodles and top with more spinach, mushrooms and cheese. Repeat layering with sauce, noodles, spinach and cheese 2 more times, ending with noodles on top. Sprinkle remaining 1 1/2 cups of Parmesan over top, cover tightly with foil and bake until noodles are tender and lasagne is hot and bubbly, about 30 minutes. Uncover and continue baking until golden brown on top, about 10 minutes. Let rest for 10 to 15 minutes before serving. Serve hot.

Mexicano Lasagne

Makes 8 to 10 servings

2 pounds ground chuck
1 onion, chopped
1 clove garlic, minced
2 tablespoons chile powder
3 cups tomato sauce
1 teaspoon sugar
1 teaspoon salt
1/2 cup sliced black olives
1 (4-ounce) can chopped green chiles
12 corn tortillas
Vegetable oil
2 cups small-curd cottage cheese
1 egg, beaten
8 ounces grated Monterey Jack
1 cup grated cheddar

TOPPINGS:
1/2 cup scallions, chopped
1/2 cup sour cream
1/2 cup sliced black olives

Preheat oven to 350 degrees. In a large, heavy skillet, brown meat over medium-high heat, stirring to break up lumps. Push to one side of pan, drain off any fat and add onion. Sauté 5 minutes, until translucent; add garlic and cook 1 minute longer. Sprinkle chile powder over meat and onions and mix well. Add tomato sauce, sugar, salt, olives and chiles. Simmer uncovered for 15 minutes. Oil a 13 x 9-inch baking dish. In a small skillet, heat 1 to 2 tablespoons oil and soften the tortillas by placing them, 1 by 1, in hot oil until soft and pliable. Beat together the cottage cheese and egg; set aside. Place 1/3 of meat mixture in prepared baking dish. Top with layer of half the Monterey Jack cheese. Spoon on half cottage cheese and cover with half tortillas. Repeat process, ending with meat sauce on top. Cover with grated cheddar and bake for 30 minutes, until bubbly. Allow lasagne to stand at room temperature for 15 minutes before cutting into squares. Place toppings in small bowls and let guests serve themselves.

Galisteo Street Garden, 1985, by Tom Macaione, oil on canvas, Museum of Fine Arts.

Greek Delight

Makes 8 servings

Olive oil

2 medium eggplants, 1/2-inch slices

2 pounds lamb steak, cubed

8 cloves garlic

1 (16-ounce) can crushed tomatoes
   or 1 large chopped tomato

1 large onion, sliced

1 large red pepper, sliced

1 large green pepper, sliced

8 ounces crumbled feta

Preheat oven to 300 degrees. Use a 3 or 4-quart casserole dish, about 4 inches deep with straight sides. Grease bottom of pan with olive oil. Leave skin on eggplants and brush with olive oil; fill in eggplant rounds with small pieces. Layer everything as noted at left. Cook 4 hours in oven. Add feta cheese 30 minutes before done. Serve with cumin-flavored rice and top with pine nuts, french bread and mixed green salad.

Novelli Polenta with Sausage

Makes 4 servings

POLENTA:

4 cups water

1 teaspoon salt

1 cup cornmeal

2 to 4 tablespoons butter or
  margarine, softened

RED SAUCE:

2 tablespoons olive oil

2 cloves garlic, as needed

2 to 3 Italian sausages, hot or mild,
  sliced

1 (35-ounce) can peeled Italian plum
  tomatoes with juice

Pinch hot red pepper flakes, optional

2 tablespoons chopped parsley

POLENTA:

In top section of double boiler, bring water and salt to a boil. With whisk, to prevent lumping, gradually add cornmeal. When all cornmeal is added, bring to a boil, reduce heat and simmer for 5 minutes. Place top section of double boiler over boiling water and continue to cook cornmeal for 50 to 60 minutes. Add butter. Portion onto plate and spread sauce over. Turn leftover polenta into buttered loaf pan, and refrigerate. To serve, slice and fry in butter and cover with sauce. May also be served at breakfast with syrup.

RED SAUCE:

Heat olive oil in skillet, add garlic and cook until lightly brown. Take out garlic. If using sausage, cut into bite-size pieces, cook until brown, about 15 minutes, turning frequently. Pour out any fat from pan. Add all remaining ingredients and simmer until heated through. Serve with Parmeggiano-Reggiano cheese.

VEGETARIAN SAUCE:

Add garlic, onion, chopped celery, 1/2 green pepper, tomatoes and 1 to 2 tablespoons of capers, 2 tablespoons red wine, 2 tablespoons tomato paste, parsley to taste, and 1/4 cup of olives, sliced.

Reuben Sandwich Casserole

Makes 6 servings

16 ounces sauerkraut, rinsed and
  drained from jar or package

2 large tomatoes, sliced

12 ounces corned beef,
  sliced in 1-inch strips

3 to 4 tablespoons Deluxe Thousand
  Island Dressing (see page 100)

12 ounces natural Swiss cheese,
  grated

1 tablespoon butter

1 can refrigerator layered biscuits

4 to 6 rye crisps, crumbled

1/2 teaspoon caraway seed

Preheat oven to 400 degrees. Layer in a greased 8 x 11-inch baking dish, sauerkraut, tomatoes, corned beef, Deluxe Thousand Island Dressing (see page 100) and Swiss cheese. Dot with butter. Bake for 15 to 20 minutes. Remove from oven and raise oven temperature to 425 degrees. Separate biscuits into layers and cover top of casserole with them. Sprinkle with cracker crumbs and caraway. Bake for additional 15 to 20 minutes until biscuits are light brown.

Ham, Bean and Red Wine Casserole

Makes 6 servings

8 strips bacon

1/4 cup butter

1 green bell pepper, seeded, sliced

4 to 5 cups ham, cooked and cubed

2 scallions, sliced

4 ounces tomato paste

2 cups red wine (pinot noir)

1 (15-ounce) can red kidney beans,
  drained

Sea salt and black pepper, to taste

Preheat oven to 350 degrees. In a medium stockpot, gently cook bacon strips. Remove bacon before it browns and set aside. Leave drippings in pot. Add butter; sauté pepper and ham, 4 minutes. Wash and slice scallions (just before use, to avoid soapy flavor), add to peppers and ham. Add tomato paste and mix thoroughly. Mixture will be thick. Cook mixture without burning, stirring as needed, for 7 minutes. Add wine and stir to blend smooth, cook 5 more minutes. Add beans; stir and heat through 1 minute, season with salt and pepper. Rub inside of casserole dish with strip of bacon to coat, and pour mixture into casserole. Lay bacon strips over top. Bake 30 minutes until bacon is cooked. Bacon may not completely crisp. Remove from oven and cool 5 minutes.

Use good ham, preferably leftovers from a bone-in ham. Recipe will leave 2 glasses of wine from bottle, to be enjoyed with dish. Serve over buttered white rice with green vegetable and baguette.

Michael S. Williams, chef and instructor at Albuquerque Technical and Vocational Institute

Side Dishes and Accompaniments

Snow in Santa Fe, 1935, by Paul Lantz, oil on masonite, Museum of Fine Arts.

Ancho Rellenos

Makes 6 to 8 servings

6 ounces ancho (dried poblano)
   chile pods

FOR FILLING:
5 ounces smoked tofu
8 ounces fat-free cream cheese (at
   room temperature)
Nonfat milk, if needed
1/2 cup chopped walnuts
1/2 cup raisins
1 cup shredded low-fat cheese

Preheat oven to 350 degrees. Briefly rinse chile pods in colander and put into bowl. Pour boiling water over pods and soak for 20 minutes, making sure they remain submerged. Meanwhile, chop tofu into 1/2-inch pieces. Drop tofu and softened cream cheese into a blender and mix thoroughly. You may need to add a small amount of milk at this point to help the ingredients blend, but the mixture should remain thick. Scrape into bowl. Mix in walnuts and raisins.

Carefully split chiles lengthwise and rinse out seeds. Lightly pat dry each chile with paper towel. Stuff each pepper with filling and place them in lightly oiled baking dish. Sparingly sprinkle cheese over chiles. Bake for 15 minutes, or until filling is warmed through and cheese is melted. Serve on bed of your favorite red chile sauce with boiled yams or grilled squash mashed and drizzled with white truffle oil.

Variations and substitutions:
While this recipe produces a rich and delicious low-fat dish, whole-fat versions of cream cheese, milk and cheese may be used. Smoked mozzarella or other cheeses would work well as filling too. Almonds, pine nuts or other nuts may be used instead of walnuts. Other ingredients besides raisins may be added, such as onions, garlic and even grated orange peel. A dark mole makes a good sauce for this dish. The important idea for this recipe is the use of anchos instead of green chiles and baking instead of deep-frying.

Asparagus and Sun-Dried Tomato Pasta

Makes 4 servings

1 bundle asparagus

4 sun-dried tomatoes, cut in 1/2-inch
    strips

1 (14-ounce) can chicken broth

1 pound vermicelli

1 tablespoon cooking oil, added to
    pasta water

1 1/2 teaspoons salt

4 tablespoons pine nuts

6 ounces goat cheese cut into
    1/2-inch rounds, floured and
    browned in butter

Wash asparagus, break off tough end and cut into bite-size pieces. Boil asparagus and sun-dried tomatoes in chicken broth for about 15 minutes, or until they are tender. Meanwhile, cook pasta, with salt, according to package instructions. Drain pasta, return to pot and add asparagus, tomatoes and broth, toss. Serve on hot plates heated in the microwave for 1 minute. Garnish with pine nuts and warm goat cheese croutons.

Haricots Verts in Plum Tomatoes

Makes 4 servings

4 plum tomatoes

48 haricots
    (or very thin green beans)

3/4 cup olive oil

1/3 cup red wine vinegar

1 tablespoon Dijon mustard

Salt and pepper, to taste

Slice off top and bottom of each tomato. Remove pulp with spoon to create hollow cylinders; set aside. Trim stem ends of green beans. Steam beans in saucepan for 3 to 5 minutes, or just until tender; do not overcook. Place 12 green beans, or as many as will fit, in each tomato; arrange tomatoes on serving plate and combine the olive oil, vinegar, mustard, salt and pepper in blender and process until smooth. Drizzle 1 teaspoon of vinaigrette over each tomato.

Eggplant with Goat Cheese

Makes 6 servings

1 eggplant, unpeeled

1 cup unbleached white flour,
    seasoned with salt and pepper

3 eggs, lightly beaten

1 cup fresh bread crumbs

Olive oil

6 ounces goat cheese,
    cut into rounds

Preheat oven to 350 degrees. Slice eggplant into 1/4-inch slices. Using a 2-inch round cutter, cut each slice into round shapes. Put seasoned flour, lightly beaten eggs and bread crumbs into 3 separate bowls. Dip each eggplant round first into flour, then egg and then bread crumbs. Put small amount of olive oil into skillet. Sauté eggplant rounds on both sides until brown. Put half of eggplant rounds onto baking sheet. Top with 1/2-inch slice of goat cheese. Top with remaining rounds of sautéed eggplant. Can put dish in oven to keep warm until ready to serve.

Brussels Sprouts with Malted Cream

Makes 12 Servings

4 ounces slab bacon, cut in 1/4-inch
   dice

1 large onion, cut in 1/4-inch pieces

1/4 cup malt vinegar

2 cups sour cream

1 teaspoon Worcestershire sauce

Salt and pepper, to taste

2 pounds brussels sprouts, trimmed

Heat a large nonreactive skillet over moderate heat. Add bacon and cook, stirring occasionally, until just beginning to brown and fat is rendered, about 5 minutes. Add onion and cook, stirring, until softened, about 8 to 10 minutes. Pour off excess fat from skillet. Increase heat to moderately high, add malt vinegar and boil until almost evaporated, about 2 minutes. Stir in sour cream and Worcestershire. Season with salt and pepper and keep warm. In a large saucepan with a steamer basket, bring 3 cups water to boil. Meanwhile, score root ends of brussels sprouts with an X. Halve sprouts if they are large. Steam brussels sprouts until just tender, about 12 to 15 minutes. Transfer sprouts to serving bowl. Add malted cream and toss to coat. Serve hot.

Elegant Five-Cheese Macaroni

Makes 8 servings

6 tablespoons butter

1/2 cup flour

5 1/2 cups whole milk

2 teaspoons salt

1/4 teaspoon pepper

1/4 teaspoon nutmeg (optional)

1/4 teaspoon cayenne pepper,
   or to taste

1 teaspoon dry mustard

1 pound elbow macaroni

4 1/2 cups sharp cheddar, Parmesan,
   fontina, and Swiss combination,
   grated

1 1/2 cups (8 ounces) grated Gruyère

Preheat oven to 350 degrees. Melt butter. Add flour. Cook and whisk a few minutes to eliminate raw taste. Gradually add warm milk and whisk till bubbly and thick. Remove from heat and add seasonings. Set aside. Cook macaroni and drain well. Mix cheese mixture with macaroni and put into greased casserole dish. Cover with sauce. Bake for approximately 30 minutes.

Note: Add 1 small can of green chiles for spicy taste. Also may add 1 cup lightly toasted bread crumbs sprinkled over top.

Kitchen from home in Sierra del Norte area of Santa Fe.
Photography by Daniel Nadelbach,
photographic styling by Gilda Meyer-Niehof.

Tamale Dressing for Turkey

Makes 8 to 10 servings

1 cup chopped onion

1/4 cup butter

2 packages yellow corn bread mix

4 cups pork or beef tamales, crumbled

1/3 cup sugar, follow directions on corn bread mix, adding sugar

2 cups chicken broth

3 eggs, slightly beaten

1/4 cup fresh parsley, chopped

1 tablespoon cumin

1 teaspoon garlic powder

Fresh ground pepper

Preheat oven to 350 degrees. In a skillet, sauté onions in butter until soft. In a large bowl, crumble corn bread and tamales. Add sugar, broth, eggs, parsley and seasonings. Bake in 9 x 13-inch pan for 40 minutes.

Crispy Polenta with Gorgonzola Sauce

Makes 4 to 8 servings

3 1/2 cups salted water

1 cup polenta (not instant)

2 ounces unsalted butter

1/3 cup Parmesan, grated

1/8 cup chopped rosemary

Red wine vinegar, to taste

Salt and black pepper, to taste

Cayenne pepper, to taste

Olive oil

2 cups heavy cream

1 sprig rosemary

3 to 4 ounces Gorgonzola

Lemon juice

Parsley, chives and bread crumbs

POLENTA:

Bring salted water to a boil. Slowly whisk in polenta. Cook gently 20 minutes. Add butter, Parmesan and rosemary. Finish by adding red wine vinegar, salt and cayenne pepper to taste. Pour polenta into 8 x 8-inch baking pan to 1 to 1 1/2 inches thick. Cool, slice into desired shape. Cover bottom of heated sauté pan with oil and fry polenta until crispy. Remove and pat dry.

GORGONZOLA SAUCE:

Reduce heavy cream by 1/2 with 1 sprig rosemary. Whisk in Gorgonzola, season with salt, black pepper and lemon juice to taste. Pour Gorgonzola sauce onto plate and place polenta on top. Garnish with parsley, chives and bread crumbs. The polenta and sauce can be made ahead. The polenta can be fried to order and sauce can be reheated.

Andiamo! A Neighborhood Trattoria—Joan Gilbert, owner; Esteban Parra, chef

Scalloped Onions and Nuts

Makes 6 servings

12 small white boiling onions

1 cup cooked celery, diced

4 tablespoons butter

3 tablespoons flour

1 teaspoon salt

1 1/8 teaspoons pepper

1 cup milk

1/2 cup light cream

1/2 cup blanched almonds or Spanish
    peanuts, with skins

Paprika

Grated Parmesan

Preheat oven to 350 degrees. Wash and peel onions and cook in boiling salted water until tender. Drain. Prepare celery same way. Melt butter in saucepan, add flour, salt and pepper; cook over low heat until bubbly. Add milk and cream a little at a time, and cook until thick, stirring constantly. Place onions, celery and almonds in layers in buttered casserole dish. Cover with cream sauce and sprinkle with paprika and Parmesan. Bake until bubbly and golden.

Cauliflower Almond Gratin

Makes 6 servings

3/4 cup half-and-half

1/2 cup whole roasted almonds with skin, plus 2 tablespoons coarsely chopped almonds

4 tablespoons butter

2 tablespoons all-purpose flour

1 cup whole milk

3/4 cup plus 2 tablespoons finely shredded Manchego or other mildly nutty semi-aged sheep's or cow's milk cheese, such as Gouda

Pinch freshly grated nutmeg

1 (2-pound) head cauliflower, cut into 1 1/2-inch florets

1 medium onion, finely chopped

1/4 teaspoon paprika

Salt and pepper, to taste

Preheat oven to 400 degrees. In a small saucepan, heat half-and-half until steaming; transfer to food processor/blender, add 1/2 cup of whole almonds and process until finely ground. Let stand 10 minutes. Strain half-and-half in fine sieve, pressing on almonds to extract as much liquid as possible. Discard ground almonds. In a medium saucepan, melt 2 tablespoons butter. Add flour and whisk over moderately high heat for 1 minute. Add milk and half-and-half, and cook, whisking constantly, until thickened. Remove from heat. Add 3/4 cup of cheese and whisk until melted. Whisk in nutmeg. Keep warm. In a large skillet, bring 1/2 inch of water to boil. Add pinch of salt and cauliflower, cover and cook over high heat until crisp-tender. Drain cauliflower in colander. Melt remaining 2 tablespoons of butter in skillet. Add onion and cook, stirring until lightly brown. Add cauliflower and cook, stirring until golden brown. Season with salt and pepper, to taste. Transfer to a 7 x 10-inch baking dish and spread cheese sauce on top. Sprinkle gratin with remaining cheese, 2 tablespoons of chopped almonds and paprika. Bake for 20 minutes or until bubbling and brown on top. Let stand for 10 minutes before serving.

Amy's Easy Potatoes

Makes 8 servings

1 (10-ounce) can mushroom soup

1 cup sour cream

1 pound sweet onion, diced

3 cups Italian Mix grated cheese

1 (32-ounce) bag Ore-Ida hash brown potatoes

1 teaspoon lemon pepper

1 (6-ounce) can chopped green chile

1 (5-ounce) can french-fried onion rings

Preheat oven to 350 degrees. Mix all ingredients except onion rings. Place in a flat, buttered 9 x 11 1/2-inch baking dish and bake for 1 hour and 10 minutes. Remove from oven and put onion rings on top. Return to oven and bake 10 to 15 minutes more or until top is golden brown.

Note: May use crushed corn flakes with melted butter as topping.

Baked Blue Cheese Potatoes

Makes 8 servings

15 tiny new potatoes
1/4 cup Canola oil
Coarse sea salt
4 ounces blue cheese

1/2 cup sour cream
3 slices bacon, crumbled
2 tablespoons chopped chives or
    green chiles

Preheat oven to 350 degrees. Clean potatoes and put in a bowl. Add oil to bowl and coat potatoes generously. Add coarse salt and coat potatoes lightly. Place potatoes on baking sheet and bake 50 minutes or until softened. In bowl, add blue cheese, sour cream, and bacon together and blend. Remove potatoes from oven and cut a cross in top of each potato. Be sure to gently press potatoes open enough to hold topping. Top each potato with a dollop of cheese mixture. Sprinkle with chives or chopped green chiles and serve immediately.

Two-Rice Stuffing

Makes 12 servings

1 stick butter
4 large onions, chopped
3 large celery stalks,
    chopped, including leaves
2 pounds mixed mushrooms, sliced
7 cups low-salt chicken broth

1 tablespoon thyme
1 tablespoon sage
8 ounces wild rice
8 ounces white rice
1 cup parsley, chopped
Salt and pepper, to taste

Preheat oven to 350 degrees. In a large pot over medium heat, put in half of butter and sauté onions and celery until tender. Remove to large bowl. To pot, add remaining butter and sauté mushrooms until dark brown. Remove to bowl with onions and celery. In a large pot, bring broth, thyme and sage to boil. Add wild rice, cover, and reduce heat to simmer for 30 minutes. Add white rice, cover and simmer until rice is tender. Remove rice and liquid to bowl with onions and mushrooms. Add parsley, and salt and pepper, to taste, and mix. Put mixture in a 9 x 12-inch buttered baking dish, cover, and place in oven for 30 minutes. Uncover, and bake until golden crust forms on top.

Spinach and White Beans

Makes 8 to 10 servings

2 pounds fresh spinach
4 tablespoons butter
1/2 cup finely diced cooked ham
2 cups cooked (or canned) white
    navy beans, drained

2 tablespoons whipping cream
Salt and pepper, to taste
Nutmeg

Wash spinach and cut away heavy stems. Cook 1 minute in a covered container. Drain and put in food processor until finely chopped. Melt butter in large skillet. Add spinach, ham and beans. Stir in cream and cook until the consistency of mashed potatoes. Correct seasonings and add just a whiff of nutmeg.

Lemon Southwest Rice

Makes 6 to 8 servings

2 tablespoons butter

1 cup leeks, white part only, cleaned
    and thinly sliced

1 tablespoon finely minced garlic

2 cups white rice

3 1/2 cups chicken broth, defatted

1/2 cup lemon juice, freshly squeezed

2 teaspoons freshly
    grated lemon rind

1 teaspoon azafran

1 teaspoon toasted and freshly
    ground coriander seeds

1 teaspoon salt

White pepper, to taste

1/2 cup green chiles, roasted,
    peeled and chopped

1/4 cup finely minced cilantro
    (optional)

In a nonstick saucepan, heat butter until sizzling and sauté leeks over medium heat until softened. Add garlic and sauté 1 minute, stirring often. Add rice and stir to coat. Add chicken broth, lemon juice, lemon rind, azafran, coriander seeds, salt and pepper. Bring to a boil, cover and reduce heat. Simmer slowly for approximately 20 to 30 minutes. Remove pan from heat, allow to rest for 5 minutes; add chiles and cilantro, if desired, stirring well to combine.

Santa Fe School of Cooking—Nicole Ammerman

Spinach Cheddar Soufflé

Makes 8 servings

2 tablespoons grated Parmesan

8 tablespoons butter

6 tablespoons flour

2 cups warm milk

6 egg yolks

1 pound cooked spinach, finely
    chopped

1 3/4 cups grated cheddar

1 teaspoon red chile powder

Salt

1 teaspoon nutmeg

10 egg whites

Parchment paper

Preheat oven to 400 degrees. Take parchment paper and line a 2-quart soufflé dish 2 inches above rim. Butter soufflé dish and paper, and dust with Parmesan, set aside. Melt butter in a 2-quart saucepan, whisk in flour and stir for several minutes. Add 1/3 of warm milk to flour mixture and stir until smooth, repeat this process 2 more times. Remove from heat and whisk in egg yolks, one at a time, until well incorporated. Squeeze spinach until very dry, and stir into milk mixture with cheddar, chile, salt and nutmeg. In a separate bowl, beat egg whites with pinch of salt until they hold soft peaks. Fold egg whites into spinach mixture and pour into prepared soufflé dish. Bake until soufflé has risen and is nicely browned but still has a slight quiver to it when shaken gently. Serve immediately.

Las Campanas Country Club—Jeff Moses, executive chef

Potato Gnocchi with Brown Butter and Parmesan

Makes 6 servings

3/4 pound Idaho potatoes

3/4 pound Yukon gold potatoes

1 cup all-purpose flour, plus a little
    extra for rolling out the dough

3/4 teaspoon kosher salt

1 egg yolk

3 tablespoons unsalted butter

1/4 cup grated Parmesan

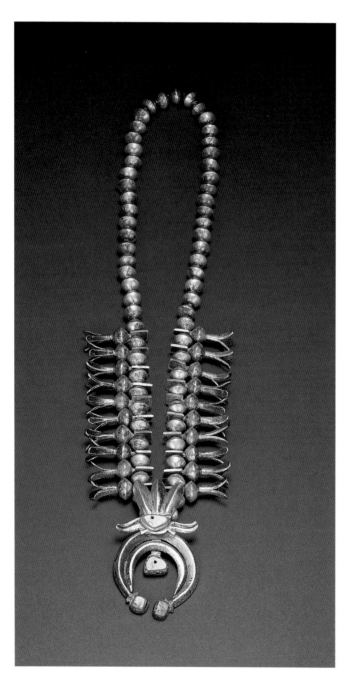

Preheat oven to 375 degrees. Wash and dry potatoes. Do not peel potatoes. Pierce potatoes on all sides with tip of knife and place on baking sheet. Place baking sheet in oven and roast potatoes for 90 minutes. The potatoes are ready when they give easily to your touch. Remove potatoes from oven and allow to cool slightly. Remove skins and run potatoes through a ricer. Place potatoes in mixing bowl and add flour, kosher salt and egg yolk. Mix ingredients by hand until all are thoroughly incorporated. Lightly flour work surface. Pull off small piece of dough and roll it out between palms of your hands and work surface until you have a long tube about 1/2 inch in diameter. Flour blade of knife and cut tube into 3/4-inch pieces. Repeat process using all of dough. Be mindful to lightly flour your work surface and blade of knife continuously during this process.

Put on a pot of water and add some salt. Bring water to a boil and then reduce heat so the water is at soft simmer. Add gnocchi. Heat a sauté pan over low to medium heat and add butter. Allow butter to melt and then brown. The butter should have a sweet, nutty smell to it. Remove sauté pan from heat and whisk butter, scraping brown bits off bottom. When gnocchi float to top, wait another 30 seconds, then with slotted spoon, remove them from water and add them to brown butter. Toss lightly in pan. Place gnocchi in a serving bowl and sprinkle with Parmesan.

Trattoria Nostrani—Eric Stapelman, owner/chef; Nelli Maltezo

*Squash Blossom Necklace, from the Collection of
the Museum of Indian Arts and
Culture/Laboratory of Anthropology.*

Potato and Yam Gratin

Makes 8 servings

1 pound russet potatoes

1 pound yams or sweet potatoes

3/4 cup whipping cream

3/4 teaspoon salt

3/4 teaspoon pepper or white pepper

1/6 teaspoon freshly grated nutmeg

1/3 cup snipped fresh chives

1/2 cup freshly grated
   Parmesan reggiano

Preheat oven to 350 degrees. Peel both kinds of potatoes and slice thinly into ice water. Drain and pat dry before assembling. Cover bottom of well-greased 8-inch square casserole dish with a layer of potatoes, then yams. Blend cream, salt, pepper, and nutmeg and drizzle over potatoes. Continue to layer potatoes, yams and cream mixture. Top with chives and Parmesan. Cover casserole dish with foil and bake for 30 minutes. Remove foil and bake an additional 15 minutes, being sure potatoes are cooked through. Cut in squares to serve after letting rest for 10 minutes.

Pickled Green Chile

Makes 2 cups

1 cup vinegar

1 cup sugar

1/2 teaspoon dill seed

1/4 teaspoon mustard seed

1/2 teaspoon pickling spice

Salt and pepper

3 cloves garlic, in slices

2 cups green chile, chopped

Boil vinegar, sugar and spices for 5 minutes. Cool about 5 minutes. Place garlic slices in chile and cover with syrup. Refrigerate 3 days.

Note: May use whole green chiles. The chopped chiles are great served with cream cheese and crackers. The whole ones are delicious with sandwiches.

New Mexico Calabacitas

Makes 6 to 8 servings

3 tablespoons butter or
  bacon drippings
1 small onion, chopped
4 medium-size summer squash
  and/or zucchini, chopped
3/4 cup green chile, chopped
1 clove garlic, chopped
1 (12-ounce) can
  corn, drained

1 cup half-and-half
Salt and pepper, to taste
1/2 cup Monterey Jack, grated
1 small sweet green pepper, finely
  diced (optional)
1/4 cup shelled pine nuts or
  sunflower seeds (optional)

Preheat oven to 350 degrees. Melt butter in a large skillet. Sauté onion until soft. Add squash, chile, garlic, corn, milk, salt and pepper. When squash is almost cooked, pour into casserole dish and cover with cheese. Bake about 30 minutes or until bubbly and cheese melts. Can also add sweet green pepper, pine nuts or sunflower seeds, if desired.

Pico de Gallo Pineapple

Makes 3 cups

1 cup crushed pineapple, drained
3/4 cup pineapple juice (use what
  you drained)
3/4 cup bell pepper, chopped
1/4 cup white onion, chopped

1/4 cup cilantro, chopped
1/3 cup jalapeno peppers, chopped
1 clove garlic, diced
1/4 teaspoon salt
1/4 teaspoon white pepper

Use as many fresh ingredients as possible. Combine all ingredients into a bowl, mixing well. Refrigerate. Serve with tortilla chips or as relish for fish, chicken, fajitas, etc. Adjust ingredients for personal taste. Substitute pineapple and pineapple juice with tomatoes and tomato juice for a tomato-based pico de gallo.

Chipotle Salsa

Makes 1 quart

1/2 cup dried whole chipotle chiles (packed down)

1 teaspoon Mexican oregano

2 teaspoons garlic, minced

1 white onion, minced

1 (28-ounce) can diced tomatoes with juice

1/4 cup apple cider vinegar

1/4 cup olive oil

1 teaspoon honey

1/2 teaspoon salt

Cut stems from chiles. Chop with blender or spice grinder into a coarse powder. Toast oregano in dry skillet until fragrant (about 30 seconds). Crush after toasting. Combine ingredients in food processor and chop until somewhat smooth (about 20 seconds). Pour mixture into saucepan and heat over medium-low heat until bubbling. Reduce heat to low and simmer 10 to 15 minutes. Allow to cool before serving or pouring into a jar.

Chipotle Cranberry Sauce

Makes 1 quart

1/2 small onion, diced

2 tablespoons shallots, minced

1 ounce olive oil

2 cups brown sugar

1 to 2 tablespoons chipotle chile powder or 1 or 2 dried red chiles, soaked and pureed

2 cups fresh orange juice

4 tablespoons raspberry or white vinegar

1/2 teaspoon ground cinnamon

1 teaspoon salt

1 pound fresh cranberries

Sauté onion and shallots in oil until soft. Add rest of ingredients and cook until cranberries pop and sauce thickens.

Apricot Chutney

Makes 8 cups

8 cups apricots, halved

1 lemon, chopped

1/2 cup currants

1/4 pound candied ginger, sliced

4 yellow onions, sliced

2 cloves garlic, minced

2 cups brown sugar

1 cup white sugar

1 1/2 cups red wine vinegar

2 tablespoons mustard seed

1 teaspoon powdered ginger

2 teaspoons salt

3 Japanese chiles, finely minced

1 teaspoon cayenne red pepper

In a nonreactive pan, combine first 6 ingredients. Add next 3 ingredients and bring to a boil. To that mixture, add next 5 ingredients (the spices) and simmer uncovered 1 1/2 hours. You may substitute small dried red chile peppers, crumbled fine, for the cayenne. Put in a glass container and refrigerate. Serve on bread or crackers, or with pork or chicken.

Creamy Chipotle Red Chile Sauce

Makes 8 servings

2 cups onion, chopped

2 tablespoons butter

4 cloves garlic

4 medium dried guajillo chiles

2 dried chipotle chiles

1 (16-ounce) can organic fire-roasted tomatoes

Sauté chopped onion in butter until translucent. Roast garlic until golden brown. Remove stems and seeds from chile pods. Boil in just enough water to cover them, until soft. Place all ingredients in blender and blend at high speed for 3 minutes. Recipe can be used for enchiladas, on top of burritos or as a dip for chips. Cooking time is 20 minutes.

Pasilla Negro Chile Sauce

Makes 8 to 10 servings

4 ounces sun-dried tomatoes

1 red onion, grilled

6 ounces whole peeled garlic, sautéed

1 1/2 cups olive oil, plus additional oil for soaking later

1 teaspoon thyme

1 teaspoon tarragon

1 teaspoon oregano

1 teaspoon salt

12 dried pasilla negro chiles

Soak the sun-dried tomatoes until softened (about 15 minutes), then remove from water. Grill onion until blackened on all sides. Sauté garlic in pan with some olive oil until brown. Slice onion and garlic just enough for easy blending. Puree sun-dried tomatoes, onions, garlic and olive oil in blender. Grind chiles to a powder and add to mixture in blender. Add thyme, tarragon, oregano and salt. Blend again until all ingredients are thoroughly mixed. Sauce can be used immediately with sautéed shrimp or fish or stored in refrigerator until needed. To store sauce, add enough olive oil to completely cover mixture in container.

Mucho Gusto Authentic Mexican Food—Alex Castro, owner and chef

New Mexican Pecan-Pumpkin Salsa

Makes 2 to 3 cups

1/2 teaspoon brown sugar

1/2 teaspoon salt

1 1/2 pounds pumpkin, peeled, seeded and diced

1/4 cup toasted pecans

1/4 cup dried cranberries

1/4 cup maple syrup

1 tablespoon New Mexican red chile powder

1/4 cup water

2 tablespoons apple cider

1 teaspoon apple cider vinegar

1 teaspoon fresh sage, minced

Bring a large pot of water to boil, add sugar, salt, and pumpkin and cook until tender (about 5 minutes). Drain in a colander and reserve. In a saucepan, add pecans, cranberries, maple syrup, chile powder and water, and cook for 5 minutes over medium heat. Add this mixture to pumpkin with apple cider, vinegar and sage. Adjust seasoning and serve with chicken, pork or grilled halibut.

Coyote Cafe—Mark Miller, owner; Bradley Borchardt, chef

Pear Chutney

Makes 6 cups

18 hard pears
3 green bell peppers, chopped
1 large onion, chopped
1 1/2 cups tart jelly
1 1/2 cups raisins
1 1/2 cups sugar
3 cups vinegar

Juice of 4 lemons
1 1/2 tablespoons ginger, ground
1/2 teaspoon cloves, ground
1/2 teaspoon allspice
1/2 teaspoon nutmeg
2 bay leaves
Salt and pepper, to taste

Peel, core and dice pears. Add green pepper and onion. Mix with jelly, raisins, sugar, vinegar and lemon juice. Add spices and boil all together until thick. Add salt and pepper, to taste. Serve on bread, crackers or chicken.

Canyon Road Butter

Makes 1/2 cup

1/2 cup unsalted butter, softened
2 tablespoons minced fresh cilantro
   (also called fresh coriander)
1 1/2 teaspoons minced
   grapefruit zest

1 1/2 teaspoons minced lime zest
1 teaspoon minced fresh jalapeno
   chile pepper
1 teaspoon fresh lime juice
1 teaspoon fresh grapefruit juice

Combine all ingredients in a medium-size bowl. Using an electric mixer, beat ingredients until creamy. Press butter into a small ramekin or mold. Keep refrigerated.

Santa Fe Kitchen. Photography: Daniel Nadelbach,
photographic styling: Gilda Meyer-Niehof.

Breads

Dance Costume, *Northwestern Igbo people, Nigeria, twentieth century. Embroidery, cotton and felt appliqué on plain weave cotton. Museum of International Folk Art, Neutrogena Collection.*
Photo: Pat Pollard.

Indian Corn Muffins

Makes 12 muffins

1 1/4 cups yellow cornmeal

1 cup wheat germ (or 1/2 cup wheat germ and 1/2 cup soy flour)

1/3 cup powdered milk

3 teaspoons double-acting baking powder

1 teaspoon salt

1 teaspoon nutmeg (optional)

1 cup milk or yogurt

2 eggs, beaten

1/3 cup honey

2 tablespoons vegetable oil

2/3 cup golden raisins

1/2 cup pine nuts or pecans

1 grated rind of orange (optional)

Preheat oven to 400 degrees. In a large bowl, stir together dry ingredients except fruit and nuts. In another bowl, mix liquid ingredients. Blend into dry ingredients. Add fruits and nuts and blend. Fill well-greased muffin tins or paper baking cups 2/3 full. Bake 15 to 20 minutes, or until tops lightly brown.

VARIATIONS:

If a lighter texture is desired, separate eggs, with egg yolks added as above, and stiffly beat the whites, and add them immediately before baking. Cranberries may also be substituted for raisins.

Indian Fry Bread

Makes 8 servings

4 cups flour

2 tablespoons baking powder

1 teaspoon salt

1 1/2 cups warm milk or water

1 tablespoon oil

Mix flour, baking powder and salt. Add warm milk and oil. Knead dough until soft but not sticky. Flour your hands and knead dough until springy. Shape into 3-inch ball, then stretch and pat dough until thin and 10 to 12 inches across. Poke a large hole in middle and fry in kettle of very hot cooking oil or lard until puffy and golden on both sides. Serve hot. Make next 3-inch ball and repeat steps. Do one at a time. This is a wonderful bread with beans and stews, by itself, or with honey or powered sugar.

Banana and Butternut Squash Bread with Mace and Pecan

Makes 1 loaf

1 cup granulated sugar

1/2 cup unsalted butter, softened

3/4 cup (1 to 2 bananas) mashed, very ripe banana

1 cup cooked and mashed butternut or other winter squash

2 large eggs

1 teaspoon vanilla

2 cups flour

1 teaspoon baking soda

1/2 teaspoon baking powder

1/2 teaspoon salt

1 teaspoon ground mace

1/2 teaspoon freshly grated nutmeg

1 cup chopped pecans or walnuts

Preheat oven to 350 degrees. Butter a 9 x 5-inch loaf pan, preferably glass. In a large bowl and using an electric mixer set on medium speed, beat together sugar and butter until light. Beat in banana and squash. Add eggs, beating until smooth, and then mix in vanilla. In another bowl, stir together flour, baking soda, baking powder, salt, mace and nutmeg. Add flour mixture to butter mixture, beating until smooth. Stir in nuts. Spread batter into prepared pan. Bake for 50 to 60 minutes, or until a toothpick inserted in center comes out clean. Let cool completely on rack before slicing.

Chocolate Cherry Pecan Muffin Cakes

Makes 6 large or 12 small muffins

1/2 cup butter

3/4 cup light brown sugar

2 eggs

1 3/4 cups all-purpose flour

2 teaspoons baking powder

1/2 teaspoon baking soda

1 cup buttermilk

1/2 cup dried cherries

1/2 cup chopped pecans

1/2 cup semisweet chocolate, chopped into 1/4-inch pieces

GLAZE:

1/4 cup powdered sugar

1 tablespoon water

1/2 teaspoon vanilla

Preheat oven to 375 degrees. In a bowl with an electric mixer on medium speed, beat butter until creamy. Add brown sugar and continue beating until blended. Add eggs, one at a time, and continue mixing into butter mixture. In a small bowl, mix together flour, baking powder and baking soda. With wooden spoon, stir half of flour mixture into wet ingredients. Then stir in buttermilk, being careful not to overmix. Carefully fold in remaining flour mixture, cherries, pecans and chocolate. Drop batter by spoonfuls into ungreased muffin pan. Bake for 20 minutes. Let cool for 5 minutes in pan. To make glaze, in a small bowl, mix together powdered sugar, water and vanilla until smooth. Drizzle approximately 1 tablespoon of glaze over each muffin. Remove from pan and serve.

Apple Bread

Makes 10 to 15 slices

2 large eggs

1 cup sugar

1/2 cup unsalted butter

1 teaspoon vanilla

2 cups chopped apples

1 tablespoon warm water, with
   1 teaspoon baking soda
   dissolved in it

2 cups flour

1 teaspoon baking powder (at high
   altitude reduce to 1/2 teaspoon)

1/2 teaspoon salt

1/2 cup chopped walnuts

*Note: All ingredients should be
at room temperature for at least
1 hour before using.*

Preheat oven to 350 degrees. Combine eggs, sugar and butter: beat well until mixture is smooth–no lumps. Add vanilla, apples and baking soda water. Sift flour, baking powder and salt together, and mix well. Stir into egg mixture and add nuts. Prepare a 9 x 5-inch bread pan: cut waxed paper to fit flat on bottom of pan. Grease and flour bread pan. Put waxed paper in bottom of pan. Scrape batter into bread pan–it will be very stiff. It helps to wet hands, and using fingers, spread batter until it is distributed evenly in pan.

Place uncovered in oven. After approximately 1 hour, cover pan with sheet of aluminum foil. This keeps top of loaf from getting too brown. Bake another 15 to 20 minutes. Poke toothpick into loaf and remove. If toothpick comes out clean, loaf is done. Place loaf pan on cooling rack. Let pan cool 30 or more minutes. When pan is warm to the touch, run knife blade around edges of loaf, and turn out apple bread. Remove waxed paper. Continue cooling on rack.

The Mary Austin Compound of Camino del Monte Sol.
Photography: Daniel Nadelbach,
photographic styling: Gilda Meyer-Niehof.

Corn Muffins with Squash and Sweet Onions

Makes 12 large muffins

1 1/2 cups coarse-grind
    yellow cornmeal

1/2 cup all-purpose flour

1 1/2 teaspoons baking powder

1 teaspoon baking soda

1 teaspoon salt

1/2 teaspoon sage

1/4 teaspoon rosemary

1 small Vidalia (or other sweet
    onion), finely diced

2 large eggs

3/4 cup sour cream or plain yogurt

4 tablespoons unsalted
    butter, melted

1 cup cooked and mashed acorn
    squash (or butternut or pumpkin)

Preheat oven to 425 degrees. Grease 1 standard-size 12-cup muffin tin or 2 miniature muffin tins and set aside. In a large bowl, stir together cornmeal, flour, baking powder, baking soda, salt, sage and rosemary. Stir in onion and set aside. In a second bowl, beat eggs lightly, stir in sour cream and melted butter. Stir in squash until smooth. Add squash mixture to cornmeal mixture and stir to mix fully. Spoon batter into muffin cups until each cup is 2/3 full. Bake in oven 20 to 25 minutes, or until golden brown and toothpick inserted into center comes out clean. Let cool a few minutes, then turn out tins and serve hot.

Corn Fritters

Makes 20 fritters

3 eggs, separated

1 (14-ounce) can creamed corn

1 1/2 cups pancake mix

1 inch oil, in pan for frying

Beat egg yolks slightly, add corn and pancake mix, blend gently. Beat egg whites until stiff. Blend egg whites into mixture of yolks, corn and pancake mix. Next, spoon your preferred size fritter into hot oil. Fry over medium-low burner until fritter is golden brown. Spoon onto several layers of paper towel, and blot. Serve hot. You can prepare ahead and microwave on paper towel before serving.

Mexican Corn Bread

Makes 12 servings

2 cups white cornmeal (stone ground
    is best)

2 cups buttermilk

1 1/2 teaspoons baking soda

1 teaspoon salt

4 eggs

1 1/2 cups cream-style corn

6 jalapenos, chopped and seeded or
    3/4 cup diced green chile

1/3 cup oil (bacon drippings,
    vegetable oil or Canola oil)

1 1/2 cups grated cheese (cheddar or
    Monterey Jack)

Preheat oven to 400 degrees. Mix all ingredients except cheese. Pour 1/2 of batter in well-greased, preheated skillet, and spread cheese over batter in skillet and top with remaining batter. Cook for 30 minutes or until set and browned on top. After cooking, let stand to set. Serve from skillet. Do not try to turn out.

Senator Jeff Bingaman Oat Muffins

Makes 3 dozen

Vegetable shortening spray
1 cup stone-ground whole-wheat flour
1 cup rolled oats
1/2 teaspoon cinnamon
1/4 teaspoon cloves
1/4 teaspoon nutmeg
1/2 teaspoon baking powder
1/2 teaspoon baking soda

8 ounces plain (nonfat or low-fat) yogurt
1/4 cup plus 1 tablespoon vegetable oil
2 egg whites, slightly beaten
1 tablespoon molasses or brown sugar
1/2 cup raisins (optional)

Preheat oven to 375 degrees. Spray muffin tins. Combine flour, oats, cinnamon, cloves, nutmeg, baking powder and baking soda. In a separate bowl, mix yogurt, oil, egg whites and molasses or brown sugar. Add raisins, if desired. Add yogurt mixture to dry ingredients and mix lightly, just until dry ingredients are moistened. Spoon batter (it will be thick) into muffin tin and bake 17 minutes or so, until tops are brown and toothpick comes out clean. Remove from oven and cool 5 minutes. Remove muffins from tin. Serve warm, or cool and wrap tightly for storage. These freeze wonderfully!

Sun-Dried Tomato Bread

Makes 1 large loaf or 3 mini loaves

2 cloves garlic
1/3 cup oil-packed sun-dried tomatoes
1 bunch scallions
2 1/2 cups all-purpose flour
2 teaspoons baking powder
1 1/4 teaspoons salt
1/2 teaspoon baking soda

5 ounces provolone cheese, grated
3/4 teaspoon dried rosemary
3/4 teaspoon ground black pepper
1/3 cup pine nuts, lightly toasted
2 tablespoons solid vegetable shortening at room temperature
2 tablespoons sugar
2 large eggs
1 1/4 cups buttermilk

Preheat oven to 350 degrees. Grease one 9-inch loaf pan. In a small saucepan, cook garlic in boiling water and cover for 15 minutes. Meanwhile, drain and chop tomatoes, reserving 2 tablespoons of oil. Slice scallions thin, and include 1 inch of green part. In a large bowl, stir together flour, baking powder, salt and baking soda. Add cheese, scallions, rosemary, pepper, sun-dried tomatoes and pine nuts. Toss mixture until combined. In a small bowl, blend together shortening, reserved oil and sugar until mixture is smooth. When garlic has finished cooking, drain, peel and mash it with a fork. Add to shortening mixture along with eggs and buttermilk. Add shortening mixture to flour mixture and blend until well combined. Pour batter into prepared pan. Bake until toothpick comes out clean, about 45 to 50 minutes for a large loaf. Cool bread in pan on a wire rack for 5 minutes. Turn onto rack and cool completely.

Radio Active Reds, 1986, by Patrick Nagatani, polacolor II photo, Museum of Fine Arts.

Starry Night Variation #2, 1977, by Betty Hahn, serigraph,
Museum of Fine Arts.

Caramelized Onion Basil Bread

Makes 3 loaves

2 packages dry active yeast

2 1/4 cups water at 110 degrees

1 egg

6 1/2 to 7 cups unbleached flour

1 extra-large onion

1 tablespoon olive oil

1/4 cup butter

1 tablespoon salt

1/4 cup chopped fresh basil

2 egg whites (plus 1 teaspoon of
    water), slightly beaten

Preheat oven to 350 degrees. Mix 2 packages of yeast in 2 1/2 cups warm water (110 degrees) and lightly whisk egg into warm water. Add 3 cups of flour to water and yeast. Stir and let stand. Sauté onion in skillet with 1 tablespoon of olive oil until sweet and caramel colored (not burned!). Combine butter and salt. Melt in warm oven. After onions, butter and salt have cooled to touch, combine these ingredients with chopped basil (do not cook basil), and add to yeast and flour mixture. Stir in 2 cups of flour and turn out on floured table. Add remaining flour while kneading. At high altitude, if you don't knead enough, you'll get hockey pucks!

Place bread in lightly buttered bowl and cover with clean towel. Let rise in warm location until doubled. Punch down and let the dough rest 2 minutes. You might have to add a little flour at this point if dough is sticky. Form into desired shapes, sealing bottom with fingertips. Remember that loaves will triple in size. Place on baking sheet with parchment paper. Sprinkle paper with water, and lightly butter top of loaves. Cover with clean towel. Let rise in warm location approximately 1 1/2 hours until side of dough when gently pushed, stays in. Bake for 20 minutes. Pull out and brush tops with lightly beaten egg whites. Finish baking for about 5 minutes until brown and loaves sound hollow. Place on wire rack to cool. Heat in oven 10 minutes before serving.

Dinner for Two—Andrew Barnes, chef

Tortillas

Makes 6

3 cups flour

2 teaspoons salt

2 teaspoons baking powder

2 tablespoons lard or shortening

Mix all ingredients by hand until crumbly. Add 1 cup hot water and knead until smooth. Pull apart handfuls of dough, make into ball and roll out individually. Cook on each side on hot skillet or griddle until golden brown.

New Mexico Governor Bill Richardson

Sweet Potato Bread

Makes 2 large loaves

1/4 pound butter

1/2 cup yogurt

1/2 cup honey

1 teaspoon cinnamon

1 1/2 cups chopped pecans

2 cups grated raw sweet potatoes

3 1/2 cups flour

3 cups sugar

2 teaspoons baking soda

2 teaspoons salt

1 teaspoon nutmeg

1 teaspoon cinnamon

1 cup cooking oil

3/4 cup water

4 eggs, beaten

Preheat oven to 350 degrees. Combine first 4 ingredients in a saucepan and boil 1 minute. Stir in 1 cup pecans and cool. Mix remaining pecans with sweet potatoes. In a large mixing bowl, combine dry ingredients and stir in potato-nut mixture. Blend oil, water and eggs. Add to potato-nut mixture, mixing only enough to moisten. Line two 9 x 5-inch loaf pans with greased foil. Place 1 cup batter in each pan. Top with 1/2 cup of cooled butter and pecan mixture. Cover with another cup of batter. Repeat each again. Bake for 65 to 75 minutes, until center cracks. Cool 15 minutes.

Scones with Raisins and Chocolate Chips

Makes 12 servings

1 3/4 cup all-purpose flour

2 1/4 teaspoons baking powder

1 tablespoon sugar

1/2 teaspoon salt

1/4 cup butter

1/2 cup white chocolate chips

1/4 cup golden raisins

1/2 cup plain yogurt

2 eggs, beaten

1/3 cup heavy cream

Preheat oven to 400 degrees. Sift all dry ingredients together. Add butter, chocolate and raisins. Place the flour mixture in mixer. Mix yogurt and eggs until well blended. Add to flour mixture and slowly blend. Slowly add cream until just mixed. Place mixture on a floured cool surface and roll out into 1-inch square. Cut into 2 triangles and place on parchment-lined cookie pan. Brush tops with heavy cream and sprinkle with sugar. Bake for 5 to 7 minutes. Turn oven down to 375 degrees and finish baking for 10 to 12 minutes. When finished baking, remove from trays immediately to a cool tray. Let sit for 5 to 10 minutes before eating.

Las Campanas Country Club—Jeff Moses, executive chef

Desserts

Santa Fe Hills, *1917, by Leon Kroll, oil on canvas, 34 x 40 1/4 inches, Museum of Fine Arts.*

Delicate Almond Frosties

Makes 3 dozen

1 cup butter
2/3 cup sugar
1 egg yolk
1 teaspoon almond extract
1/4 teaspoon salt
2 1/3 cups flour

ICING:
Milk
2 cups powdered sugar
Drop vanilla
Food coloring or paste

Preheat oven to 350 degrees. Cream butter and sugar until fluffy. Beat in egg yolk, almond extract and salt. Blend well. Gradually beat in flour to form dough. Use low speed and mix until flour is incorporated. Do not over-beat. Refrigerate dough. Bake on ungreased baking sheet or on parchment paper–lined baking sheets. Bake 8 to 10 minutes. Do not get too brown.

ICING:
Add small amounts of milk to powdered sugar until it is of spreading consistency. Add a tiny drop of vanilla. Color icing with food coloring or colored paste. Spread with small spatula or knife on cookies. You can also spoon carefully melted chocolate into small pastry tube and pipe onto cookies for decoration.

Apricot Nut Bars

Makes 5 dozen

4 eggs
1 1/2 cups brown sugar
1 (10 1/2-ounce) can
    evaporated milk
2 tablespoons lemon juice
1 1/2 cups sifted flour
1 1/4 teaspoons baking soda

1 teaspoon cinnamon
1/2 teaspoon salt
1 cup dried apricots, chopped
1 cup walnuts, chopped
1 cup flaked coconut
Confectioners' sugar

Preheat oven to 375 degrees. Combine beaten eggs, sugar, milk and juice in large bowl. Sift together flour, baking soda, cinnamon and salt. Add flour mixture to egg mixture all at once. Stir just until blended. Fold in apricots, walnuts and coconut. Do not overmix. Smooth batter evenly into 2 well-greased 15 x 10 x 1-inch jelly roll pans. Bake 20 minutes. Cool in pans before sprinkling with a light topping of confectioners' sugar. Cut into bars and store in airtight containers. Can be frozen, well wrapped.

Jonathan Apple Squares

Makes 32 squares

2 cups sifted flour

2 teaspoons baking powder

1/2 teaspoon salt

1/2 cup butter

1 1/2 cups sugar

2 eggs

2 teaspoons vanilla

1 tablespoon powdered sugar

1/2 teaspoon cinnamon

1 cup raw Jonathan apples, chopped

1 cup coarsely broken walnuts

Preheat oven to 350 degrees. Sift flour, baking powder and salt. Melt butter, add sugar and cool. Beat eggs into batter. Add vanilla and dry ingredients. Add apples and walnuts. Pour into greased 9 x 13-inch pan and bake for 30 minutes. While warm, cut into squares and dust with powdered sugar and cinnamon mixture. These are best when they are covered with plastic wrap while still warm.

Triple-Ginger Biscotti

Makes 30 to 40

2 1/4 cups flour

3/4 cup sugar

3/4 teaspoon baking soda

1/4 teaspoon salt

2 teaspoons ground ginger

2 tablespoons fresh ginger, minced

2 eggs

2 tablespoons molasses

1/2 teaspoon almond extract

3/4 cup toasted almonds

1/2 cup candied ginger, chopped

Preheat oven to 350 degrees. In a large bowl, combine flour, sugar, baking soda, salt and ground ginger, mixing until well combined. In a small bowl, mix fresh ginger, eggs, molasses and almond extract, stirring until well combined. Add to flour mixture, beating until a dough is formed. Stir in toasted almonds and candied ginger. Turn dough out onto slightly floured surface. Knead it several times and divide in half. Working on a buttered, floured baking sheet, form dough into 2 flattish logs, at least 3 to 5 inches apart. Bake for approximately 20 minutes until golden. Cool about 10 minutes. Transfer carefully to a cutting board and slice diagonally. Bake an additional 6 to 8 minutes each side. Cool on racks. Store in airtight containers.

Biscochitos

Makes 5 dozen

2 cups lard (shortening or butter may be substituted)

1 1/2 cups sugar

2 eggs

1 1/2 tablespoons anise

6 cups flour

1 teaspoon salt

3 teaspoons baking powder

2 teaspoons vanilla

1/4 cup warm water as needed (can be half wine)

Preheat oven to 350 degrees. Mix lard and sugar. Add eggs and anise. Sift flour, salt and baking powder. Combine ingredients. Dough will be sticky, but do not add flour. Flour rolling pin. Roll out on a floured pastry board to a thickness of 1/2 inch. Form by hand or cut out with cookie cutter. Sprinkle or dip cut-out cookies in sugar-cinnamon mixture. Bake 10 to 12 minutes.

Red Chile Chocolate Chip Cookies

Makes 6 dozen

3 sticks margarine

2 cups brown sugar

1 cup sugar

3 eggs

Dash salt

1 tablespoon vanilla

3 tablespoons hot red chile powder

1 teaspoon baking soda

3/4 cup cocoa

4 cups flour

3 cups chocolate chips

Preheat oven to 350 degrees. Mix first 6 ingredients by hand or with mixer on low speed until blended. Blend in chile powder, baking soda and cocoa. Stir in flour and add chocolate chips. Scoop onto baking sheets (parchment lined is best). Bake 14 minutes for small-size cookies, 16 minutes for larger cookies.

Craven Cookies, Albuquerque, New Mexico—Barb Hively, her signature cookie

Still Life, *by Donald Beauregard, oil on canvas, Museum of Fine Arts.*

Cowgirl Cookies

Makes 100 cookies

2 cups butter or margarine

2 cups sugar

1 1/2 cups brown sugar

3 cups white flour

2 teaspoons salt

2 teaspoons vanilla

2 teaspoons baking soda

4 large eggs

6 cups old-fashioned oats

12 ounces chocolate chips

1 1/2 cups flaked coconut (optional)

1 1/2 cups raisins or dried cranberries (optional)

1 1/2 cups nuts (optional)

Preheat oven to 350 degrees. Grease 2 large baking sheets. Cream butter and sugars. Add flour, salt, vanilla and baking soda. Beat in eggs 1 at a time. At low speed, beat in oats. Slowly add chocolate chips and then add other options. Drop by heaping teaspoon onto greased baking sheets. Space cookies as dough spreads. Bake 10 to 15 minutes. Place on racks to cool.

Navajo at Dance, by Harrison Begay, from the Collection of the Museum of Indian Arts and Culture/Laboratory of Anthropology.

Double Lemon Delights

Makes 32 bars

1/2 cup butter

1 1/2 cups sugar

2 eggs

1 teaspoon vanilla

2 teaspoons lemon juice

1 cup flour

2 teaspoons baking powder

1/2 teaspoon salt

3/4 cup coarsely chopped walnuts

1 cup candied lemon peel, finely chopped

1 tablespoon lemon zest

Powdered sugar

Preheat oven to 350 degrees. Cream butter and sugar. Add eggs, one at a time, beating well after each egg. Add vanilla gradually. Add lemon juice (use fresh lemons). Sift dry ingredients and add to creamed mixture, blending well. Stir in walnuts, candied lemon peel and fresh lemon zest. Spread in 13 x 9-inch pan. Bake 30 to 35 minutes. Cool. Dust with powdered sugar from a small strainer.

Chocolate Mint Sticks

Makes 8 servings

2 eggs, beaten

1/2 cup melted butter

1 cup sugar

2 squares unsweetened chocolate, melted

1/2 teaspoon peppermint extract

1/2 cup flour

1/2 cup pecans, chopped

FROSTING:

2 tablespoons soft butter

1 cup powdered sugar

1 tablespoon cream

1 square semisweet chocolate, melted

1 tablespoon butter, melted

Preheat oven to 350 degrees. Combine eggs, butter and sugar. Beat well. Add melted chocolate and peppermint extract. Mix well. Add flour and chopped nuts. Stir until blended. Pour into greased 9 x 9-inch pan. Bake 25 to 30 minutes. *Do not* overbake. This is a cross between a brownie and fudge. Cool before frosting. Blend butter, powdered sugar, and cream and spread over cooled baked layer. When frosting is firm, pour melted chocolate and butter over it.

Crackly Gingersnaps

Makes 48 cookies

3/4 cup oil

1 cup sugar

1/4 cup molasses

1 egg

2 cups flour

1/4 teaspoon salt

2 teaspoons baking soda

1 teaspoon cinnamon

1 teaspoon ground cloves

1 teaspoon ground ginger

Small bowl sugar, for dipping

Preheat oven to 375 degrees. Grease baking sheet. Beat oil and sugar until creamy. Add molasses and egg, and beat. Sift together flour, salt, baking soda, cinnamon, cloves and ginger. Add to sugar mixture and mix well. Roll dough into teaspoon-size balls. Dip balls in bowl of sugar to coat tops. Place 2 inches apart on baking sheet. Bake 9 to 12 minutes, until cracked and lightly browned.

Holiday Brownies

Makes 2 dozen

BOTTOM LAYER:

1 square unsweetened chocolate
1/4 pound butter
1 cup sugar
2 eggs
1 cup flour
1 teaspoon baking powder
1 teaspoon vanilla
1/2 cup walnuts, chopped
3/4 cup chocolate chips

MIDDLE LAYER:

6 ounces cream cheese
1/2 cup sugar
2 tablespoons flour

1 egg
1/2 teaspoon vanilla
1/4 cup walnuts, chopped

TOP LAYER:

1 square unsweetened chocolate
1/8 pound butter
2 ounces cream cheese
2 tablespoons Kahlua
1 teaspoon vanilla
2 tablespoons milk
2 1/2 cups powdered sugar

Preheat oven to 350 degrees. Melt chocolate and butter. Add other ingredients of bottom layer and mix well. Spread in greased 9 x 13-inch pan. Combine ingredients for middle layer and spread over chocolate. Bake 20 to 25 minutes. Cool. For top layer, melt chocolate, butter and cream cheese. Add Kahlua, vanilla and milk. Add powdered sugar. Spread when cooked layers are cool. Delicious frozen too! Slice when cool and freeze.

Green Chile Brownies

Makes 12 to 16 brownies

1/3 cup butter-flavored shortening
2 squares unsweetened baking
    chocolate
1 cup sugar
2 eggs
1 teaspoon vanilla
3/4 cup flour
1/2 teaspoon baking powder
1/2 cup pine nuts
1/2 cup medium green chiles,
    chopped

FROSTING:

1/2 cup milk
1/8 cup cocoa
1 tablespoon butter
1 cup powdered sugar

Preheat oven to 350 degrees. Melt shortening and chocolate. Cool. Add sugar, eggs and vanilla. Add sifted flour and baking powder. Add nuts and green chiles. Put into a 9-inch greased pan. Bake 20 to 25 minutes. Cool.

FROSTING:

Combine milk, cocoa, butter and sugar. Boil until soft, and frost brownies. Sprinkle with nuts.

Homesteaders Cookies

Makes 25 cookies

1 cup butter, melted

1 cup brown sugar

1 egg, beaten

1 teaspoon cinnamon

3 cups flour

1/2 teaspoon salt

1/2 teaspoon baking soda

1/2 cup nuts, finely chopped

FROSTING:

2 tablespoons butter, melted

1 cup powdered sugar

1/2 teaspoon vanilla

2 to 3 teaspoons warm milk

Preheat oven to 375 degrees. Combine butter, brown sugar, egg and cinnamon. Sift flour, salt and baking soda. Blend wet and dry ingredients. Add nuts. Line a 9-inch loaf pan with plastic wrap. Press cookie mixture into pan and freeze 1/2 hour or chill 2 hours. Remove from pan and slice 1/4 inch thick. Bake on ungreased baking sheets for 8 to 10 minutes. Remove and cool. Put cookies on surface, touching. Mix frosting ingredients and drizzle over cookies. Dough freezes well.

Yogurt Ice Cream

Makes 4 servings

8 ounces yogurt

3 ounces sugar

3 ounces heavy cream

Juice of 1 lemon

Note: This recipe requires an ice cream maker.

Combine all ingredients together, then blend and transfer to ice cream maker. Freeze according to manufacturer's instructions.

Fuego Restaurant, Maxim Boureou, pastry chef at La Posada de Santa Fe

Tequila Sherbet

Makes 6 servings

1 1/2 cups sugar

3 cups water

1/2 teaspoon lime zest

1/2 cup lime juice

1/3 cup tequila

1 egg white

1/4 teaspoon coarse salt

Stir together sugar and water and boil for 5 minutes. Add lime zest and boil 1 more minute. Stir in lime juice and pour into freezer tray. Freeze until mixture is thick. Remove and place mixture in a blender. Add tequila, egg white and salt, and blend together. Return to freezer and leave until firm.

Piñon Crisps

Makes 24 to 30

1/2 cup plus 2 tablespoons piñons
1/4 cup unsalted butter
1/4 cup solid vegetable shortening
1/2 cup powdered sugar
2 tablespoons granulated sugar plus
    extra for topping

1 teaspoon vanilla
1 cup flour
1/2 teaspoon ground cardamom
1/4 teaspoon baking powder
3/4 teaspoon salt

Preheat oven to 350 degrees. Toast piñons in oven for 10 minutes, or until golden. Set aside 2 tablespoons for later use. Grind remaining nuts in food processor until finely textured. Mix butter, shortening, sugars and vanilla until well combined. Sift together flour, cardamom, baking powder and salt. Add flour mixture along with ground nuts, mixing until well combined. Chill for 30 minutes or longer. Place 1-inch balls of dough on baking sheet 2 inches apart. Flatten balls with bottom of glass that has been dipped in granulated sugar. Decorate with reserved piñons. Bake at 325 degrees for 15 to 20 minutes, or until just beginning to color around edges. Leave on baking sheet for 20 to 30 minutes before removing to rack.

Piñon Nut Cookies

Makes 3 dozen

1 1/2 cups slivered blanched almonds
3 1/2 cups piñons
6 tablespoons sugar
3 egg whites

1/4 teaspoon cream of tartar
1 1/2 cups sugar
1/4 teaspoon almond extract

Preheat oven to 375 degrees. Grind almonds, piñons and 6 tablespoons sugar to a fine powder in a food processor with a metal blade. Set aside. Beat egg whites and cream of tartar until soft peaks form. Add sugar, 1/2 cup at a time, and beat until soft peaks form. Add almond extract, ground almonds and piñons. Drop by teaspoon onto greased baking sheet and bake until golden brown.

Toffee Bars

Makes 5 dozen

1 1/2 cups butter
1 3/4 cups brown sugar
1/2 teaspoon vanilla

2 cups sifted flour
1 cup walnuts or pecans, chopped
6 ounces chocolate chips

Preheat oven to 350 degrees. Cream butter, sugar and vanilla. Stir in flour. Stir in nuts and chips. Spread in ungreased jelly pan. Bake 20 minutes. Cut while warm. Freezes well.

Ricotta Nuts

Makes 2 dozen

1 (15-ounce) package whole Ricotta
cheese
1 1/4 cups sugar
1 (7-ounce) can flaked coconut
1/2 cup unsweetened cocoa

Drain Ricotta in a strainer over a bowl for several hours in refrigerator. Add sugar and 1/2 can coconut to Ricotta and mix well. Separate mixture into 2 equal parts and mix cocoa into 1/2 of cheese mixture. Shape non-cocoa mixture into walnut-size balls and roll in remaining coconut. Do the same for cocoa mixture and place in decorative pastry cups and refrigerate until 1 hour before serving time.

OTHER COMBINATIONS:
Mix drained, crushed pineapple with coconut
Orange extract and chocolate with orange zest coating
Lemon zest, lemon extract and coconut
Chocolate and crushed hazelnuts or other nuts
Instant espresso and chocolate rolled in chocolate beads

Nedra Matteucci Galleries—Nedra and Richard Matteucci

Berry Butter Cake

Makes 8 to 12 slices

1 1/2 sticks unsalted butter, softened
1 cup sugar
1 extra-large or jumbo egg and
   1 yolk
1/2 teaspoon fresh lemon zest

1 cup flour (unbleached)
1/2 cup berries (blueberries,
   raspberries, etc., fresh or frozen)
Powdered sugar for decoration

Preheat oven to 375 degrees. Beat butter until smooth. Cream in sugar. Beat in eggs, until fluffy and lemon colored (a long time). Add lemon zest and mix well. Mix in flour. Beat only until blended. Pour into pre-buttered cake pan. Place berries randomly on top of batter and poke down. Bake 45 minutes or until center tests done. Cool. Remove from pan and sprinkle with powdered sugar.

The Plaza in Winter, *Santa Fe, New Mexico, ca. 1914. Photograph by Jesse L. Nusbaum, courtesy of the Palace of the Governors Photo Archives. Negative 61463.*

Chocolate Mousse Cake

Makes 10 to 14 servings

1/2 pound sweet butter

8 squares unsweetened chocolate

8 eggs, separated

1 1/4 cups sugar

2 tablespoons Gran Marnier
    or other liqueur

1 tablespoon lemon juice

Powdered cocoa

Powdered sugar

Preheat oven to 250 degrees. Butter 9-inch springform pan. Melt butter and chocolate in a double boiler and cool. Beat egg yolks with sugar until light and lemon colored. Add chocolate mixture and liqueur. Beat 7 egg whites and add lemon juice. Continue beating to form stiff peaks. Fold 3/4 of egg whites into chocolate mixture. Bake 2/3 of chocolate mixture in a buttered pan for 1 1/4 hours. Cool. Fold rest of egg whites into remaining chocolate mixture and frost cake. Sprinkle with cocoa and powdered sugar before serving.

New Mexico Adobe Cake

Makes 12 or more servings

1 cup butter

1 cup sugar

4 eggs

1 teaspoon vanilla

1 1/2 cups flour

1/3 cup cocoa

1 cup pecans, chopped

1 (7-ounce) jar marshmallow crème

FROSTING:

1/2 cup butter

1 box confectioners' sugar, sifted

1/3 cup cocoa

1/2 cup condensed milk

1 teaspoon vanilla

1 cup pecans, chopped

Preheat oven to 350 degrees. Using an electric mixer, cream butter well. Add sugar and mix again. Add eggs one at a time, mixing after each addition. Add vanilla. Add flour and cocoa and mix well. Add nuts. Batter will be thick. Spread in well-greased and floured 9 x 13-inch pan. Bake 25 to 30 minutes. Remove from oven and spread with marshmallow crème while cake is hot (put dollops of crème all over cake and spread with a spoon dipped in cold water). Let cool completely.

FROSTING:

Cream butter and slowly add all sifted confectioners' sugar and cocoa a little at a time, adding condensed milk as needed to achieve a spreading consistency. Add vanilla and nuts. Cut in small pieces (very rich). Freezes well.

Carrot Cake with Cherries

Makes 8 to 10 servings

1/2 cup (or more) dried tart cherries, chopped

2 cups flour

1 tablespoon dry unsweetened cocoa

2 teaspoons cinnamon

1 teaspoon baking soda

1 teaspoon salt

2 teaspoons baking powder

4 large eggs

2 teaspoons vanilla extract

1 cup sugar

1 cup brown sugar, packed

1 1/4 cups vegetable oil

4 cups packed grated carrots

1 cup nuts, chopped (optional)

Cherries

Preheat oven to 350 degrees. Grease three 9-inch pans and line with waxed paper or grease a 9 x 13-inch pan and a small loaf pan or muffin tin. Combine dry ingredients in a bowl. In another bowl, beat eggs and add vanilla, sugars and oil. Mix well. Mix in dry ingredients until just blended and then stir in carrots, nuts and cherries. Divide and spoon batter into desired pans and place in center part of oven. Bake 35 to 40 minutes until tops of cakes spring back when touched and edges have begun to pull away from sides of pans. Cool and frost with favorite frosting.

Apple Cocoa Cake

Makes 9 to 12 servings

3 eggs

2 cups sugar

1 cup butter, softened

1 teaspoon vanilla

1/2 cup water

2 1/2 cups flour

1 teaspoon baking soda

2 tablespoons cocoa

1 teaspoon cinnamon

1 teaspoon allspice

1 1/2 cups chocolate chips or 1 cup chocolate chips and 1/2 cup chopped nuts

2 apples, grated

GLAZE:

1 tablespoon cocoa

1 1/2 cups powdered sugar

2 to 3 tablespoons milk

1/2 cup finely chopped nuts

Preheat oven to 325 degrees. Grease and flour a Bundt pan. Beat together eggs, sugar, butter, vanilla and water until fluffy. Sift together flour, baking soda, cocoa and spices. Add to creamed mixture and mix well. Fold in chocolate chips, nuts and apples. Pour batter into prepared pan. Bake 60 to 70 minutes. Cool 15 minutes. Remove from pan. When completely cool, frost with glaze and top with nuts.

GLAZE:

Mix cocoa and powdered sugar together. Add milk, one tablespoon at a time. The glaze should be thin enough so that it runs a little down side of cake, but not too thin.

Sautéed Strawberries in Red Wine-Pepper Sauce

Makes 6 servings

1 1/2 cups good-quality cabernet sauvignon

7 tablespoons sugar

1/2 teaspoon freshly ground pepper

1 (2-inch-long) piece vanilla bean, split lengthwise

1 tablespoon cornstarch

2 tablespoons unsalted butter

1 cup strawberries, hulled and quartered lengthwise

Pinch pepper

Vanilla ice cream

6 sprigs fresh mint

Combine 1 cup wine, sugar and 1/2 teaspoon pepper in heavy, medium-sized saucepan. Scrape seeds from vanilla bean into wine sauce; add bean. Stir over medium heat until sugar dissolves. Whisk remaining 1/2 cup wine and cornstarch in a small bowl to blend. Add this to wine sauce, and whisk constantly until it comes to a boil and thickens, about 2 minutes. Remove vanilla bean pieces from sauce. Set aside. (Sauce can be made a day ahead. Cool; then cover and refrigerate.) Melt butter in a large skillet over high heat. Add berries; sauté 1 minute. Add sauce and a pinch of pepper; bring to boil. Divide berries and sauce among 6 martini glasses. Top each with a scoop of vanilla ice cream. Garnish with mint.

Kathryn Huelster, professional cooking instructor

Lemon Goat Cheese Cake

Makes 8 servings

6 eggs, separated

1 1/4 cups sugar plus 2 tablespoons
or more for the pan
(can substitute Splenda)

1 1/2 pounds goat cheese

2 tablespoons rum

2 tablespoons flour

Grated zest of 2 large lemons (organic are best)

1 tablespoon plus 1/4 cup fresh lemon juice (3 to 4 large lemons)

2 teaspoons vanilla extract

1/4 teaspoon kosher salt

2 pints fresh raspberries

Appliqué with Figures, *wall hanging by Samual Ojo Omonaiye, Nigeria, ca. 1960, appliquéd and embroidered fabric. Girard Foundation Collection in the Museum of International Folk Art. Photo: Blair Clark.*

Preheat oven to 325 degrees. Place rack in middle of oven. Spray an 8-inch springform pan with nonstick cooking spray and sprinkle bottom and sides with sugar or Splenda, shaking out excess.

Beat egg yolks and 1 cup sugar (or Splenda) until yolks are very pale. Slowly beat in goat cheese, 1 cup at a time. Add rum, flour, lemon zest, 1 tablespoon lemon juice, vanilla and 1/8 teaspoon salt. Beat until creamy. In another bowl, whisk egg whites and 1/8 teaspoon salt until foamy. Add 2 tablespoons sugar and whisk until soft-peaked meringue consistency. Working in 2 batches, gently fold whites into cheese mixture. Pour batter into prepared pan. Place pan in a baking dish large enough to contain batter comfortably. Pour enough hot water into baking dish to reach approximately 1 inch up sides of pan. Cover entire baking dish with foil and carefully place in oven. Bake 35 to 40 minutes. When done, cake will begin to rise slightly and will be somewhat set in middle. Remove foil and bake an additional 5 to 10 minutes or until cake is completely set. Remove cake from oven and allow it to cool in baking dish for several minutes. Meanwhile, combine remaining 1/4 cup lemon juice and sugar in saucepan and bring to a boil. Boil rapidly until thickened. Remove from heat and set aside to cool.

Note: This mixture can quickly become too thick and harden. After cooling, and just before using this glaze, add a couple of additional tablespoons of lemon juice and heat mixture in microwave for about 30 seconds. Then stir. Heat a little more if you don't have right consistency for spreading glaze on cake.

When cake has cooled slightly, remove pan from baking dish. Refrigerate cake until completely chilled. Remove sides of springform pan. Using a pastry brush, lightly brush glaze evenly over cake top and sides. Cut into wedges and serve with berries. Any leftover cake must be refrigerated. Cake is better 1 day old.

Fruit Torte

Makes 10 to 12 servings

CAKE:
1/2 cup butter
1/2 cup sugar
4 egg yolks
1/2 cup cake flour
 plus 2 tablespoons
4 tablespoons milk
1 teaspoon baking powder
1/2 teaspoon salt

MERINGUE:
4 egg whites
1/4 teaspoon cream of tartar
3/4 cup sugar
1/3 cup pecans, chopped

FILLING:
1 cup heavy cream
1/4 teaspoon vanilla
1 cup fresh fruit (sliced strawberries
 are excellent)

CAKE:
Butter and flour two 9-inch cake pans. Cream butter and sugar. Add egg yolks, beaten lightly. Sift 1/2 cup cake flour 3 times and add alternately with milk. Add remaining cake flour, sifted with baking powder and salt. Divide batter between 2 pans.

MERINGUE:
Beat egg whites until stiff, adding cream of tartar while beating. Fold sugar into beaten egg whites. Spread equally over 2 cake pans. Sprinkle with nuts. Bake 25 minutes.

FILLING:
Whip cream, adding vanilla while beating. Mix fresh fruit into whipped cream. After cakes have completely cooled and are ready to be served, place filling between layers.

Chocolate Cherry Cheesecake

Makes 12 to 16 servings

1 1/2 cups graham cracker crumbs
1 cup sugar
1/4 cup butter, softened
2 (8-ounce) packages cream cheese
1/2 cup plain yogurt
2 extra-large eggs

Dash salt
1 teaspoon vanilla
1 cup chocolate chips
1 cup frozen sweet cherries,
 defrosted

Preheat oven to 350 degrees.

CRUST:
In a large bowl, blend graham cracker crumbs, 1/4 cup sugar and butter. Press over bottom of 9-inch springform pan.

FILLING:
Using an electric mixer, blend softened cream cheese, yogurt, 3/4 cup sugar, eggs, salt and vanilla until smooth. Gently, fold chocolate chips and cherries into mixture. Pour into pan over crust and bake in center of preheated oven for 30 to 40 minutes, until center is just set. Cool on rack before removing rim of pan.

Doña Flora's Cake

Makes 20 servings

8 ounces butter or margarine
2 scant cups sugar
5 eggs
2 teaspoons vanilla
4 teaspoons baking powder

4 cups flour (plus 2 tablespoons
   for high altitude)
1/4 teaspoon salt
1 cup milk
2 teaspoons orange rind

Preheat oven to 375 degrees. Cream butter. Add sugar and beat until fluffy and light. Add eggs one at a time, beating after each one. Add vanilla. Sift dry ingredients and add alternately with milk to butter and sugar. Mix in orange rind last. Pour into a greased and floured Bundt or rectangular cake pan. Bake 50 minutes.

Fifteen-Lemon Layer Cake

Makes 10 to 12 servings

ICING:
10 large eggs
1 1/2 cups sugar
1 cup unsalted butter
1 cup fresh lemon juice
Zest of 4 lemons

CAKE:
3 cups flour
3 teaspoons baking soda
1/2 teaspoon salt
1 cup butter, unsalted, at room
   temperature
2 heaping cups sugar
5 large eggs
1 cup milk, cold
Nonstick vegetable spray

ICING:
Beat eggs and sugar. Cook mixture in double boiler over medium heat until sugar dissolves, about 2 to 3 minutes. Add butter, lemon juice and zest. Cook, whisking constantly, for 5 minutes. Refrigerate icing 1 to 2 hours until cold, then store in freezer. If icing begins to freeze, return to refrigerator. Icing should be very cold.

CAKE:
Double sift together flour, baking soda and salt. Cream butter and sugar. Add eggs one at a time, blending well after each addition. Add 1/2 flour mixture and blend well. Stir in cold milk and mix well. Add remaining flour mixture and mix until very smooth.

Grease and flour four 9-inch cake pans. Spray lightly with vegetable spray. Put 2 heaping tablespoons cake mixture into each pan and smooth with spoon. Bake, watching closely, until layers brown around edges, for 3 to 5 minutes. Remove from oven and quickly turn warm layer out onto cake plate. Ice cake layer with 2 1/2 tablespoons cold icing. Repeat with remaining 3 layers, working very quickly. Return icing to freezer and put assembled cake in refrigerator. Re-grease, re-flour and re-spray pans and repeat baking, icing and layering procedure for 15 layers.

When assembly is complete, ice top and sides of cake. Cover and refrigerate at least 1 day, preferably 3 to 4 days, before serving.

Fourth-Generation Pound Cake

Makes 10 to 12 servings

8 ounces butter

2 cups sugar

6 eggs

2 cups flour

1 teaspoon vanilla

1 tablespoon almond flavoring

Preheat oven to 325 degrees. Cream together butter and sugar. Add 4 eggs, one at a time, mixing well after each. Add 1 cup flour and 1 egg. Mix well. Add last cup of flour, remaining egg and flavorings. Mix well. Pour into a prepared tube pan and bake 50 to 60 minutes.

Olive Oil Cake with Orange-Lavender Syrup

Makes 10 to 12 servings

2 eggs

1 cup sugar

Zest of 1 lemon

1/4 teaspoon salt

1/3 cup dry Marsala

1/3 cup milk

1/2 cup vegetable oil

1/4 cup extra-virgin olive oil plus extra
    to oil pan

1 tablespoon baking powder

1 1/2 cups flour

1/2 cup orange juice

3 slices orange peel

2 teaspoons lavender, or to taste

Preheat oven to 400 degrees. Beat eggs and 1/2 cup sugar until they become lemony yellow. Add lemon zest, salt, Marsala, milk, oil and olive oil. Mix to combine. Stir baking powder into flour. Add flour to other ingredients and mix thoroughly. Smear inside of a 2 1/4-quart tube pan with olive oil. Add batter and bake 25 minutes or until cake is nicely browned. Place 1/2 cup sugar, orange juice and orange peel in small saucepan. Place lavender in cheese cloth and tie tightly with kitchen twine. Bring syrup to a boil and place lavender sachet in syrup. Allow to simmer until sugar is completely dissolved and syrup thickens slightly, about 10 minutes. Discard lavender and orange peel. Cool slightly. Pour syrup over warm cake. Serve garnished with crème de fraiche or sour cream.

Coconut Pound Cake

Makes 4 small loaves

3 cups all-purpose flour

2 cups sugar

1 (5-ounce) can evaporated milk (plus
    water to make 8 ounces)

3/4 pound butter, melted

1 teaspoon vanilla

5 large eggs

1 (7-ounce) package Bakers Dream
    Fluff Coconut

Preheat oven to 300 degrees. Mix together flour and sugar. Pour milk into a 1-cup liquid measuring cup and add enough water to make 8 ounces. Pour butter, milk and water combination, and vanilla into flour and sugar mixture. Stir with a wooden spoon until smooth. Add eggs one at a time, stirring well after each addition. Fold in coconut. Grease and flour four 2 1/4 x 2 1/4 x 6-inch small loaf pans. Divide batter equally into pans. Place in center of oven and bake 40 minutes until golden brown. Remove from pans and cool on rack. These keep well if wrapped in foil and placed in a plastic bag in freezer.

The Village Lamplighter, *by Joseph Sharp,*
oil on canvas, Museum of Fine Arts.

Stahlman Pecan Cake

Makes 15 to 20 servings

1 pound butter, softened

2 cups sugar

6 eggs, beaten

1 tablespoon lemon extract

4 cups flour

1 1/2 teaspoons baking powder

4 cups pecan halves

2 cups canned, drained white grapes or golden raisins (optional)

Preheat oven to 300 degrees. Blend butter and sugar in a large mixing bowl. Gradually add eggs and lemon extract. Sift flour and baking powder 3 times. Add to sugar and eggs. Add nuts and grapes or raisins. Blend and put in a greased and floured angel food cake pan. Bake 1 1/2 to 2 hours. Cool 15 minutes before removing from pan. Cake is very dense.

Raspberry Cheesecake

Makes 12 servings

1 cup finely crushed graham crackers

1/4 cup finely chopped almonds

3/4 cup sugar

4 tablespoons flour

2 tablespoons butter, melted

3 (8-ounce) packages cream cheese

1/4 cup raspberry liqueur, red or black

1 tablespoon vanilla

2 eggs

2 (8-ounce) containers raspberry yogurt

Raspberry jam

2 pints raspberries or blackberries (can mix)

Confectioners' sugar

Preheat oven to 375 degrees.

CRUST:
Combine cracker crumbs, almonds, 1/4 cup sugar, 2 tablespoons flour and butter. Press into springform pan.

FILLING:
In mixing bowl, combine 1/2 cup sugar, 2 tablespoons flour, cream cheese, liqueur and vanilla. Beat until fluffy. At low speed, add eggs and yogurt until just combined. Pour into springform pan. Place on center rack in oven. Bake 50 to 55 minutes or until center is nearly set when shaken. Cool 20 minutes. Loosen side of pan. Wait 30 minutes. Remove sides. Chill at least 4 hours. Top with thin spread of jam and fresh berries. Dust with confectioners' sugar.

Home of Randy Travis. Photography: Daniel Nadelbach, photographic styling: Gilda Meyer-Niehof.

Raspberry Almond Cake

Makes 9 servings

1 1/3 cups flour
1 teaspoon baking powder
1/3 cup sugar
1/2 cup butter or margarine
1 egg
1/2 cup raspberry jam

FILLING:

1/2 cup butter or margarine
2/3 cup sugar
1 cup finely chopped almonds
1/2 teaspoon almond extract
2 eggs

Mix first 5 ingredients in processor. Press on bottom of an 8 x 8-inch or 9 x 9-inch square pan. Cover with jam and chill.

Preheat oven to 350 degrees. Blend all ingredients and pour filling over chilled base and bake 45 to 50 minutes. Cool. Sprinkle with powdered sugar and cut into squares. Can also be used as cookies.

Apple Almond Tart

Makes 6 to 8 servings

PASTRY SHELL:

2 cups flour
1 stick butter
1/4 teaspoon salt
1/2 cup cold water

FILLING:

1 stick butter
1/2 cup sugar
2 eggs
1/4 pound almonds, finely ground
2 teaspoons flour
1 teaspoon almond extract
2 teaspoons rum
2 Gala or Granny Smith apples,
   thinly sliced

Preheat oven to 400 degrees.

PASTRY SHELL:
Combine flour, butter and salt. Cut in butter or use fingers until mixture becomes like coarse meal. Add water gradually. When dough comes together in a ball, do not mix more. Divide dough in 2 portions, wrap in plastic wrap and refrigerate for 2 hours.

FILLING:
Cream butter and sugar, and beat in eggs 1 at a time. Add almonds, flour, almond extract and rum. Mix well. When ready to bake tart, roll out pastry on a floured surface to make a 10-inch circle. Place in a 9-inch tart pan with removable bottom. Cover pastry with cream mixture, then place sliced apples in a swirl pattern on top. Bake at 400 degrees for 30 minutes.

Optional Glaze: 2 tablespoons apricot preserves, melted with 1 teaspoon water. Then brush over surface of tart as soon as it comes out of oven.

Chocolate Pecan Pie

Makes 6 servings

1 1/2 cups sugar
2 eggs, beaten
1/2 cup milk
1 stick butter, melted
1/4 cup flour

3 tablespoons cocoa
1/2 teaspoon salt
1 teaspoon vanilla
3/4 cup pecans, chopped
1 unbaked piecrust

Preheat oven to 275 degrees. Mix all ingredients together. Pour into unbaked piecrust and bake at 275 degrees for 1 hour. May be served with whipped cream.

Coffee Toffee Pie

Makes 6 to 8 servings

1 square unsweetened chocolate

2 teaspoons instant coffee granules

1/4 pound butter, softened

3/4 cup sugar

2 eggs or egg substitute

1 (9-inch) prebaked piecrust

2 cups whipping cream

2 tablespoons instant coffee granules

1/2 cup powdered sugar

Shaved chocolate

Melt chocolate and 2 teaspoons instant coffee together in a double boiler. Allow to cool. Beat butter and sugar together in a mixing bowl until light and creamy. Blend in cooled chocolate mixture. Add eggs, one at a time, beating 5 minutes after each addition. Turn mixture into a pastry shell; cover and refrigerate overnight. Combine whipping cream, 2 tablespoons instant coffee and powdered sugar in another mixing bowl and refrigerate for 1 hour. When thoroughly chilled, whip until stiff. Spread over top of pie, mounding toward center. Garnish with shaved chocolate.

Creekside Bar and Grill

Liqueur-Spiked Pie

Makes 8 to 10 servings

1 1/2 cups cookie crumbs, see note

1/4 cup melted butter

1/2 cup cold water

1 (4-ounce) package unflavored
    gelatin

2/3 cup sugar, divided

1/8 teaspoon salt

3 large eggs, separated

1/2 cup liqueur, see note

1 cup heavy cream

Food coloring, if necessary

Preheat oven to 350 degrees. Combine crumbs with butter, and form in pan. Bake 10 minutes. Cool. Pour water in saucepan, sprinkle with gelatin. Let stand 5 minutes. Add 1/3 cup sugar, salt and egg yolks, and stir. Cook over low heat until gelatin dissolves and mixture thickens. *Do not boil!* Stir in liqueur and chill until it mounds slightly, approximately 30 minutes. Beat egg whites stiff, add remaining sugar, and beat until peaks form. Whip cream. Using a whisk, gently blend cream-liqueur mixture, egg whites and whipping cream with an upward motion. Turn into crust and garnish as desired. Chill. Best made a day ahead and carefully covered. It also freezes very well.

Note: Match the crumbs (vanilla wafers, chocolate wafers or ginger-snaps) to the liqueur of choice for best flavor blend. Be imaginative. Match brandy with chocolate crumbs, blend fruit-flavored liqueurs or use just 1 liqueur for total flavor. Possible combinations: Brandy Alexander Pie: cognac and crème de cacao, Grasshopper Pie: crème de menthe (white, green or both), Eggnog Pie: Rum, Chocolate Eggnog Pie: crème de cacao and triple sec.

Piñon and Honey Tart

Makes 8 servings

Preheat oven to 350 degrees.

SWEET DOUGH:

8 ounces flour

3 ounces powdered sugar

3 ounces butter, room temperature

1 egg

2 tablespoons corn syrup

FILLING:

4 eggs

4 ounces powdered sugar

4 ounces melted butter

6 ounces honey

10 ounces toasted piñons

SWEET DOUGH:

Combine flour, powdered sugar and butter in bowl of a mixer. Set on medium speed. Continue mixing butter into dry ingredients until no large chunks of butter remain visible. Add egg and corn syrup (do not add water) to mixture and keep mixing until dough holds together and is smooth. Form dough into a ball and wrap it in plastic wrap. Let dough rest in refrigerator for at least 1 hour.

Using Pam spray or melted butter, coat a 12-inch round tart mold or tart ring, then dust with flour. Roll dough on a lightly floured surface. Line tart mold with dough and leave 10 minutes in freezer until it gets hard. Cover dough with parchment or baking paper and fill with pie weights or dried beans, to keep pastry flat while baking. Bake for 10 to 15 minutes at 350 degrees or until edge of crust is light golden brown.

FILLING:

Combine eggs, powdered sugar, and melted butter in a bowl and beat until well mixed. Add honey and piñons, and keep beating until blended. Set aside. Pour filling into prebaked tart shell and bake again for 15 minutes or until all of tart is golden brown. It is now ready to eat. This delightful piñon tart goes perfectly with a scoop of yogurt ice cream, a few slices of ripe white peach and a cold glass of muscat.

Fuego Restaurant at La Posada de Santa Fe—Maxim Bouneou, pastry chef

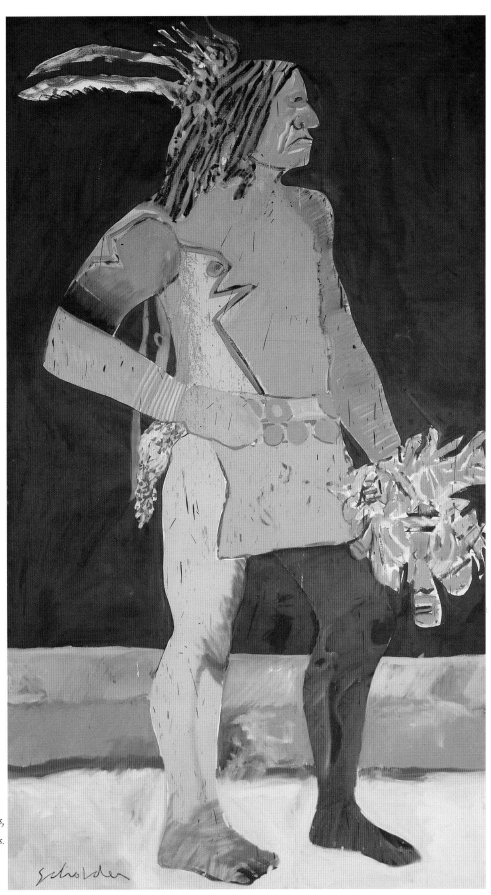

Super Indian, *by Frita Scholder, oil on canvas,*
102 x 68 inches. Museum of Fine Arts.

Chewy Pecan Pie

Makes 8 servings

3 egg whites
1/2 cup powdered sugar
1 cup graham cracker crumbs
1 cup sugar

1 cup chopped pecans
1/2 teaspoon baking powder
1 teaspoon vanilla

Preheat oven to 350 degrees. Beat egg whites with powdered sugar until stiff. In a separate bowl, mix graham cracker crumbs with sugar, then fold into egg whites. Add pecans, baking powder and vanilla. Spoon mixture into a greased 8-inch pie plate. Bake for 30 minutes. May be topped with whipped cream and pecan halves.

Pumpkin Praline Pecan Pie

Makes 6 to 8 servings

1 (9-inch) unbaked piecrust with
   high-fluted sides
1/3 cup pecans, chopped
1 cup brown sugar
1 tablespoon melted butter
2 eggs
1 cup minus 2 tablespoons canned
   pumpkin
2/3 cup brown sugar

1 tablespoon flour
1/4 teaspoon ground cloves
1/8 teaspoon ground mace
1/2 teaspoon each cinnamon
   and ginger
1/2 teaspoon salt
1 cup half-and-half
Whipping cream and pecan halves
   for garnish

Preheat oven to 375 degrees. Keep crust covered until filling is prepared.

PRALINE:
Mix well-chopped pecans, brown sugar and butter. Spread evenly over bottom of prepared piecrust.

FILLING:
Beat eggs well. Add remaining ingredients and mix until just blended. Pour over praline and bake for 45 to 50 minutes. Cool. Serve topped with whipped cream and pecan halves.

Kathryn Huelster, professional cooking instructor

Rhubarb Pie

Makes 6 to 8 servings

2 1/2 cups raw rhubarb,
   chopped fine
1 1/3 cups sugar
4 eggs, beaten

2 tablespoons flour
Juice of 1 large lemon
2 tablespoons butter, melted
1 unbaked piecrust

Preheat oven to 400 degrees. Place rhubarb in a bowl. Add sugar, eggs, flour, lemon juice and melted butter. Mix well and let stand for a few minutes. Pour into unbaked piecrust. Bake for 10 minutes, then lower temperature to 325 degrees and bake until firm, about 20 minutes.

Borrego House Apple Pudding

Makes 6 to 8 servings

1/2 cup butter

2/3 cup honey

1 large egg, beaten

1 cup flour

1/2 teaspoon salt

1 teaspoon cinnamon

1/2 teaspoon ground nutmeg

1 cup soaked raisins

1 cup pecans, chopped

2 cups apples, chopped

Preheat oven to 350 degrees. Cream butter and honey, and add beaten egg. Then add flour combined with salt, cinnamon and nutmeg. Beat to blend. Add raisins and chopped ingredients and mix. Spread in a greased 8 x 8-inch baking pan and bake 1 hour. Serve warm with whipped cream. Serve small servings as this is quite rich.

Note: Whip cream with 4 tablespoons honey and a pinch of cinnamon.

Borrego House Restaurant

Texas Cream Pie

Makes 6 to 8 servings

2 tablespoons cornstarch

2 tablespoons flour

1 cup sugar

2 cups milk

2 eggs, separated

1 teaspoon vanilla

Pinch salt

1 tablespoon butter

1/2 pint whipping cream

1 teaspoon powdered sugar

1 (9-inch) baked piecrust

In large saucepan, combine cornstarch, flour and 3/4 cup sugar. Add milk into which 2 egg yolks have been beaten. Cook over medium-high heat, stirring constantly until very thick. Remove from heat and add vanilla, salt and butter. Cool. Beat egg whites with 1/4 cup sugar until stiff. Fold whites into custard. Chill in cooked 9-inch pie shell. When ready to serve, top with whipped cream that has been whipped with powdered sugar.

Brandied Apricot Mousse

Makes 6 to 8 servings

1 (16-ounce) can apricot halves (or sliced peaches), reserve syrup

1 envelope unflavored gelatin

1 (7-ounce) jar marshmallow crème

1/4 cup sliced almonds, lightly toasted

2 tablespoons brandy

1 cup heavy cream, whipped

Drain apricots, reserving 1/2 cup syrup. Chop apricots. Soften gelatin in reserved syrup, and then stir over low heat until dissolved. Gradually add syrup to marshmallow crème, mixing until well blended. Stir in apricots, almonds and brandy; fold in whipped cream. Pour into 1 1/2-quart serving bowl; chill until firm. Garnish with additional apricot slices (canned, dried or fresh) and mint sprigs, if desired.

Pumpkin Roll

Makes 12 to 16 servings

3 eggs
1 cup sugar
2/3 cup pumpkin
1 teaspoon lemon juice
3/4 cup flour
1 teaspoon baking powder
1 teaspoon cinnamon
1/2 teaspoon ginger
1/4 teaspoon nutmeg
1/2 teaspoon salt
1 cup walnuts, finely chopped

FILLING:
1 cup powdered sugar
6 ounces cream cheese
4 teaspoons butter, softened
1/2 teaspoon vanilla

Preheat oven to 375 degrees. Beat eggs on high speed for 5 minutes. Gradually beat in sugar. Stir in pumpkin and lemon juice. Stir together flour, baking powder, cinnamon, ginger, nutmeg and salt. Fold into pumpkin. Spread in greased and floured 15 x 10 x 1-inch pan. Top with finely chopped walnuts. Bake for 15 minutes. Turn out on towel sprinkled with powdered sugar. Starting lengthwise, roll towel and cake together, cool and unroll for filling.

FILLING:
Combine powdered sugar, cream cheese, butter and vanilla. Beat until smooth. Spread over cake. Roll and cool.

Rhubarb and Peach Crisp

Makes 6 to 8 servings

TOPPING:
2/3 cup old-fashioned oats
2/3 cup dark brown sugar, packed
1/2 cup all-purpose flour
3/4 teaspoon ground cinnamon
1/4 teaspoon salt
1/2 cup chilled, unsalted butter,
    cut into pieces
1/2 cup pecans or almonds, chopped

FILLING:
4 cups 3/4-inch-thick slices fresh
    rhubarb (about 1 1/2 pounds)
6 fresh peaches or 1 (16-ounce)
    package frozen sliced peaches,
    thawed, drained
1 cup sugar
2 tablespoons quick-cooking tapioca
2 teaspoons fresh lemon juice
1 teaspoon ground cinnamon
1/8 teaspoon ground nutmeg

Preheat oven to 375 degrees.

TOPPING:
Combine first 5 ingredients in medium bowl. Add butter and cut in using pastry blender or rub with fingertips until mixture begins to clump together. Mix in nuts. (Can be prepared 3 hours ahead. Cover and chill.)

FILLING:
Combine all ingredients in a large bowl. Let stand 1 to 3 hours. Position rack in center of oven and preheat to 375 degrees. Butter 8 x 8 x 2-inch glass baking dish. Transfer filling to prepared dish. Sprinkle topping evenly over filling in dish, covering completely. Bake until fruit is tender, and juice bubbles thickly around sides and topping begins to brown slightly, about 40 minutes. Remove crisp from oven. Preheat broiler. Broil until topping is crisp and golden, watching closely, about 2 minutes. Serve warm with frozen vanilla yogurt or pistachio ice cream.

Note: May use all rhubarb, increasing to 6 cups.

Museum Hill Cafe Bread Pudding

Makes 12 servings

1/2 cup dried cranberries
3 tablespoons orange juice
10 eggs
1 quart heavy cream
1 1/2 cups sugar
2 tablespoons vanilla extract
1/2 cup toasted pine nuts
1 large loaf rustic bread (1 quart)

TOPPING:
1/4 cup sugar
1/2 tablespoon cinnamon
1 teaspoon ground ginger
1 ounce cold butter

Preheat oven to 350 degrees. Combine cranberries and orange juice. Let soak 1/2 hour.

Whisk eggs, cream, sugar and vanilla. Add to above mixture, then add pine nuts. Remove crust from bread and discard. Cut remaining bread into cubes. Place cubes into a buttered 9 x 12-inch dish. Pour cream mixture over bread cubes and mix well with spoon. Top with sugar, cinnamon, ginger and cold butter cut into bits. Bake until firm and puffy in center.

Note: Great served with caramel whipped cream. May add other dried fruit or fresh apple slices.

Walter Burke Catering—Stacy Pearl, executive chef

Capirotada (Mexican Bread Pudding)

Makes 8 servings

3/4 cup brown sugar
1/2 teaspoon cinnamon
3/4 cup water
6 slices day-old bread, toasted and cubed
1/2 cup peanuts

1/2 cup raisins
1 banana, cubed
1/4 pound goat or Mexican-type cheese, cubed
Pinch salt
1 tablespoon butter

Preheat oven to 350 degrees. Mix together brown sugar, cinnamon and water in saucepan. Bring to a boil and set aside. In a casserole dish, put layer of toast cubes, peanuts, raisins, banana and cheese. Sprinkle with a pinch of salt. Repeat until ingredients are used. Over this, pour sugar, water and cinnamon mixture, dot with butter and bake in oven for 20 minutes. Serve hot or cold with cream.

Wood Vendors, *Burro alley at San Francisco Street, Santa Fe, New Mexico, ca. 1900. Photograph by Royal Hubbell, courtesy of the Palace of the Governors Photo Archives. Negative 87028.*

Berry, Berry Sorbet

Makes 10 to 12 servings

2 (16-ounce) packages frozen
    strawberries, without sugar
1 (16-ounce) package
    frozen raspberries, without sugar
1 cup sugar

1 cup water
1/2 cup orange peel
1 tablespoon orange liqueur,
    per serving

Partially thaw berries in their plastic bags. Place sugar, water and orange peel in a saucepan, bring to a boil–do not stir. Reduce heat and continue cooking until all sugar has dissolved. Remove from heat and let cool to the touch. Place all partially frozen berries in a food processor, turn on and begin adding sugar mixture in a steady stream. Continue processing until all berries have been pureed. Place in a plastic container and put in freezer. May be made a few hours before serving. May be served in individual compotes with a tablespoon of orange liqueur over each. (This sorbet becomes very hard when frozen for a long period of time.)

Chocolate Cream Cheese Mousse

Makes 12 servings

2 cups semisweet chocolate chips
2 (8-ounce) packages Original
    Philadelphia cream cheese, room
    temperature

1/4 cup sugar
1/4 cup Gran Marnier
2 cups heavy cream, whipped

Melt chocolate chips in double boiler and set aside to cool slightly. In food processor, mix in softened cream cheese, sugar and Gran Marnier till no lumps are left, scraping bowl with rubber spatula a few times, approximately 5 minutes. Add melted chocolate to food processor and mix till combined. Whip heavy cream until peaks form and gently fold in chocolate mixture with a rubber spatula. Pour mixture into a small serving bowl, cover with plastic wrap and chill overnight. (May be made in advance and frozen for several weeks). Top with whipped cream, ganache, raspberry sauce, fresh raspberries or whatever you choose.

Cuisine Justine—Justine Witlox-Becker, owner

Chocolate Ganache Torte

Makes 6 servings

CRUST:
6 tablespoons melted,
  unsalted butter
1 1/2 cups graham cracker
  or Oreo crumbs

FILLING:
12 ounces chocolate chips
5 egg yolks
3 tablespoons brandy
1 teaspoon vanilla
12 ounces heavy cream

CRUST:
Combine mixture and pat into bottom of fluted 9-inch tart pan with a removable bottom. Chill until ready to use.

FILLING:
Put chocolate chips, yolks, brandy and vanilla into a food processor fitted with a steel blade attachment. Process mixture until it looks slightly pureed, approximately 2 minutes. In the meantime, bring cream just below boiling point, keeping a good watch as it will want to boil over. While food processor is still running, slowly add cream through top and mix for 2 minutes, stopping once to scrape down mixture with a rubber spatula. Pour mixture into chilled crust and refrigerate at least 3 hours until firm. When chilled, decorate with whipped cream and chocolate shavings. This is a very rich torte, so a little goes a long way.

Note: Other flavorings can be used such as peppermint extract instead of vanilla, or rum instead of brandy.

Walter Burke Catering—Stacy Pearl, executive chef

Coffee Parfait

Makes 6 servings

1 1/2 pints coffee ice cream
3 tablespoons brandy
4 tablespoons crème de cacao
3 tablespoons Kahlua

Whipped cream
Grated semisweet chocolate
  for garnish

Set out ice cream at room temperature for about 20 minutes, to soften. Blend in brandy, 3 tablespoons crème de cacao and Kahlua. Fold remaining 1 tablespoon crème de cacao into whipped cream. Divide ice cream mixture among 4 parfait glasses. Top with flavored whipped cream and sprinkle with grated chocolate. Return to freezer until ice cream is re-frozen, at least 1 hour.

New Mexico Crème

Makes 6 servings

1/2 cup granulated sugar
1 pint light cream
1 tablespoon gelatin

1 cup cold water
1 pint sour cream
2 teaspoons vanilla

Add sugar to light cream in double boiler. Stir until dissolved. Sprinkle gelatin over cold water. Let stand 5 minutes. Add gelatin mixture to cream mixture until dissolved. Refrigerate until cool, and then fold in sour cream and vanilla. Pour into fancy mold and chill overnight. Un-mold and surround with fresh berries.

Three-Fruit Sherbet

Makes 6 servings

Juice of 3 lemons
Juice of 3 oranges
3 ripe bananas, mashed
3 cups sugar
3 cups water
1 cup heavy cream

ALSO NEEDED:
Ice cream freezer
Ice
Coarse-ground ice cream salt

Mix all ingredients together except heavy cream and let sit for 1 hour for flavors to meld. Add 1 cup heavy cream to fruit mixture and freeze in a traditional ice cream freezer.

Frozen Mango Supreme

Makes 16 servings

7 to 8 large fresh mangos (or 2 large cans mangos or peaches)
2 cans Eagle Brand condensed milk
Pinch salt

50 lady fingers
Whipped cream
Slivered almonds

Place mangos, condensed milk and salt in blender. Puree until smooth. Alternate layers of lady fingers with the mango mixture in an attractive freezer-safe serving bowl. Place in freezer, covered, overnight. To serve, cover with whipped cream and garnish with slivered almonds.

Fresh Peach Flan

Makes 6 to 8 servings

CARAMELIZED
SUGAR:

1 cup sugar

3 tablespoons water

FLAN:

1 (14-ounce) can sweetened
   condensed milk

5 eggs

2 tablespoons sugar

1 cup water

5 to 6 tablespoons brandy or
   Gran Marnier

1/4 teaspoon salt

1/4 teaspoon nutmeg

1/2 teaspoon lemon juice

Grated zest of 1 lemon

4 to 5 ripe peaches, peeled
   and diced

GARNISH:

3 peaches, peeled and sliced

Blueberries

Mint sprigs

1 tablespoon toasted almonds

Preheat oven to 150 degrees. Heat 2-quart soufflé dish in oven while caramelizing sugar. To caramelize sugar, place sugar and water in a heavy saucepan. Swirl pan to dissolve sugar and bring to a rolling boil over medium-high heat. Cook until syrup is a nut brown. Pour into heated soufflé dish and rotate dish to cover bottom and sides with syrup. Set aside. To make flan, combine condensed milk, eggs, sugar, water, liqueur, salt, nutmeg, lemon juice and zest in food processor. Add diced peaches. Pulse 3 to 4 times to chop and blend. Pour mixture into prepared soufflé dish. Set in a shallow pan. Pour hot water into pan, about 2 inches deep. Change oven temperature to 350 degrees and bake for 75 to 90 minutes. Test with a knife for doneness. Refrigerate 4 hours or overnight. When ready to serve, run a knife around inside of dish and invert onto serving platter. Arrange peach slices and blueberries around base of flan with sprigs of mint. Place almonds in center.

Plum Tart

Makes 8 to 12 servings

2 cups all-purpose flour

3/4 cup finely chopped walnuts

3/4 cup light brown sugar,
   lightly packed

12 tablespoons cold unsalted
   butter, diced

1 egg yolk

2 pounds firm, ripe plums,
   pitted and quartered lengthwise

Preheat oven to 400 degrees. Combine flour, walnuts and sugar in a large bowl. Add butter and egg yolk. Mix, either by hand or with an electric mixer, until crumbly.
Press 1 1/2 cups of crumb mixture in an even layer into bottom of a 9-inch tart pan. Arrange plums in pan, skin side down, to form a flower pattern; begin at outside and work your way in. Sprinkle rest of crumb mixture evenly over plums. Bake tart for 40 to 50 minutes, or until it is lightly browned and plum juices are bubbling. Remove from oven and cool for 10 minutes. Remove from pan and transfer to a flat plate. Serve warm with vanilla ice cream or frozen yogurt.

Note: Also wonderful made with 6 cups peeled, pitted and sliced peaches and 2 cups blueberries.

Day of the Dead Altar Model, *David Villafañez, Oaxaca, Mexico. Carved and painted wood, ca. 1960. Girard Foundation Collection in the Museum of International Folk Art. Photo: Michel Monteaux.*

Buttermilk Panna Cotta

Makes 6 servings

2 tablespoons cool water
2 tablespoons unflavored gelatin
1 cup heavy cream
7 tablespoons sugar

2 cups buttermilk
3/4 teaspoon vanilla
6 (3/4-cup) custard ramekins

Place water in bowl. Sprinkle gelatin over water and let stand for 10 minutes. Combine cream and sugar in medium saucepan. Stir over medium heat until sugar dissolves and mixture is hot. *Do not boil.* Remove from heat and add gelatin mixture, stirring gently until gelatin dissolves. Let mixture come to room temperature. Add buttermilk and vanilla to cream mixture. Pour mixture into ramekins and refrigerate at least 6 hours until set. Quickly place ramekins, 1 at a time, into hot water to loosen, turn custard out onto a serving plate.

Optional: Garnish with fresh berries and/or serve with tea cookies.

Las Campanas Country Club—Saul Baca, pastry chef

Holiday Date Pudding

Makes 6 servings

1 egg
1 cup sugar
2 teaspoons baking powder
1 cup flour

1/2 cup pecans, chopped
1 1/2 cups dates, chopped
3/4 cup milk

Preheat oven to 350 degrees. Mix all ingredients together and pour into an 8 x 10-inch casserole dish and cover with following mixture: 2 1/2 cups boiling water, 2 cups sugar, 1 teaspoon vanilla and 1 tablespoon butter. *Do not mix!* Bake at 350 degrees for 35 minutes. Serve from casserole dish and top with whipped cream or ice cream. Very rich! Definitely a holiday dessert.

Santa Fe Mocha Torte

Makes 12 servings

1 (12-ounce) package semisweet
　chocolate chips
2 tablespoons instant coffee
2 tablespoons sugar
2 tablespoons water

7 eggs, separated
1 teaspoon vanilla
Dash salt
1 (8-ounce) package Nabisco
　chocolate wafers, crumbled

Using a double boiler over medium heat, stir chocolate chips, coffee, sugar and water until melted. Cool. Add 7 yolks, one at a time. Beat egg whites with electric beater and add vanilla and dash of salt, and beat until stiff. Fold into chocolate mixture. Arrange chocolate wafer crumbs in 9 x 13-inch pan. Layer with mocha mixture. Top with another layer of crumbs. Chill several hours or overnight. This torte freezes well. Cut in small squares to serve.

Home of artist Miguel Martinez. Photography: Daniel Nadelbach,
photographic styling: Gilda Meyer-Niehof.

Special Thanks and Acknowledgments

Amaya, Hotel Santa Fe–Patrick Kline, chef

Andiamo, A Neighborhood Trattoria–Joan Gilcrist, proprietor; Esteban Parra, chef; Kathryn Huester, professional cooking instructor

Back Street Bistro–David Jacoby, proprietor and chef

Bagelmania–Mike Shirley

CK's, Hailey, Idaho–Chris and Rebecca Kastner, proprietors

Coyote Café–Mark Miller, proprietor and chef; Bradley Borchardt, chef

Cravin' Cookies, Albuquerque, New Mexico–Barb Hiveley, proprietor

Cuisine Justine–Justine Witlox-Becker, proprietor

Dinner for Two–Andrew Barnes, proprietor and chef

El Farol–David Salazar, proprietor; James C. Caruso, chef

For the Love of Lavender–Clint Alcott

Fuego Restaurant–Bouneou Maxime

Harry's Roadhouse–Harry Shapiro, proprietor

Jane Butel Cooking School–Jane Butel, proprietor and author

Jinja Café–Lesley Allin, proprietor and chef

Las Campanas Country Club–Jeff Moses, executive chef; Brad Gallegos, chef; Saul Baca, pastry chef

Los Pinos Guest Ranch, Pecos–Alice M. McSweeney, proprietor and chef

Marigold Art–Barbara Marigold

Monica's El Portal–Monica K. Baca

Mozzarella Co., Dallas–Paula Lambert

Mucho Gusto Restaurant–Alex Castro, proprietor

Osteria D'Assisi–Lino Pertusini, proprietor; F. Ventricini, chef

El Meson Restaurant and Chisp! Tapas Bar

Peas "N" Pod Catering, Inc.–Catherine O'Brien, Glenda Griswald

Rooney's Tavern–Jack Shaab, proprietor; Malik Hammond, chef

Santa Fe School of Cooking–Nicole Ammerman

Santacafé–Judith Ebbinghaus, proprietor; David Sellers, chef

The Shed–Carswell Family, proprietors; Josh Carswell, chef; Nelli Maltezos

Trattoria Nostrani

Walter Burke Catering–Stacy Pearl

Zia Diner–Elizabeth Draiscol, proprietor; Ahmed Obo, chef

William Berra, artist, Nedra Matteucci Galleries

Dan Dodelson, artist, Nedra Matteucci Galleries

Paula Lambert, author, *The Cheese Lover's Cookbook and Guide*

Douglas Johnson, artist, Nedra Matteucci Galleries

Gary Niblett, artist, Nedra Matteucci Galleries

Dan Ostermiller, artist, Nedra Matteucci Galleries

Ford Ruthling, artist

Betty Sabo, artist

Elizabeth and Randy Travis, 2004 Grammy Award Winner

Governor Bill Richardson

Senator Pete Domenici

Senator Jeff Bingaman

Katherine Carruthers, former First Lady of New Mexico

Cookbook Committee

CHAIRMAN
Dorothy Black

VICE CHAIRMAN
Dixie Burch

COMPILING CONSULTANTS
Jane Bacchus
Joan Black
Carla Bressan
Susan Buddendorf
Beth Forrester
Harlene Geer
Colleen Harris
Suzanne Ortiz

CREATIVE COORDINATOR
Donna Hankinson

FOOD CONSULTANTS
Sherry Ferguson
Louis Chiarito
John Daw
Richard Matteucci
Gena McKee
Judy Womack

RECIPE COMMITTEE
Jane Buchsbaum
Gail Bush
Pat Eitzen
Julie Gamble
Cindy Johns
Mary Ann Larsen
Lynn Villala Holaday
Liz Crews
Frauke Roth
Eileen Wells

MUSEUM OF NEW MEXICO FOUNDATION PROJECT ADVISOR:
John Stafford

Contributors

te Adams
sie Adams
nnie Adler
dith Alger
argaret S. Allen
arshall C. Allen
harmay Allred
hea Alper
ary Altenberg
elanie Alter
hom Andrewz
nn Applebaum
oris Jean Armstrong
hrista Assad
ffrey Dean John Baca
ie Bacchus
hel Ballen
be Banstorp
ndra Banstorp
nthia Barber
arriet Barber
eloras Barry
ahilea Barry
tsy Barry
ail I. Bass
berta Batchelor
rnie Bayless
sie Bedingfield
tty Bellamy
ancy Palmer Bellue
sa T. Bemis
aron C. Bennett
thleen Beres
verly Berger
hn Berl
ristine Beukert
llian Bidal
orothy Black
lly Blair
"Snooky" Blakemore
ay Block
ren Bloom
nnie Blough
ancesca Blueher
ne Boden
arsha Bol
net Bostelmann

Lucy Boulanger
Adele Breech
Eleanor P. Brenner
Sallie Brewer
Jenelle B. Brock
Frances Brown
Jerry Brown
Patti Brown
Suzanne Brown
Gail A. Bryant
Leslie Bryant
Susan S. Buddendorf
Dixie L. Burch
Jane K. Buchsbaum
Alanna Burke
Billie Burke
Earle Bursum
Gail Bush
Freda Caballero
Eleni Cahn
Britta Carlson
Emma & Michael Carroll
Jacqueline Cates
Peter Cate
Phillip T. Cate Jr.
Jacquelyn K. Cattaneo
Dianne Chalmers
Denise Chase
Joan Chodosh
Arlen Westbrook Clinard
June Cochrell
Kathie Cole
Helen Conklin
Edward P. Connors
Kelli Cooper
Sanford C. Cox, Jr.
Joanne Craig
Liz Crews
Hector Cruz
Sandra S. Culver
Patty Dakhli
Pat Dalton
John Daw
Melanie Dean
Ilse Delman
Leslie DeVera-Duncan
Ruth H. Dillingham

Mimi Doherty
Rosalind Doherty
Thelma Domenici
Barbara Doroba-Ogg
Elizabeth Dorrell
Malka Drucker
Christine Drumright
Nancy du Bro
Karen B. Dunn
Frances Dye
Lawrence Edwards
Ben Egel
Sarah Bishop Egel
Pat Eitzen
Jo A. Ellett
Bambi Ellis
Karen E. Evans
Marilyn M. Farquhar
Pat Farr
Carol Y. Farwell
Victorio Flores
Gloria Fondiller
Joanna Fox
Sigrid H. Freese
Fran Fresquez
Sue Frow
Pawnee Furra
Jamie Gagan
Julie Gamble
Tammy Garcia
Margaret O. Garrett
Mary B. Gavin
Harlene Geer
Nancy Moore Gehman
Joan Gibbons
Phoebe Gilmore
Ms. Kenny L. Goering
Peter Gonzalez
Marti Goodman
Rita Goodman
Lance Gordon
Mary Grana
Joyce Green
Ginger Grossetete
Gretchen Guard
Mary Lou Guerra
Blaine Gutermuth

Heidi Ann Hahn
Dianne Hall
Robert A. Hall
Randi Halsell
Mary Lou Hammett
Donna Hankinson
Colleen Harris
Sali Mauzy Harrison
Dorothy S. Harroun
Nancy Hart
Marie B. Hayden
Barbara Hester
Eva Valencia de Himmerich
John & Glenda Hodgson
Gabrilla Hoeglund
Lynn Villella Holaday
Barbara Homer
Elberta Honstein
Jane Hootkin
Barbara Hoover
Mrs. Gerald Hotchkiss
Mary Hulings
Paula Hutchison
Elizabeth M. Hutz
John Ireland
Eileen Irish
Glenda Jackson
Nancy E. Jacobs
Cindy Johns
Robert Johnson
Jean M. Jones
Robert W. Jones
Sara Julsrud
Meriom Kasther
Beverly C. Katz
Carol Keeffe
Barbara R. King
Carol Kinney
Alicia Kitzman
Rona Kramer
Marcia Krebs
Pat Kuhlhoff
Michelle Kulish
Marcia Kuska
Judith Lackner
Bruce Larsen
Mary Anne Larsen

Diana Lautens
Louise M. Laval
Evelyn LaVoi
Teresa P. Leary
Flora L. Lee
Iona M. Lee
Nancy M. Lee
Lisa Leinberger
Patricia Joseph Lewis
Tamara Lichtenstein
N. Lipton
Alice Liska
Donald Liska
Claire Lissance
Cathy Long
Lynne Loshbaugh
Sue Fox Lovitz
Doris D. Machtinger
Michael Mahaffey
Lois K. Mandros
Alice R. Mann
Alexis Martin
Don Martin
Billie Mason
Richard Matteucci
Laura Mattoon
Donald F. McCann
Sue McClane
Carol M. McDonald
Mimi McGarrity
Laura McGowan
James McGrath
Gena McKee
Patricia Metropolis
Doris Meyer
Rima Miller
Sharon Miller
George Miller
Lora Miller
Carolyn Minton
Carolyn Mitchell
Pat Mora
Marjorie Morehead
Nora N. Morse
Sally A. Morse
Linda Morsman
Janie A. Moseley

Edgar Mueller
Sandra Neal
Judith Nelson
Tony Nethery
Dana Newmann
Joyce M. Nicholson
Barbara Nordhaus
Joan Nordstrum
Nancy Black Noyes
Jodi Odland
Michael Odland
Barbara Oldehoeft
Roy Oldehoeft
Susan Conway Oliphant
Melinne Owen
Evita Ortega
Susanna C. Orzech
Dan Ostermiller
Sharon Parcel
Dianne Parker
Thomas Patin
Nancy Taylor Payne
Lucy Peterson
Ron Peterson
Diane Pinter
Letty B. Plikerd
Dana Pratt
Helen West Pynn
Hermine Quintana
Victoria Rabinowe
Nina M. Rangel
Nina Hinson Rasmussen
Agnesa Reeve
Jack Reeve
Genevieve Regas
Penny Rembe
Jerry Rightman
Joan Rigney
Beatriz Rivera
Laura Robb
Bill Robertson
Bud Robinson
Barbara Rochford
Susan Rojas
Doris Rosen
Dena Ross
Gilbert Roybal

Yvonne Russell
R. Calvert Rutherford
Magdalena Salazar
Lorraine Schechter
Ann Scheflen
Gary Schermerhorn
Hermalee Herzstein Schmidt
Ursula B. Schorn
Cita Schuster
Jack Schwarz
Teresa Seamster
Jo Seasholes
Carolyn Sedberry
Lisa Sheppard
Marian Silver
Martha Simonsen
Gail Sirna
Jennifer Smith
Mary Ann Snider
Eric Stapelman
Janet Stickel
Damaris Rocha Sumner
Josephine T. Takaki
Barbara Templeman
Margot Tewes
Henry Thomas
Enid Tidwell
Judith Tobin
Paula W. Torres
Kitty Trask
Sally Traub
Joseph Traugott
Elizabeth & Randy Travis
Adelina Tryon
Jill Cooper Udall
Benedicte Valentiner
Diane Stanley Vennema
Wanda Vint
John Vollertsen
Jane Warmbrodt
Cecelia Webb
Claire Weiner
Antoinette G. Weiser
Sarah Weld
Eileen Well
Virginia Westray
Wayne White

Grace Whitecotton
Isla Whorton
Sue Widdows
Nancy Wilbur
Phyllis S. Wilson
Suzanne H. Wise
Judy Womack
Judy Worcester
Donna Wortham
Svaja V. Worthington
Sharon Wright
Marcia Zimmerman
Stephanie Marie Zone

Index

Santa Fe